# Sinatra and Me

# SINATRA AND ME

## IN THE WEE SMALL HOURS

# TONY OPPEDISANO
# WITH MARY JANE ROSS

**THORNDIKE PRESS**
A part of Gale, a Cengage Company

3 3210 2821235

Copyright © 2021 by Anthony J. Oppedisano.
Thorndike Press, a part of Gale, a Cengage Company.

**ALL RIGHTS RESERVED**
Thorndike Press® Large Print Nonfiction.
The text of this Large Print edition is unabridged.
Other aspects of the book may vary from the original edition.
Set in 16 pt. Plantin.

**LIBRARY OF CONGRESS CIP DATA ON FILE.
CATALOGUING IN PUBLICATION FOR THIS BOOK
IS AVAILABLE FROM THE LIBRARY OF CONGRESS.**

ISBN-13: 978-1-4328-9075-9 (hardcover alk. paper)

Published in 2021 by arrangement with Scribner, a Division of Simon & Schuster, Inc.

Printed in Mexico
Print Number: 01     Print Year: 2022

Frank Sinatra never really came alive until the nighttime. On countless evenings, the sky over his Rancho Mirage home would fade to blue and gold, then burst into brilliant orange and flame out into darkness. Despite pinpoints of light from surrounding homes, there was a sense of isolation and comforting serenity in the Palm Springs desert.

We'd venture outside so Frank could have a smoke, then sit by the pool in the warm stillness, sipping Jack Daniel's and talking. From late in the night until early in the morning, oftentimes greeting the sunrise, Frank and I would just talk.

That scene or one like it was repeated night after night, from Manila to London and countless places in between. One by one, wherever we were, the people around us would drift off to bed until only Frank and I remained. In the wee small hours of the morning, we'd converse — about music, family, friends, great loves and loves lost, failures and successes, triumphs and disappointments, the lives we'd led and the lives we wished we'd led. Frank wanted to understand and be understood. He wanted someone to remember.

I *remember,* Frank. Every hour. Every word. This book is for you.

# CONTENTS

# Prologue:
## 'Scuse Me While I Disappear

A half-body follow spot picked him out of the darkness, illuminated only by a soft blue ambient glow. It was a classic pose, the whiskey glass I'd filled earlier in one of his hands, a cigarette in the other, smoke drifting languidly from its tip. A perfectly knotted bow tie against a pristine white shirt, a black tuxedo blending into the ambient dusk. With the soft notes of Bill Miller's piano underneath, he began to sing. "So drink up, all you people . . ." His voice was melancholy, filled with longing for his "Angel Eyes," the woman he'd lost for reasons he still didn't understand. He'd already sung the songs they expected, decades of standards that bore his name. This song felt different — personal, autobiographical. As the energy that had carried him through the evening ebbed, the performer's mask seemed to slip. The muscles of his face relaxed; circles appeared under his eyes; lines and hollows of sadness defined his face. Sorrow and loneliness dimmed those startling blue eyes. Standing as always in the wings at stage right, I watched him take a long drag on his cigarette, exhaling slowly as he sang the final line: " 'Scuse me while I disappear." With the last syllable, he stepped out of the light, and only the smoke was left, floating like a specter. Frank Sinatra was gone.

*May 14, 1998*

I was at my mother's house that evening, giving a dinner party for friends, when the first call came. I'd spent the earlier part of the day at Frank's Foothill house and would be back the next day. Meanwhile, my friends and I had gathered to eat dinner and watch the last-ever episode of *Seinfeld* with my mother, Rose. The phone rang just as the show started. It was Frank's girl Friday, a tall Creole woman named Vine who was devoted to her boss. She was in a blind panic, almost unable to speak.

I said, "Calm down. Take it easy. Breathe! What's the matter?"

In the background, I could hear Frank in a tirade. His wife, Barbara, had gone out with friends again, leaving Frank behind for the fourth night in a row. Frank hated being left out, especially at night. Going to dinner was one of the few pleasures he had left. He

was seeing red, and I could hear him shriek-
ing obscenities with those powerful lungs.

"What kind of life is this? What kind of
BS?"

I tried to help Vine calm him down enough
to get the situation under control. With
Frank's recent heart episodes, this wasn't
safe. Then, all of a sudden, Vine screamed.

I tried to get her attention. "Vine. Vine!
Tell me what's happening!"

"Tony! His face turned beet red, and his
eyes rolled back in his head. He just fell
back onto the bed." I could hear the terror
in her voice.

"Call the paramedics, right now!"

"I can't! You know I'm not allowed to. I've
got to ask Barbara first."

"There's no time. Listen to me. I'm calling Dr. Kennamer. I'll have him call the
paramedics, so Barbara won't be mad at
you. Call me back when the paramedics get
there."

Rex Kennamer was Frank's physician and
personal friend in Beverly Hills. I called him
at home, and Rex said he'd call the ambulance. He told me to call him back as soon
as I knew what the assessment by the
paramedics was. He'd meet us at the hospital if Frank was transported. When I hung
up from talking to Rex, I called Vine and let

11

her know.

A few minutes later, Vine called back and said, "They're taking him to Cedars." Cedars-Sinai was the hospital to the stars, a landmark in Beverly Hills, as familiar to me by then as the back of my hand. I'd been there with Frank several times before.

I said, "Okay, I'll meet you there."

I threw on my white windbreaker with the Desert Inn logo, grabbed my car keys, and apologized to my guests, telling them only, "Frank's having a problem. I'm sorry, but I gotta go."

I rushed out the door and ran to my car. By then, it was dark and drizzly, and my gunmetal-gray Jaguar blended into the gloom. Climbing in, I started the engine and pulled onto Niagara Street, then down to Riverside Drive. I called Rex on my cell phone and told him what was happening. He said he'd meet us at Cedars. Meanwhile, Vine would be with Frank in the ambulance.

Minutes later, I turned onto Coldwater Canyon Avenue, one of the main mountain roads that link LA with the San Fernando Valley. Coldwater Canyon is dark and treacherous at night, twisting and turning its way through the Hollywood Hills, but it was the fastest way to the hospital. The rush-hour traffic had died down by then, and there were few cars ahead of me. My windshield wipers kept the glass clear of mist as I drove. As I left Studio City and started to climb the hill, the Valley faded in my rearview mirror, and civilization with it. The Jag took the curves like a race car, hugging the road. The rising hills loomed over me, lined with pine trees, ghostly outlines in the darkness.

I gripped the mahogany steering wheel firmly as I concentrated on the road ahead. Frank's gold ring bearing the Sinatra family crest, the gift that symbolized my position in his life, gleamed on my right pinky finger. The weight of that responsibility hung on me as I drove. I was laser-focused on the clock. If I could just get there, I could defuse the situation. If I could just get there, it would be like all the other trips to the hospital. I could calm Frank down, put my arms around him, help him breathe, reassure him that everything was going to be all right. I would make it all right. That was my job. I couldn't entertain the thought of a world without Frank. I refused to let my mind go there. It was inconceivable. And it sure as hell wouldn't do Frank any good.

I forced myself to focus on the road as the events of the past week spun through my head. Barbara in Frank's face, waking him

13

from a deep sleep when she got back from dinner. Frank, startled and disoriented, red faced and screaming. Barbara walking out of the room to her suite upstairs. The silence at the other end when I tried to call her on the intercom. Frank, slumped on the side of his bed, asking me for a hug, saying, "This isn't a life," his arms around me like a child's. Frank and I eating pizza and getting "drunk" together on nonalcoholic beer. Laughing together. I could always make him laugh. Me putting him to bed as he mumbled, "Guess I'll put it in the bag." If I could just get there, everything would be all right.

After what felt like an eternity, the towers of Cedars-Sinai finally came into view, a glowing oasis in a city just starting to sleep. Pulling in front of the emergency entrance, I left the car by the security guard, shouting that I'd left the keys in the ignition. I pushed through the doors to the big circular desk, the epicenter of Cedars Emergency.

*I'm here, Frank, I'm here. Everything's going to be all right.*

I had no idea I was there to say goodbye.

■ ■ ■ ■

# PART I
# FRANCIS ALBERT
# AND THE KID

■ ■ ■ ■

# CHAPTER 1
# OF ALL THE GIN JOINTS
## THE BEGINNING OF A FRIENDSHIP

It was November 1974, the end of Frank Sinatra's self-imposed "retirement." He'd walked away from his performing career in 1972, believing his music was no longer relevant to the younger generation. Two years later, twenty thousand people bought out Madison Square Garden to see Sinatra on his comeback tour. ABC sportscaster Howard Cosell was emceeing that night. The concert was billed as the Main Event, and Cosell announced it like a boxing match. I was twenty-three years old, sitting a few feet from the stage, in the block of seats Frank reserved at concerts for his friends and family. I'd known him for two years by then. Spending time with him at Jilly's, a Manhattan club, I'd gotten to know the private Sinatra. I was about to see a very different man. I knew about the power he radiated onstage, but seeing it up close was a different matter. The dichotomy of the two Sinatras, onstage and off, was mind-blowing. My pulse raced with excitement.

The crowd was restless, waiting for the moment when Frank would appear. Then suddenly he was there, materializing in the center of the arena, and I felt the air electrify. The crowd came to its feet and roared loudly enough to shake the walls. Frank was dressed in an impeccable black tuxedo, black bow tie, and orange silk pocket handkerchief. I knew that the handkerchief bore his likeness and signature. He wore one at every performance to give to fans who brought him flowers onstage. A small thank-you. He began to sing "The Lady Is a Tramp" as the crowd gradually quieted to hear him. In spite of the large arena, it felt intimate, personal. Frank had a knack for making everyone in the audience feel like he was singing just to them. I was riveted. It was magic, and I was a part of it.

My father once told me he should have known I'd end up hobnobbing with the rich and famous. He liked to kid me about it.

"From the time you were born, you liked classy things."

"What do you mean, Dad?"

"Two hours out of your mother, you had to have a private suite."

The private suite in question was my incubator.

I was a preemie, arriving two months early, on September 27, 1951, at Brooklyn Hospital. In a large extended family of brown-eyed, dark-haired, olive-skinned Italian-Americans, I was a standout. My fair freckled skin, blue eyes, and flaming red hair made me easy to identify in family pictures. I got teased about my coloring, but it was never mean-spirited. The only time my parents mentioned my hair was when I'd done something truly bad. When they got frustrated with me, instead of switching to my full name, Anthony Joseph, they'd start referring to me as the "redheaded guinea." Even at the time, I knew it was tongue-in-cheek. But I also knew I was in trouble.

In many respects, I had the childhood Frank wanted. Until I was twelve, we lived in a two-story brownstone on Brooklyn's Eldert Lane. Our working-class neighborhood was a mixture of Italians, Jews, Germans, and a couple of Irish families. Like every Italian-American family of the time, our brownstone had pictures on the wall of the Pope and generations of our relatives. Once I discovered Sinatra at age thirteen, there was a photo of him on the wall as well. My godfather, Uncle Joe, lived upstairs with

Aunt Fran and their two daughters. Dad and Mom and my brothers and I had the main floor, and we all shared the basement.

There was a reassuring rhythm to our weeks. Every Friday night, the whole family went down into the basement for parties with lots of food and music. I'd carry food up and down the stairs from the kitchen, where my mother, aunts, and paternal grandmother were cooking. The men supplied the music. With my uncle Joe strumming the mandolin and my dad on guitar, they played a lot of popular tunes from the twenties, thirties, and forties, mixed with a few Italian tunes like "Santa Lucia." Sometimes Uncle Al chimed in on his banjo. What they lacked in skill, they made up for in enthusiasm. On Sundays, my big brother Pete and I got up early to be at Blessed Sacrament, where we were choirboys.

On weekday nights, if we got our homework done, we could watch TV until nine. My favorites were always the variety shows, like *Ed Sullivan, Red Skelton, The Dean Martin Variety Show,* and later *Carol Burnett.* Even at that age, I had a strong affinity for show business. I loved watching comedians like Jackie Gleason and George Burns. I enjoyed guessing where they were going with a joke and noticed how they were developing a specific bit. I had a secret hope that some Hollywood agent would discover me. In later years, I teased Frank about it. I told him I could have played the Eddie Hodges part, the little redheaded boy singing "High Hopes" with Frank in the movie *A Hole in the Head.*

Frank laughed and said, "Well, you're probably right, but I didn't know you then."

I put on my sad face, sighed, and said, "I know."

In many ways, we were the typical all-American family of the Eisenhower years, but I was also fiercely proud of my Italian heritage. People knew that the best way to get my attention was to call me Irish. A teacher of mine would spell my name O'Ppedisano just to get my goat. As the only family member who didn't really look Italian, I knocked myself out to make my ethnicity clear. I was the only one of my paternal grandmother's twelve grand-children to learn Italian. My first words to Frank were in Italian. I learned *everything* Italian, from the music to the cooking. When I grew up and started playing in the New York clubs, I'd switch over to the mandolin and strum Italian songs when the wiseguys showed up, just to make it clear that though I might not have *looked* Italian-

21

American, we shared a heritage.

I also learned the Old Country superstitions. The most feared superstition was *malocchio,* the evil eye. When people gave you the evil eye, bad things could happen. If you got a headache, it was because someone was talking badly or enviously about you. If you were complimented by people who were jealous of you, you were in danger of *malocchio.* There were several ways to prevent it. You could put your hand in your pocket and shape your fingers like a horn. Or you could wear a horn on a chain around your neck along with a crucifix. Every Italian neighborhood had those guys wearing "wifebeater" shirts and gold chains with crosses and horns. The color red also warded off the evil eye.

Aunt Fran was the only one in the family who knew the ceremony to dispel *malocchio.* The neighbors would come to see her when they were the victims of *malocchio.* She'd fill a soup bowl with water and a small bowl with olive oil. Taking two drops of olive oil, she'd say a prayer, murmur something in Italian, and drop the oil in the bowl. When the oil hit the water, it would form shapes, and I'd see a pair of eyeballs. I can't explain it, but I really did see eyeballs. Within a half hour of Aunt Fran's performing the ceremony, the person's headache nearly always went away. I asked her to teach me the ceremony, but she said it could only be taught on Christmas Eve — and in the excitement of Christmas, I always forgot. Too bad. It would have come in handy in Hollywood.

Did I actually *believe* all this stuff? Not really. On the other hand, what could it hurt to take a few precautions? When I had my very first tuxedo made, I had it lined in fire-engine red just to be safe.

Our lives were also shaped by the Catholic Church. We attended mass regularly, and all the kids in our family went to parochial school through sixth grade. I was a good student, but I found school boring. It didn't challenge me. I never took notes. At an early age, I discovered that I possess a somewhat photographic memory. It's been both a blessing and a curse. Most of my teachers were nuns. You do *not* mess with a nun. You have to grow up Catholic to understand. Catholic boys learn at an early age to respect women, even more so when they're Italian-American and raised by strong mothers and grandmothers. Frank understood that. He didn't respect anybody as much as he respected his mother, Dolly.

I was an independent kid, always my own

person, and I never worried very much about what other people thought of me. Maybe it was the hair. I was never going to fit in, so why even try to be like everyone else? Even as a small boy, I had my own sense of style. In the summer, I'd wear shorts if I was playing a game, but otherwise, whether or not it was a school day, I wore cotton or wool pants with a crease and a dress shirt with long sleeves. Sometimes I'd add a bow tie. I didn't even own a pair of jeans until I moved to California when I was twenty-four. Frank got ridiculed with the nickname "Slacksie" when he was a kid for always wearing dress slacks. I never acquired a nickname, but I was easy to find in a crowd of kids. I'd be the only one playing baseball in slacks with a crease.

I was something of a loner. Sometimes I'd find myself feeling lonely even in the midst of all those loving family members. It was like loneliness was a disease, and music was my medicine. When I was happy, I turned to music. When I was sad, I turned to music. It was always in my head, and I couldn't turn it off. I needed it like most kids need food.

At age four, I started to play the piano. We had an old player piano in the basement of our brownstone, and I'd go downstairs and noodle around on it. When I heard music on the radio, I could figure out how to translate it to the keyboard. At one Friday-night party when I was about five, I sat down on the piano bench and played a popular Lawrence Welk song called "Sailor" that I'd learned from the radio. My family was astonished. They knew I liked to fool around on the piano, but they didn't realize how much I'd learned on my own. As I practiced more, the structure of music came naturally to me. The piano made sense to me because it was the most wide-open instrument, all right there in front of you, measured in exact intervals. When I was about nine, I moved to the accordion. I initially took up the guitar because of the song "Sleep Walk," by the Ventures, an instrumental group that was very popular at the time. I loved the song, and I wanted to play it, so my uncle Joe loaned me his guitar. I was about twelve years old. I learned the guitar literally one string at a time. Once I unlocked the transition be-tween the piano and guitar, figuring out what the comparable keys and intervals were, I could play it. The mandolin was next. The violin, viola, and cello were each a different challenge since notes aren't measured on them like they are on a piano or a guitar, which has frets. You have to rely on your ear. Once I made that transition, the rest was easy. The bass and banjo followed. If it had strings, I could play it.

We moved out of Brooklyn to Long Island when I was thirteen, and I made the transition from Catholic school to public school. The change of schools came at just the right time for me musically. In junior high, I met Joe Costanzo, a music teacher who taught during the week and did weekend gigs on keyboard. He inspired me to pursue my passion for music. The year I turned thirteen was also the year I discovered Frank Sinatra's music. My rendezvous with fate occurred at a Woolworth's department store in Franklin Square. I was looking through record albums after school one day when I stumbled across one of Sinatra's and bought it for $3.95. When I got home, I immediately went down to the basement and put it on the record player. On the first cut, Frank started a cappella with the title song, "The Nearness of You." The piano then joined him, followed by the entire orchestra. At that, I went, "Wow!" It was a rich, deep, full-textured sound, and there was an electric buzz in Frank's voice. From then on, I was hooked.

I started thumbing through the stacks of

78s that my father kept in the basement. He'd collected a wealth of Sinatra tunes performed with Tommy Dorsey's orchestra and even a couple with Harry James. Whenever I had the money, I'd buy another one of Frank's albums. I bought out everything they had at Woolworth's. I still own over one hundred Sinatra vinyls, a good number of which I acquired in junior high and high school. Listening to the records was a fascinating journey back to Frank's roots. I found that I wasn't enthralled with the timbre of Frank's voice on the early albums, not only because of the primitive recording technology, but also because his voice was a lot higher and thinner then. Listening to Frank's later songs, I could hear how far he'd come in perfecting his craft.

The year I entered my teens there was another big change in the Oppedisano family. After growing up with two brothers, I acquired a sister. Angela was born in 1964 and came to us at three weeks old as a foster child. When she was five, we adopted her. Angel, as we came to call her, and I had a special bond from the very beginning. Because of the age difference, I was more like a father than a brother to her. We may not have been related biologically, but Angel and I had such similar personalities, it drove me crazy sometimes. She was a little pistol. Losing her twenty-five years later was one of my life's hardest losses. It left a hole in my heart that remains unfilled.

I started high school in Floral Park, Long Island. School was still easy for me, and I usually got all of my homework done in study hall. If I finished early, I'd go to the music room and practice on the various instruments. I also sang in the choir, where I became a soloist and the student head of the choir. In those years, I formed an especially close relationship with Fran Walker, the literature teacher. Because there wasn't a full-time drama teacher, Fran was assigned the job of producing that year's musical, *Bye Bye Birdie.* Knowing of my interest in show business, she asked me to help. I rolled up my sleeves and went at it. It was the first thing I ever produced, and I tackled it with the confidence of a teenager who has no idea what he's getting into. It meant working with an orchestra, putting together a light scheme, rehearsing elaborate choreography, and coordinating everything else that goes into a musical.

The play calls for an Ed Sullivan voice-over, and one of my first jobs was to get someone to voice Sullivan's part in the play. He had one of the most famous voices in show business, and unfortunately, there was no one in school who could do his voice well enough to suit my taste. So, being young, stupid, and fearless, I decided to call *The Ed Sullivan Show* and see if they'd help me out.

The guy who answered the phone that afternoon was named Santullo, a fellow Italian-American. I explained that I was producing *Bye Bye Birdie* for my high school out on Long Island and needed some help.

"Here's my predicament. I have a lot of respect for Mr. Sullivan and wouldn't want to have someone impersonate him badly. So I thought I'd call and see if you could help."

Mr. Santullo started laughing.

"Did I say something funny?"

He answered, "No, no. I was just impressed with your level of professionalism. Hold on a second. I think I might be able to solve your problem."

He put me on hold. I was drumming my fingers, listening to the canned music, when a different person came on the line.

The man said, "So, young man, what's the problem?" You couldn't miss the voice. It was Ed Sullivan. Mr. Sullivan listened to my explanation, then said, "No problem. We'll remedy that right away. Give me your address."

A few days later, I received a package containing a quarter-inch tape reel with the lines from the play, recorded for me by Ed Sullivan himself. When I played it, the familiar voice boomed throughout the theater: "And now, right here on our stage . . ." It was terrific.

I learned an important lesson about producing that day, one that served me well later: It's amazing what you can get if you're willing to ask for it. Especially if you have a lot of moxie and don't know any better.

It turned out I'd need that edge, because despite having top grades, I almost didn't graduate from high school. The teacher who taught my computer class threatened to flunk me because I spent my extra time in the music room rather than the computer lab.

He knew I left study hall whenever I finished my homework early, and one day he asked me, "What are you doing leaving study hall?"

I answered, "That time's my own. I use it to go down to the music room and play the piano to clear my head."

"What for?"

"Well, because I love music, and I love show business."

He looked down his nose at me and said

pointedly, "Show business is superfluous."

I still remember his words, and I remember replying, "No, *you're* superfluous."

He wanted his revenge. He threatened to flunk me so I wouldn't have enough units to graduate, even though I was doing well in the class. Luckily, Fran Walker campaigned on my behalf, and I ended up graduating with flying colors.

It was also during high school that I experienced my first real tragedy. My godfather, Uncle Joe, no longer lived upstairs from us, but we'd remained close after the move from Brooklyn. An amateur musician himself, he'd always encouraged me in my music. From the day I was born, he'd always been there, just up the stairs when I was little, his arm around me in family pictures, his guitar or mandolin in my hands. Then, when I was sixteen, he was diagnosed with lung cancer. Every male Oppedisano before him had died of cancer. He'd been a lifelong smoker. The cancer was already very advanced and was untreatable. The doctor told him to make the most of the time he had left by traveling and enjoying himself. Uncle Joe wouldn't accept the doctor's advice. He'd watched family members die in pain, and he knew what it had done to them and the family. He wanted to spare himself and our family that ordeal, either by dying quickly or by getting better. Uncle Joe asked the doctor to perform surgery on his lungs, but his doctor refused, saying he probably wouldn't survive the operation. The doctor told Uncle Joe it would be unethical to operate on him. Uncle Joe then started seeing doctor after doctor, all of whom refused to operate.

Finally, he found a doctor who agreed to do the surgery. The family suspected that Uncle Joe hoped he wouldn't survive the operation. It was pretty clear the *doctor* didn't think he would, either, because full payment was demanded up front.

Against the odds, Uncle Joe survived the surgery, but it would have been better if he hadn't. He was unable to take care of himself anymore and lived in constant agony. Aunt Fran couldn't cope, so I began taking care of him. I cooked for him, helped him eat, dressed him, helped him in and out of bed. He was too weak to stand in the shower by then, so I gave him sponge baths. Afterward, I'd dry him off, dress him again, and put him to bed. I had no idea at the time that taking care of Uncle Joe would enable me to help Frank someday. Near the end of Frank's life, as his health failed, he'd reach out to me for assistance with some of those same things. Frank was very private, and it was easier for him to accept help from a friend and surrogate family member than from a caregiver. It was my honor to help him through those difficult times.

When classes started again that fall, I'd call from a pay phone at school every day, to check on Uncle Joe, before I walked home. In the second week of October, I called him as usual when school got out. Aunt Fran told me Uncle Joe wasn't up to talking, but I could talk to *him,* let him hear my voice. What she didn't tell me was that Uncle Joe had almost died that morning but had been hanging on, waiting for my call. Ten minutes after I hung up, on October 11, 1968, my godfather, Joseph Oppedisano, passed away.

The funeral was at St. Catherine's of Sienna. It was the first time I attended a funeral for someone I loved like a part of myself. I was stunned with grief, and most of the day remains a blur. The only thing I remember is, after the service, walking down the aisle with my father, following the coffin. My dad, who'd always struggled to show me affection, reached out and took my hand as we walked, squeezing it tightly. I held on for dear life. I'm not sure which of us needed the other one more in that moment, me or my dad.

I sought refuge from the pain of Uncle Joe's passing the way I always coped, by throwing myself into my music. I formed a little trio with my older brother, Pete, and another kid from school, Gary Berzolla. We started performing at sweet sixteen parties and other local gigs. The band didn't last long. I'd had great hopes in the beginning, but after a while, it just wasn't challenging me enough. I'd begun to explore more complex music. I knew by then, with absolute certainty, that music was my destiny. It would be many years before my *father* accepted that, but I already knew where my path would take me.

When I was seventeen, I started going into the city and making money doing gigs as a jazz guitarist in some of the clubs. We moved to Ronkonkoma the next year. New York driver's licenses didn't require pictures in the sixties, so it was easy enough for me to get a "license" saying I was eighteen, the minimum age to play in the clubs. All the clubs had pianos at the time, and I could always double as a pianist if they needed one. My father still didn't like my chosen profession, and he pushed hard to get me to go to engineering school. That was never going to happen. New York beckoned, and with it, my dreams of making it in show business. I didn't know it yet, but my life would soon change forever. Forty-seven miles down the Long Island Expressway and over the Fifty-Ninth Street Bridge, my future was waiting in a reserved booth at Jilly's.

It was December 8, 1972, and I was twenty-one years old the night I met Frank Sinatra. Frank was in the middle of his self-imposed (and short-lived) retirement at the time. I, on the other hand, was just getting started. By then, I'd been performing in clubs professionally for four years. I was already making a bit of a name for myself working all over the tristate area. Some close friends and I had put together a little band that included a keyboard player, Les Stanco, and a drummer, John Bonelli. I was also working as a vocalist by then. I'm a baritone with, coincidentally, the exact same range as Sinatra, note for note. It made it easy for me to sing the standards I'd always loved.

The early seventies were an amazing time for a musician in New York City, which boasted a wealth of nightclubs. There were clubs that leaned toward jazz, and also society rooms like Danny's Hide-A-Way. These nightspots appealed to the New York upper crust and were destinations for celebrities, artists, writers, and wealthy people in general. A good number of the elite hotels had showrooms. Even at the Waldorf, they had the Empire Room, where Sinatra, Ella Fitzgerald, and Sarah Vaughan had played. Nowhere else on earth could a musician have experiences like I was having almost every night. Of all the clubs, though, Jilly's was, to me, the most special.

At 256 West Fifty-Second Street, just off Ninth Avenue, Jilly's was on "Jazz Street" in the Manhattan club district. Jilly's always offered terrific music, the best musicians, and an eclectic crowd. There'd be "twenty years of good behavior" at one table, a senator at another, and a concert pianist at another. It wasn't unusual for people like Tony Bennett and Judy Garland to sit in with the band for a set. Jilly ran a good club. One thing he never did was water down the booze, and he had a great reputation for playing straight with the customers. He'd once worked as a bouncer, but as he got older, he learned alternate ways to defuse situations.

A guy would come into his club, get drunk, and become abusive. Jilly would go quickly to the person and say, "Hey, come on, let's relax. Let's not do this. Come on, let's go to the bar. Let me get you a drink. And let's calm this whole situation down."

There was a code that Jilly had worked out with "Uncle Frank," his brother, who was usually behind the bar. Jilly would walk up to the bar with the troublemaker and say, "This gentleman is having a drink with us."

Uncle Frank would make the guy a very special drink. He kept some horse physic hidden behind the bar that was used to loosen an animal's bowels when it had colic. Frank would put a drop or two in the drink and hand it to the troublemaker. As Jilly said, by the time the guy could say, "Holy crap," it would be running down his legs. It's hard to be a tough guy when your shoes are filling up with shit. Jilly didn't have to throw the guy out. He couldn't get out of there fast enough.

By the early 1970s, Jilly's was one of the hottest clubs in town. Walking up the sidewalk to Jilly's, you saw an orange canvas awning, shading a glass door. Under the awning, as solid as a fixture, stood the doorman, Sy. Sy was a tough guy whom you didn't fool with: six feet four inches tall and solidly built, dressed in a uniform, cap, and long gray coat with braid that went all the way to his midcalf. If you got past Sy and through the first door, you went down a couple of steps to a second glass door that led into the club. Over the second door hung a framed magazine cover of Frank Sinatra and Princess Grace of Monaco, Frank's former costar, Grace Kelly. Inside the club and on the right was a bar, always crowded. The wall opposite the bar was covered with framed photos, some of Jilly, but most of Sinatra with various celebrities, dignitaries, and heads of state, as well as framed production stills from his films. If you looked closely, you'd notice that the frames were all screwed into the wall. Jilly knew someone would lift the photos if he turned his back.

On the left was a little open coatroom with a hat-check girl. Past the coatroom and the photo wall was a doorway that led you downstairs to where two pay phones nestled inside oversized clamshell enclosures. Beyond them on the left were a card room, men's and women's restrooms, and the kitchen. There was a metal tube going down to the kitchen like they used to have in navy submarines, allowing the waiters and maître d' upstairs to communicate with the cook downstairs. If you wanted to get the cook's attention, you'd pull out the cork at the speaking end of the tube and whistle, and he'd shout back up. There was also a service elevator downstairs that came up to street level in front of the club, to the left of the orange awning. Jilly had to use the elevator to smuggle Johnny Carson out of the place one night when Johnny had the misfortune of flirting with a mobster's girlfriend.

If you kept walking past the photo wall upstairs, you'd come to a maître d' stand in front of an archway with another door. Screwed to that door was a life-sized ply-board cutout of Frank Sinatra. If you got past Frank and the maître d', you entered the main room, scattered with round two- and four-top cocktail tables. Midway into the room, on the left-hand side, was a baby grand piano encircled on three sides by a shelf, small tables, and chairs (referred to as the "piano bar"), under a ceiling mirror that was cut in the shape of a baby grand. It was like looking at twin grand pianos on the floor and ceiling. Customers could sit around the piano and sip their drinks, taking in the music. Beyond the piano bar were three more rows of cocktail tables, and on the rear wall were tufted leather booths. The leather booth on the left was for Sinatra when he was in town. Jilly kept a special orange leather armchair for Frank's exclusive use, orange being Frank's favorite color.

The chair was normally kept in storage. If you knew Jilly's and saw that the orange chair was out, you knew Frank was in town. On the rear wall of that booth hung a large movie poster, depicting Frank as Dirty Dingus Magee, sporting a derby and long johns. It was kind of a strange choice of posters. Frank would be the first to tell you it was not one of his most stellar films. In between the booths was a pair of saloon-type swinging doors that looked like they were borrowed from an old John Wayne western. The doors opened to the busing station. That was also where the dumbwaiter came up with the food from the kitchen, and where the metal submarine-style communication tube went down.

I started going to Jilly's regularly because everyone knew it was Sinatra's favorite place and because I just liked it. A few weeks after I started coming to the club, I made the acquaintance of Jilly's brother Frank, who ran the place. Everyone called him "Uncle Frank." It didn't take him that long to notice me. I must have stood out a little with my carrot-red hair. Besides, I was always dressed in a tuxedo after my gig and usually smoking a cigar. I didn't really blend in. Uncle Frank was also a cigar smoker, and that's how we started our first conversation.

He was pouring me a drink one night and said, referring to my cigar, "That smells good. What is it?" So we started talking about cigars.

Another night, Uncle Frank said to me, "Every time you come in here, you're in a tuxedo. What do you do?"

I said, "Well, I'm an entertainer, a musician."

A few nights later, I was standing at the bar, looking at pictures of Jilly on the wall opposite, when I noticed that there was something not quite right with Jilly's eyes. I asked Uncle Frank about it.

He just said, "Well, he's got a bum blinker." He didn't tell me which eye it was.

I was at Jilly's so often by then that after a while, Uncle Frank suggested I sit in with the band. It went well, and it wasn't long before Uncle Frank was telling me, "I gotta introduce you to my brother. You know he's off with Mr. Sinatra."

And one night, Uncle Frank did.

He said, "My brother's comin' back to the city this weekend. Frank is not gonna be with him, so I'm gonna have an opportunity to put you two guys together. When are you comin' in?"

41

I said, "When do you want me to come in?"

The night finally came when I was supposed to meet Jilly. I was at the bar when Jilly came downstairs from his apartment. The bar was three deep with people. I was standing with my back to the bar, looking at the pictures on the wall that I'd looked at hundreds of times before, trying to look cool. Another guy was standing next to me, also waiting for Jilly. Uncle Frank handed me a drink.

Turning to his brother, Uncle Frank said, "Jilly, I want you to meet Tony Oppedisano."

Jilly and I shook hands, and then he shook hands with the guy next to me.

I went back to minding my business, still looking at the pictures, until Jilly said, "How you doin'?"

I looked at Jilly and then looked away and back at the pictures. I didn't say anything.

A long minute passed, and Jilly said again, "So how you doin'?"

Again I didn't say anything. Finally, Jilly slapped me on the shoulder and said, "What! Are you deaf [pronounced *deef*]? I'm talking to you!"

I blurted out, "Jeez, Jilly, I'm really sorry. Your brother and I were talking about the

42

fact that you have a bad blinker. I didn't know if it was this one or that one. I thought you were talking to *him,* " pointing to the guy next to me. I felt like a fool.

Jilly started laughing, put his arm around me, and said to his brother, "Frank, I like this kid."

He and Uncle Frank and I sat down and chatted for quite a while that night. From that first meeting, Jilly and I hit it off.

Uncle Frank told him what a good musician I was, and Jilly said, "Well, give him some work. Bring him in and put him with some people here."

So I began working at Jilly's occasionally, along with all the other clubs. I got to work with guys like Joe Petrone, who played piano. One night when I was working, Joe got sick, and Mickey Deans filled in for him. I didn't know who Deans was; I only knew he was a good piano player and a decent singer. I found out later he'd been married to Judy Garland for the last three months of her life.

As the place was closing down, Jilly said to me and Mickey, "Listen, I'm going to the after-hours joint down on Houston Street. You guys want to come along?"

We said, "Yeah," so I left my car at the club. I went with Jilly and some other people, and Mickey met us there later.

The place on Houston Street had the feel of a speakeasy, where you walk down four steps to a door and a guy opens a peephole. Everything in the world was going on inside: card games, slot machines, and plenty of drinking. I'd never seen anything like it. I was still a kid and mesmerized by it all.

When my mind finally started to clear, I noticed it was about six thirty or so in the morning, and I said to Jilly, "Listen, you heading out any time soon? Because I still have to go to Long Island."

He said, "No, I'm gonna be here for a while."

Then Mickey said, "I'll drive you back." He'd drop me at Jilly's on his way home to New Jersey.

It turned out that Mickey wasn't just being a good Samaritan. On our drive back to Jilly's, he hit on me.

I said, "Listen, I'm flattered, but no, thank you." When we got back to Fifty-Second Street, I got in my car and headed home.

I thought about the implications of that moment when I found out he'd been married to Judy Garland. Another small piece of the tragedy that was Judy Garland's final year.

Jilly had been gone from the club a lot in

the years before I'd met him, on the road with Sinatra when Frank was still touring. But from late 1971 to early 1973, Jilly was in the club more often because of Sinatra's temporary "retirement." Frank was still in and out of New York a lot during that time, and when he was in town, he'd come into Jilly's after dinner and stay until the sun came up. As I soon witnessed for myself, every time Frank arrived at Jilly's, he'd follow the same ritual.

Frank would come in the door and immediately walk through the club past the bar, the maître d', the cocktail tables, the piano bar, and his booth in the left-hand corner. He'd keep walking through the swinging saloon doors, straight to the busing station. Going to the metal tube going down to the kitchen, he'd pull the cork out, whistle into the thing, and wait for Howie to pick up. Howie was the Chinese chef who created tasty Cantonese dishes that rivaled any restaurant in Chinatown. Frank used to claim that Jilly had Howie chained to the stove downstairs. "He doesn't let him out of there, you know."

Howie could mangle the English language like no one else. When Frank whistled into the tube, Howie would answer back, "Yes, what you want?"

Frank would say, "Howie?"

"Yes, dis is Howie."

"Howie, this is Frank."

"Oh, Frant."

"Listen to me, Howie."

"Yes, what, Frant?"

Frank would say in his best impersonation of Howie, "Futt you, Howie."

And Howie would answer, "Oh, futt you, too, Frant!"

Frank did it every time he came in. When Howie retired, Frank gave him a Cartier watch, and on the back, it said, "To Howie. Futt you. Frank Sinatra."

Many years later, when Frank and I were in residence at the Waldorf Towers, we started reminiscing about the club. We got to talking about Howie, and Frank said, "I wonder what the hell ever happened to him."

I made an excuse to go in the other room and started doing a little research. This was before the Internet, but I managed to find out that Howie was still alive and living in Brooklyn with his grandson. I got the number, then went back in the other room, dialed the number, and put Frank on the phone. The minute Frank heard the voice, it was unmistakable.

Howie asked, "Who dis?"

"This is Frank Sinatra. Who is this?"

"Oh, Frant! Dis is Howie."

"Oh! Futt you, Howie."

"Futt you, Frant!"

Right off the bat. It was like no time had passed.

In December 1972, shortly before his fifty-seventh birthday, Frank was back in New York, and just as Uncle Frank had decided to introduce me to Jilly, Jilly wanted to introduce me to Sinatra. He knew I idolized the man, and he suggested it, in part, because he knew what it would mean to me. He also suggested it because, as I learned later, he thought Sinatra and I would get along well, be a "good fit." For a kid who'd been telling his friends for years that someday he'd be friends with Frank Sinatra, Sinatra's imminent arrival was like the second coming. Jilly said he'd try to set something up.

That same December, Frank Sinatra Jr. was booked for an extended run in Manhattan, four nights a week at the iconic Rainbow Room. With Frank Sr. retired, Frank Jr.'s singing career had started gaining major momentum. As the only male Sinatra out there singing, Frankie Jr. was carrying the Sinatra banner. The gig at the Rainbow

Room at 30 Rockefeller Center was a premier booking. It was a dream gig in a beautiful venue with a seventeen-piece orchestra. Junior was doing terrific business, in part because some folks in New York, including me, were hoping that Frank Sr. might show up some night to see his son. With Sinatra out of the business, any sighting of the man was an event.

Somewhere around December 6, Jilly called me and said, "Listen, Tony. Don't talk it up, but the ol' man's comin' in." Frank was coming to check out his son's show in the middle of its run — traditionally, a more relaxed time for a performer. Whatever kinks had existed in the first performances would be remedied by then, and the pressures associated with closing wouldn't have yet started. "We're gonna go to the late show Friday, the midnight show. What're you up to Friday?"

"I'm doing a gig in the city, but I'm done early 'cause it's a private function."

So Jilly said, "Well, if you can, try to make it over for the show. Either way, before the night's done, we'll end up over at my joint."

I was so excited at the prospect of actually meeting Sinatra that I was afraid to think about it, for fear I'd jinx it. One thing was sure: come hell or high water, I'd be at Jilly's

Friday night.

When December 8 rolled around, I headed into the city earlier than usual to set myself up for a seat at Frank Jr.'s show later that night. When I arrived at the Rainbow Room, I went up to the maître d' and introduced myself.

I said, "Listen, I'm doing a gig here in the city. I'm going to be done early. I'd like to have a seat wherever you can stick me to see Frank Jr.'s late show tonight. I'll be coming in just around the time that he's going on. Can you help me out?"

The maître d' said, "Fine, no sweat." So I gave the guy a twenty — a good tip at the time — to seal the deal.

As soon as I finished my gig that evening, I ducked out and rushed over to the Rainbow Room. As I stepped out of the elevator, I could hear the show starting. Frank Jr. was in the middle of his opening number, and as I approached the maître d', he motioned for me to follow him into the room. He wanted to seat me right away, but I whispered to him that it wasn't polite to walk in when a performer was in the middle of a song. I asked him to wait until the first number was over. The room was wall-to-wall people. As audiences in the Big Apple usually do, everyone in the place had dressed appropriately in sports jackets or suits and ties. Looking around the room, I was beginning to feel just a little conspicuous in my tuxedo with the red lining.

That was when I saw him, seated in the audience stage left, just outside the ring of artificial light. He was watching his son, obscured from the view of the audience in the soft darkness. Frank Sinatra. Unmistakable. I felt a surge of electricity go through my body. I was momentarily transfixed. When my mind cleared, all I wanted was to get seated quickly and quietly with no one noticing my late arrival.

A moment later, a captain appeared with a small cocktail table, complete with tablecloth. As Frankie Jr. finished his opening number, the captain said to me, "Right this way, sir."

He then proceeded to walk through the center of the audience straight toward the stage, carving a path through the press of people, carrying the table with its cloth over his head. A waiter followed with the table setting. I brought up the rear in my tuxedo. As the applause tapered out, heads turned toward us, and both the audience and Frank Jr. watched our little procession in bemused fascination as we inched our way across the room. The silence onstage seemed to stretch interminably. I kept waiting for the floor to open up and swallow me. No such luck.

The captain plunked my table down within feet of the stage. Pretending I was invisible, I sat down all by myself. I could see Jilly out of the corner of my eye, sitting near Sinatra Sr. and watching me. He was shaking his head like, *What the f\*\*\*?* The show had shifted from the stage to me.

As if it couldn't get any worse, a waiter then appeared and said, in a voice that seemed to echo, "May I take your drink order, sir?"

I whispered through slightly gritted teeth, "There's a show on! Jeez! Just bring me a Jack rocks . . . please!"

I felt certain everyone in the audience had heard what I'd be drinking that night. I was acutely aware that Frank Jr. was still standing silently onstage, staring at me as if to say, *May I continue now? Would that be okay with you?* I prayed that through some miracle, his father hadn't noticed me. Finally, after what felt like a week, Frankie Jr. started his second number, and the audience's attention switched back to the stage.

It was a great performance, though it didn't quite play to what a large portion of the audience was hoping to hear. Frankie was terrific, but they wanted to hear his father's songs. Finally, in the middle of his act, the orchestra began playing the intro to "All the Way." The audience burst into applause as soon as they heard the opening notes.

Frankie said, "This is what I lovingly call the Sinatra hour." The applause got even louder, and when it finally died down, he said, "You have no idea how happy I am that you responded like that to what we're about to do, because you're a lot closer to Frank Sinatra right now than you know."

Surprised, I glanced over to where Frank Sr. was sitting. He was glaring at his son. Those blue eyes seemed to give off a laser that could melt a lead wall. Frank Sr. did not want to be outed to that audience. Junior obviously caught the look.

Fortunately, he was quick on his feet and said, "No, you don't understand. This is Dad's tux. I borrowed it for this engagement." That got a good laugh and neutralized the excitement as quickly as it had appeared.

When the show was over, Frank Jr. received a well-deserved standing ovation. But once the lights came up and the audience had a chance to look around, the rumor started circulating that Frank Sr. was indeed in the room. Before anyone could get to him, Jilly grabbed Frank, and they quickly made their way out through the kitchen. In a routine that would become familiar to me, waiters instinctively ran interference, making it impossible for anyone to get over to where they were.

I yelled to Jilly as he hustled Frank out, and Jilly shouted back, "I'll see you over at the joint later."

I settled my tab, took the elevator down to the street, got in my car, and went over to Jilly's. Word must have gotten around quickly that Frank Sr. had been at the show. Jilly's open-air parking lot next to the club was overflowing, with Cadillacs and Lincoln Town Cars double-parked down the street. Sy had his hands full controlling the crowd as they surged toward the entrance, excitedly anticipating the "Chairman's" arrival. I threaded my way through the mass of fans to the glass door. As soon as Sy saw me, he opened the door and waved me in. I could see as I went through the second door that people were four deep at the bar. Men and women were crushed together, sporting their finest clothes and jewelry, with enough pinky rings to fill several showcases. Shortly after I entered, Uncle Frank spotted me and handed me a drink over the heads of the crowd. I kept walking, greeted the maître d', and went to sit at the piano bar. Once there, I tried to relax, but I couldn't settle. I sat there sipping Jack and waiting.

At about two thirty a.m. or so, I felt the place suddenly come alive with electric energy, and two words spread through the club like a chant: "He's here! He's here!"

Sure enough, walking down the steps with Jilly behind him, in the flesh, was Frank Sinatra. I remember the moment vividly. People turned toward him as though they were magnetized. Even those who didn't realize he was there felt the pull and looked to see what it was. For me, the moment was overwhelming.

Despite Jilly's best efforts, Frank was getting mobbed. He fought his way past the bar and into the room on his way to his booth, which was just behind me. I was sitting at the tail of the piano as he walked past me.

Somewhat to my own surprise, I heard myself saying in Italian: *"Madonna, che gran baccano!"* loosely translated as, "Mother of God, what chaos!"

Frank heard me, turned, and said to me, "Can you believe that? You'd think they'd be able to keep people from doing that to me, for crying out loud. But hey, when they stop doing that, that's when it's all over."

Then he patted me on the shoulder, smiled, and went to his booth. God bless my grandmother for teaching me Italian.

As Jilly walked past me, he leaned over and said, "We'll talk later." Then he joined Frank in his booth.

I glanced over at Frank, trying to be unobtrusive. The man was impeccable. He was wearing a dark blue suit with subtle light blue pinstripes, a pristine white shirt, and a perfectly knotted silver tie with a soft blue diamond pattern. His eyes were a startling azure no head shot could do justice to, his hair showing a few silver strands. Sitting in his usual booth, laughing and relaxed, he gave off a charisma that was like a force field.

I continued sitting at the piano bar, sipping my drink and trying not to stare. Frank's favorite waiter, John Bianculli, was serving the group. John's nickname was Johnny Smash. Johnny and I had developed a pretty tight relationship by then, so I called him over.

I said, "Listen, do me a favor. I don't know if the opportunity is going to present itself for me to meet Frank formally, and God knows when I might be in his company again. I hate to be a civilian, but could you see if you can get Frank's autograph for me?"

Johnny said, "Sure, sure."

Johnny knew without my telling him that it would be rude to interrupt Frank's dinner. When Frank's group finally finished eating, Johnny walked over to Frank and started talking. As he listened, Frank leaned forward and peeked around Johnny at me. Johnny was nodding his head. In my mind, the conversation was probably going something like this:

*"Well, who's this for?"*

*"The kid sitting at the piano bar."*

*"The kid in the tuxedo?"*

*"Yeah."*

*"Okay."*

I could only pray Frank hadn't asked, *"The kid who interrupted my son's show?"*

Then Johnny handed Frank one of Jilly's promotional mailers with a printed menu on it, and Frank proceeded to sign it. Johnny read it as he came walking back over to me, shaking his head with a bemused look on his face.

I asked Johnny, "What's the matter?"

"This guy's been coming in here twenty years. I've asked him for hundreds of autographs. I've never seen him sign his name like this."

He handed it to me, and I read, *Hi, Tony. Best, Frank Sinatra, Sr.* Johnny pointed at the *Sr.* after his name.

I knew immediately it was Frank's way of teasing me, of letting me know, *I saw you over at the Rainbow Room making your "low-key" entrance to my son's show!* It was, as I later learned, classic Frank.

By then it was past three thirty in the morning, and Jilly issued last call. Everybody was "invited" to leave except for a select group.

As the club closed, Jilly got up from Frank's booth and came over to me. He leaned in, putting his hand on my shoulder, and said, "So, you got your ax [guitar] in the car?"

"Yeah, why?"

"Well, he" — he nodded his head in the direction of Sinatra — "feels like hanging out, and I'd like him to hear you play." My mind started racing. All I could think was, *Damn, I've been sitting here drinking Jack Daniel's for the last two hours. If only I'd had a clue. I'm going to embarrass myself. Here's my big moment, and I'm going to blow it.*

I went out to my car and got my guitar and amp out of the trunk. I brought them back into the club as they were settling tabs, chasing people out wholesale, and clearing the room. By twenty minutes after four, the doors were locked, and the only people left were Uncle Frank behind the bar; Johnny Smash; me; Joe Petrone on piano; Lou Berriman, the great bass player; Jilly; Frank; and a young lady to whom I was never introduced. It was just the three of us playing: Joe, Lou, and me — piano, bass, and guitar.

I started making sure my guitar was tuned up. Like I often did in clubs, I went downstairs and lifted the telephone, tuning the guitar to the dial tone. Then I came back up and sat down on the street side of the piano, facing Frank's booth, and plugged into my amp. Joe Petrone was just finishing a tune when I sat down. Frank, Jilly, and Frank's lady companion got out of their booth and moved up to the piano.

I tried my best to put my anxiety out of my head and concentrate on going into work mode. Joe, a consummate professional, picked a tune, called a key, counted it off, and we went. We moved seamlessly from one number to the next, picking up on each other as experienced musicians — especially jazz musicians — know how to do. It was going really well. Joe and I, having played together before and each knowing how the other thought musically, instinctively knew how to stay out of each other's way. Tune after tune, the first half hour whizzed happily by. Then, just as I was relaxed and basking in the glow of the music, the unimaginable happened.

Joe turned to me and said, "Hey, Tony, why don't you play something by yourself?"

For a moment, my mind went utterly blank from sheer terror. Fortunately, I had a lifetime of music and hundreds of Sinatra songs stored away in my head, and something came to me out of the blue. I remembered an album Frank had recorded with composer/guitarist Antonio Carlos Jobim, a record I'd worn out from playing it so many times. There was one song, entitled "How Insensitive," that I knew was a particular favorite of Frank's. My fingers instinctively found the strings, and I started to play it in Frank's key, chords and melody together.

As my fingers moved over the frets, I began to hear a soft hum. It took me a moment to realize where it was coming from.

When it hit me, I almost dropped the guitar. It was coming from Frank.

I thought to myself, *Is anything* else *going to happen to me tonight?*

Here, just a few feet away from me, was that rich baritone, coming across the piano in unison with my playing. I looked up at

Frank. He had his eyes closed. He was leaning back, completely in the moment, humming the beautiful melody. Watching him, I felt myself relax with him, both of us at one with the music. I laid back as he took the melody and accompanied his voice with chords. I paused when he paused, and when I played the closing few bars, he held on to the last note, and we ended together perfectly, as though we had rehearsed it.

When the final chord faded out, he opened his eyes and looked over at me with a smile that could light up a room. Then he said, "That was very, very nice, kid."

At a loss for words, I said, "Well, thank you, Mr. Sinatra. I'm no Al Viola [Frank's longtime guitarist], but I try."

Frank turned to Jilly and started to laugh. "Al Viola? How the hell does this kid know Al Viola?" I was the wrong generation. The Ventures, yes. Al Viola, no.

Jilly responded by making a formal introduction. "Frank, this is my friend Tony Oppedisano. Tony O. Tony, Frank Sinatra." He told Frank a little bit about me, and before I knew it, we were all chatting and laughing like we'd known each other for years.

Frank began teasing me about the tuxedo, so I said, "Well, you know, I'm really very

60

Italian. When people pay me a compliment, especially a great one like you just did, my immediate reaction is, 'Is the guy trying to give me *malocchio*?' I know how to deal with that." I opened my tux jacket to reveal the fire-engine-red lining.

Frank started roaring and said, "How *old* is this kid?"

It was the first of countless nights I would spend talking with Frank Sinatra. That first night, we played music, drank, and hung out until about six thirty, a respectable hour to call it a night, even for Frank. Usually, I'd realize I'd stayed out too late when I heard the garbage trucks beginning their rounds, and that morning, I heard them working right outside. It was like a signal to all of us. I packed up my guitar and amp, and we all made our way out to the curb together. It was daylight by then, and Frank's limo was just pulling up. He was heading back to the Waldorf Towers.

Before I walked to my car, I said to him, "Mr. Sinatra, I'm not certain when I'll have the good fortune to see you again, so I want to take the opportunity to wish you a very happy birthday. I know that today" — I looked at my watch and corrected myself — "rather, yesterday, was Sammy Davis's birthday, and yours is coming up on the

61

twelfth. So I want to wish you a happy birthday, Mr. Sinatra."

Frank looked at Joe Petrone and said, laughing again, "Who *is* this kid?"

He reached out to shake my hand and said, "Let me tell you something. You're a really talented guy. This business can be cruel. It can knock you down. It can kick your teeth in, but when it's good, there's nothing like it. So if you have the passion for it, hang in there. It will be good to you."

Then he got into his limousine. It pulled away from the curb, and he disappeared from my view.

Very few people recognize the turning points in their lives until much later, if at all. I'm one of the exceptions. At four a.m. on December 9, 1972, in a club on Fifty-Second Street in New York, a page in my life story turned, and a new chapter began. As I walked back to my car that morning, barely feeling the pavement, I knew that my life would never be the same.

# CHAPTER 2
## AND ONE MORE
### FOR THE ROAD
#### CRISIS AND CROSSROADS

When Frank Sinatra made his way from backstage to the center of Madison Square Garden that October evening in 1974, he wasn't walking alone. Holding Frank's arm was a tall man with an unfocused eye and a face that radiated *Don't even think about it.* When they reached the raised stage, they walked up the steps together. As Frank took the stage to a roar of applause, the taller man stood at the top of the steps for a moment, watchful, silhouetted against the light spilling from the stage. At the end of the concert, the same silhouette would appear again, in the same place. He would take Frank's arm and make sure he made it safely back down the steps and through the audience. I smiled at the sight of the familiar figure, knowing Jilly would make certain that no one harmed Frank. Some people thought Jilly was part of Frank's security team. He wasn't. Jilly was never Frank's bodyguard. He was Frank's protector. They both knew that if he ever had to, Jilly would give his life for Frank without a second thought.

If you want to understand Jilly Rizzo's importance in Frank Sinatra's life, look at the Sinatra family burial plot. You'll find Frank; his parents, Dolly and Martin Sinatra; his "Uncle" Vincent Mazolla; his last wife, Barbara Sinatra; and Jilly Rizzo. Frank's family. From the day Jilly was laid to rest there, following his brutal and untimely death, Frank's life changed forever. As Frank's daughter Tina described it, Frank never recovered from the wound of losing Jilly. He never picked up another paintbrush. He never returned to the hobbies he'd pursued all his life. As much as Frank loved Sammy and Dean, Jilly Rizzo occupied a unique position in Frank's life. Jilly was a complex man who has been stereotyped and misjudged by virtually every Sinatra biographer. He never made it past elementary school, and he was sometimes embarrassed by his lack of education, but he was a shrewd businessman who'd pulled himself up from poverty to become a New York icon. To Frank, Jilly was the brother he'd longed for as an only child. To me, he was a mentor, pal, and one-man battalion of strength and unconditional friendship. If Jilly hadn't welcomed me into his huge Italian heart, there might never have been a Tony O. If it weren't for Jilly Rizzo, Frank Sinatra might have had to pull himself up from the depths alone.

When Jilly first met Sinatra, Frank was at an all-time low professionally. It was somewhere in the early fifties, when Frank couldn't get arrested. One night at the Copacabana, Frank noticed everyone making a fuss over a tall, jovial man, and after he left, Frank asked one of the captains, "Who was that guy? Why is everyone falling all over him?"

"Oh, his name is Jilly Rizzo. He's got a great club in Manhattan. It's a popular spot, great music."

A couple of months later, Frank was working in Florida at the Fontainebleau when who should show up again but Jilly. Once they were introduced, they became instant pals. Frank nicknamed him "CBS" after the network's logo because Jilly had only one working eye. There was no benefit to being Frank's friend when they first knew each other. Frank had bottomed out personally and professionally. His contracts had been canceled, his throat had hemorrhaged, and his fair-weather friends had vanished like shadows. Frank trusted Jilly for the rest of his life because Jilly was his friend when most "friends" had walked away.

As popular as Jilly and his club were for decades, there was one segment of society that didn't exactly welcome him early on. His blue-collar persona didn't endear him to some of New York's "elite" upper crust. They looked at Jilly with disdain, considering themselves superior to this guy who'd come up from the New York streets. As far as they were concerned, Jilly was beneath them, uneducated and uncouth. Frank knew it, and it infuriated him.

At the time, Frank was working his way up from his career slump and had to spend a lot of time networking. He didn't enjoy it, but it was a necessary evil. When he got an invitation to an Upper East Side party that was important to him professionally, he found himself forced into a corner. The host subtly made it clear that Jilly would not be welcome at the party. Frank thought, *You motherf\*\*\*\*\**, but he couldn't say so. He felt like he was being forced to choose between his career and his friend, and he was furious. His Sicilian loyalty made it impossible for him to turn his back on the friend he loved, but he needed the professional contacts he could make that evening. Fortunately, the host didn't realize who he was dealing with. Frank always thought outside the box and had years of experience with elaborate pranks. He accepted the party invitation on the host's terms and put the wheels of his plan in motion.

Frank knew two New York cops who spent a lot of time at Jilly's club and would do anything for Jilly. When Frank and Jilly explained their plan, the cops were only too happy to help. On the evening of the party, the doorman was sent on a diversionary errand about an hour into the festivities. As soon as he was gone, the two off-duty cops, dressed in dark clothing and wearing masks, knocked on the door. When the butler opened the door, the cops burst into the room with their guns drawn, shouting at everyone to get down on the floor. The terrified guests complied and stayed down while the two "robbers" relieved them of their valuables, collecting everything in two bags. Then the "robbers" made a quick exit.

Afterward, the host was beside himself, angry, embarrassed, and scared. He knew he could call the police, but he also knew that even if the police recovered their valuables, it would take weeks. He pulled Frank aside and said, "I have no idea how to handle this."

Frank said, "Well, I have connections on both sides of the law. If you want, I could make a couple of calls for you." The host agreed it was worth a try.

About an hour later, there was another knock on the door. When the butler opened the door this time, in walked Jilly with a big smile on his face, carrying two bags filled with everyone's valuables. He was welcomed with a rousing ovation, and the host proclaimed Jilly the hero of the hour. Nobody was ever the wiser, and from then on, Jilly was fast friends with the host and welcome at every party. Frank and Jilly had a lot of laughs about the whole scheme.

Jilly could always make Frank laugh, sometimes on purpose, other times without meaning to. Jilly's malaprops were legendary.

The funniest example of Jilly's tendency to misspeak was when he was in Italy with Frank, shooting *Von Ryan's Express*. Frank gave the first unit a couple of days off to relax and enjoy being in Italy, but Jilly was never very good at relaxing.

One afternoon, Jilly was sitting with Frank when Frank said, "So what do you think? Isn't it pretty over here?"

Jilly said, "Oh, yeah. It's beautiful. As a matter of fact, the agriculture that they got here in this country . . . . we don't have agriculture like that in the US."

"The what?"

"Agriculture. You know, like that place you took me where the gladiators used to fight."

"You mean the Colosseum?"

"Yeah. They don't got agriculture like that at home."

Frank chuckled and didn't say anything.

After a few minutes, Jilly said, "So what are we going to do? Are we going to sit around here all day or what?"

"Well, what do you want to do?"

"You told me you was going to take me where they got all those churches."

"Churches?"

"The fifteen churches."

Frank had to think a moment and then said, "You mean the Sistine Chapel?"

"Well, fifteen, sixteen . . . who's counting? We going or what?"

Who could keep a straight face hearing that?

Sometimes we *couldn't,* and Jilly would look like a hurt child and mumble, "Well, you know what I meant."

Frank and Jilly shared the same adolescent sense of humor. One of Frank's favorite memories was the great pie fight at Jilly's club. Unfortunately, that was before my time. Jilly always had the desserts delivered to the club, and one night, he and Frank decided to "hijack" the delivery truck. When the driver pulled up to drop off the club's desserts, Jilly said he'd "take it all" and paid the guy for all the pies he had. Then he took every single pie out of the truck, and he and Frank and the rest of the guys had a giant pie fight in the middle of the Manhattan street. The next morning, when people were on their way to work, there was so much pie residue on the pavement that it was a traffic hazard. Drivers would turn onto Fifty-Second Street and skid past the Roseland Ballroom across the street on cream filling. It was every schoolboy's fantasy.

Jilly loved pranks as much as Frank did. One night at the club, Frank said he wanted to go downstairs to the restroom. Jilly followed him, and once Frank started walking down the steps, Jilly motioned to me to come along. I had no idea why, but I followed them down the stairs anyway. Jilly went into the bathroom first, to make sure no one else was there.

He told Frank, "The coast is clear."

Frank went in and was standing in the corner at the urinal when a guy came past me and stopped in the doorway. I recognized him right away: a comedian by the name of Bernie Allen. He was dressed as a Gestapo officer, complete with a helmet.

Bernie goose-stepped into the bathroom while Frank was still standing there, blew a whistle, and shouted, "There's no pissing here!"

I'll spare you the details of what came next. Let's just say that three out of four of us were laughing our heads off.

Frank wanted Jilly around all the time, so Jilly started traveling with him on tour. Eventually, Frank put Jilly on the payroll. He would often give Jilly from 2 to 5 percent of the gate. By the time Uncle Frank introduced me to Jilly in 1972, Jilly was Frank's right-hand man.

By the mid-seventies, three years after I met Frank, the club scene in New York had begun to change. It was clear that the clubs were on a downhill path. Musical taste was changing, and the music industry was moving west. With the club scene fading, Jilly sold the New York club and spent all his time on tour with Frank. I still saw Frank and Jilly regularly, but they were spending more and more of their time in either Los Angeles, Las Vegas, or Palm Springs. I didn't know yet whether I'd be able to make it big in the business, but I wanted to give it a real shot. Los Angeles seemed like my best bet. It meant leaving my family and girlfriend behind, but if I didn't pursue my dream, I knew I'd regret it forever.

In February of 1976, I moved to California with two of my buddies, musicians Frank Goldstein and Dominic Famularo, with whom I'd formed a nice little trio. We were young and stupid and fearless. We believed in our success. It never once crossed our minds that it might not happen for us.

Our trio had signed with a new hotel for a six-nighter, so we had Monday nights off. When Frank was playing Vegas, we'd drive up and catch his act at Caesars when he was there. The Vegas trips soon fell into a regular pattern. I'd meet Jilly at a coffee shop at Caesars, and we'd catch up a little. When he had to leave to get ready for the first show, I'd follow with whoever was with me that trip, usually Dom and Frank G. Jilly always made sure we had seats near the stage, at one of Frank's tables. Jilly would usually be in the wings until Frank walked onstage, then join us once the show started. He'd join Frank backstage between shows for a quick bite and a drink — never too much, because Frank didn't want to become lethargic. After the second show, Frank and Jilly would go to dinner while my friends and I had dinner on our own. Afterward, we'd usually all meet up at a lounge in Caesars and hang out with Frank until the early morning, when we'd drive like maniacs back to Southern California.

I soon became familiar with the rhythm of Frank's performances. Frank was a master showman who was always intimately involved with planning every aspect of a performance. His shows were carefully choreographed to take the audience on an emotional journey. There was a pattern to what he unveiled. The minute he walked onstage with that incredible magnetism, the audiences would go crazy. He'd always kick things off with a couple of upbeat numbers like "Come Fly with Me" or "I've Got the World on a String," followed by something that swung, like "The Lady Is a Tramp." The middle of the show was always romantic ballads like "Strangers in the Night" or "Moonlight in Vermont." Those would lead into the saloon songs, torch songs of sorrow and regret. "Angel Eyes" was the song he chose most often. Having led the audience to an intense emotional moment, he nearly always finished upbeat with "My Way," which invariably got a huge ovation. And he chose for his encore a rousing rendition of "New York, New York" that could be counted on to bring the audience to its feet. Delighted fans would leave their seats at the end still bubbling over with joy and excitement.

The best parts of the shows, however, were sometimes unplanned. If Frank was in the mood, he loved to throw in fractured parody lyrics for his standards, catching his audience off guard. Instead of singing, "This is my first affair . . . handle my heart with care . . . ," he'd sing, "This is my first affair . . . So show me where . . ." Rather than a love song, he might sing an "anti-love song": "You're nobody 'til somebody loves you. / You're nobody and *nobody* cares . . ." Or the hilarious, "You are too beautiful / For one man alone, / So I got a group together . . ." Sometimes what started out in a performance ended up on a studio album, frequently personalized for Jilly. A duet with Sammy Davis on "Me and My Shadow" turned into "We'll wind up at Jilly's / Right after Toots Shor." In Frank's studio recording of "Star," he sings, "If they've got a drink with her name in Jilly's bar, / The chances are, the lady's a star."

One of my favorite memories is the night Frank dragged his lead guitarist, Al Viola, into the confusion. Frank and Al had both had a little too much Jack Daniel's and very little pizza in between shows. When they went on for the second show, they were feeling no pain.

Usually, when singing "Try a Little Tenderness," Frank sang the original lyrics, advising men to treat their women tenderly when they got tired of wearing the same worn-out dress. That night, however, Frank sang, "So when she's weary, / Buy her *another* shabby dress."

Everyone started laughing. So far, fine, but when Frank went on, he couldn't remember what the next lyric was because everyone was laughing, including him.

So he turned to Al, who was sitting on a stool next to Frank, accompanying him, and said, "What the hell is the next line?"

Al looked up at him, every bit as drunk as Frank was, and said to him, in Italian, *"Il salsicce sono bruciate,"* which means, "The sausages are burnt." Frank knew exactly what Al had said, but he also knew that what Al meant was, "I'm as drunk as you are. I don't know what the next line is."

Frank couldn't stop laughing. He turned to the audience, figuring they didn't understand what Al had said anyway, and pointed at Al. "Oh, what he said, I can't even translate that. They'll shut this place down." That got an even bigger laugh. The joke was even funnier if you actually spoke Italian!

I was surprised that my relationship with Frank went so quickly from, "Hi, Frank, remember me? My name is Tony Oppedisano," to Frank's greeting me, "Hey, *compare mio* [my dear friend], how are you?" I'd come to Frank through Jilly, and that meant there was instant trust. I'd been vetted by an unimpeachable source.

During this time, the trio I'd formed with Frank Goldstein and Dominic Famularo had been getting good reactions from audiences, but it was a fluid time in musical taste. In the course of a decade, music went from disco to grunge to heavy metal. The industry slammed the door shut on the American songbook we played. Turned out, it was New York all over again — only this time it was our music, not the clubs, that was disappearing. Dom and Frank went back to New York, and that was the end of our trio. I adjusted my trajectory and formed a Top 40 show band. I got very decent reviews as a vocalist and started to attract a following. For the next five years, I persevered. I traveled constantly, rotating among the venues in Las Vegas and Lake Tahoe where I was under contract, living in hotel rooms that were complimentary for performers. I eventually let my apartment go and stored my stuff at my uncle's house in Anaheim. I had plenty of friends and some short-lived dalliances but no real relationships. I was never around long enough. Frank and Jilly were two of my few constants. I was struggling, but I wasn't quite ready to give up yet.

In the early eighties, I decided to make one last effort and try my hand at recording. I picked a powerful group of tunes and hired a full orchestra. A lot of Frank's musicians were in it, guys like Bill Miller and Al Viola, whom I'd gotten to know over the years. I hoped the record would break me out from the crowd. I tried shopping the demo around with the idea of winning a recording deal, but I didn't get anywhere. I began to feel that I was deluding myself by thinking I still had a shot at the big time. I didn't want to become that fortysomething guy who's losing his hair and playing the tambourine in a lounge. I finally reached my breaking point and made the difficult decision to end my performing career. I knew I could go to Frank for career help, but I wasn't going to do that. Frank was my friend. I refused to take advantage of the friendship by becoming another hanger-on, looking for favors.

Many years later, I finally worked up the

nerve to play my album for Frank. He got a big kick out of hearing it and said, "Jesus Christ, you swing your ass off!" The album hadn't done me much good professionally, but it was almost worth it to hear Frank say that.

Giving up my childhood dream of performing for a living was one of the hardest things I've ever done, but it was the right decision. I was the wrong singer for that time and place. There was no longer a market for the kind of music I was doing. The performance years weren't wasted, however, because along the way, I'd learned a great deal about producing. After a few years of working with other partners, Jilly and I began working together. We represented some good talent and produced several projects. I also started helping Jilly with some of Frank's business. Jilly often didn't have time to return phone calls because his work for Frank kept him too busy. I tried to take some of the weight off his shoulders.

I had a condo in the San Fernando Valley, and Jilly had a house a couple of blocks from Frank's in Palm Springs. Jilly and I were staying at each other's homes a great deal by that point because it was convenient for both of us. If we finished our business in

LA, we'd spend time at my condo. If we finished the workday in the desert, we'd go to Jilly's house in Palm Springs. I was spending more and more time in the desert, usually at Jilly's and sometimes at Frank's place. If Jilly was busy, Frank might ask me to do something with him. Frank loved company, and we got along. Sometimes I'd go visit for an evening and end up spending three weeks. When I'd start to leave, Frank would say, "Hey, where are you going?"

Often when I was at home in LA and Jilly was in the desert, I'd get a call from Jilly after he left Frank's house at midnight.

I'd answer, "Hello."

He'd say, "What are you doing? I just came from around the corner [meaning Frank's house]. That tomato can [Frank's wife Barbara] is driving me crazy."

"You want me to come down and pick you up?"

"Would ya?" And I would.

Sometimes Jilly would call me and say, "You got to come down. Frank's got a house full of people coming tonight. He wants me there, and I'm not going to go by myself." Jilly liked having me around in case he needed a buffer or an excuse to get out of there. If I didn't have something going on, I'd drive out to Jilly's place in the desert.

If Frank said it was urgent, we'd leave Jilly's, cut across the golf course behind Frank's house, and hop the fence. If Frank wanted to go to a cocktail lounge down the block, we'd take the car. Frank didn't like going anywhere by himself.

Frank loved to host boys' nights, and whenever I was in the desert, I'd go. Sometimes Frank and I cooked together. Frank would announce, "Tony will be the chef of the night." The running joke was that Frank and I were both graduates of the Julia Child School of Cooking. He used to imitate her and say that the secret to cooking with wine was to pour three cups into the chef before you started. Little by little, Frank would end up doing more drinking and joking. I'd end up doing all the cooking. I didn't mind. It gave me an excuse to make the Italian dishes Frank and I both loved.

I was by far the youngest in the group of Frank's friends. Even when I started losing my hair, I remained "the kid" because not only Frank but most of his friends were two or three decades older than I was. It never bothered me because I'd always felt comfortable with older people. But my junior status did mean I came in for a lot of advice.

On one boys' night, this time at Frank's beach house, I was surrounded by the usual suspects. Frank's neighbor Dick Martin (of *Rowan & Martin's Laugh-In* fame) was there that night. Between hands of cards, Dick looked at me and said, "Well, Tony, I want to impart some wisdom your way. When you get up into your seventies or thereabouts, there are rules that you have to live your life by. Someday you're going to be our age, and you're going to remember I told you this. I want you to pay attention."

I said, "Okay, I'm paying attention."

"Rule number one: Never miss an opportunity to take a great piss. Rule number two: Never, ever waste an erection. And rule number three, last but not least, the most important one: Never, ever, under any circumstances, trust a fart."

Frank fell over laughing. Dick's advice makes more sense with every decade that passes. Rules to live by.

Frank had a lot of great friends, but Jilly remained the closest. Jilly logged thousands of hours and air miles with Frank over the forty-plus years they were together. That's a lot of time. Sometimes it was *too* much time. Because they were both Italian and had tempers, Frank and Jilly had some heated arguments. A lot of times with Frank, I could see the anger coming, like a storm on Lake Tahoe that you knew was going to be a doozy. It would come in full blast and then leave as quickly as it had arrived.

The arguments usually ended something like this:

Frank to Jilly, "Apologize for calling me an asshole."

Jilly to Frank, "Okay, I'm sorry you're an asshole." And then they'd both laugh, and that would be the end of it until the next one.

Sometimes, though, Frank would hit a real sore spot. One misunderstanding occurred when Jilly got involved with four partners in the eighties and took out a loan to develop a resort property in the Poconos. Unbeknownst to Jilly, his partners spent the money on personal luxuries like yachts instead of on property development. When the bank failed, the situation went south quickly. Once the FDIC guys started investigating, they hit gold. The Sinatra connection came up. The feds assumed there must be some kind of Mob connection and salivated at the chance to "catch" Frank and Jilly in the act.

Jilly and the four other investors were all indicted, and Jilly had to spend a lot of time in New York while the legal process played out. Frank really felt his absence. With him gone, Frank started leaning on me more. He'd say, "Hey, T, what are you doing next week? I'd consider it a favor if you could come to Vegas with me."

If I didn't have other commitments, I'd say, "Sure, Frank," and come along in an unofficial capacity, primarily as Frank's friend. I had no real responsibilities on the trips, and I enjoyed them.

Unfortunately, Frank kept needling Jilly about Jilly's legal problem. Frank wasn't always good at discerning the line between good-natured teasing and hurting somebody's feelings. Jilly already felt like he'd been made a fool of by the other investors, and he was extremely sensitive on the subject. His tough-guy exterior notwithstanding, Jilly still had a little kid inside, and Frank sometimes stepped on his feelings. That's what occurred at Thanksgiving during this period of legal troubles. Frank had invited Jilly and me over to the house. Frank loved to have a house full of people for major holidays. That year there were the Pecks (Gregory and Veronique); R. J. Wagner and Jill St. John; Louis Jourdan and his wife, Quique; and Sidney Poitier and Joanna. Jilly and I arrived at the house in the afternoon. Frank didn't like to eat until late, so everyone was hanging out, playing tennis or doing their own thing.

Frank was sitting in the den with Greg and R. J. when Jilly and I came into the room. Greg asked Jilly how the preliminary hearing had gone.

Jilly had just started to answer when Frank said, "Well, it's your own fault. You didn't listen to me. I told you what you should have done. You should have just gone before the judge and pleaded stupidity."

Greg and R. J. started to laugh — until they saw that Jilly was turning red. I could see what was coming, so I looked at Jilly and said, "Jilly, come on, let's go for a walk."

He said "*Walk?* I'm getting the hell out of here!"

He stalked off with me following a few feet behind. As he angrily passed the bar, a photograph of him and Frank on the wall above it caught his attention. He took two steps back and punched it with his left hand. It shattered, and glass fell all over the floor. I trailed him through the house and then halfway out the door. Suddenly Jilly stopped, turned on a dime, and went back inside to the kitchen.

I was starting to get worried, so I asked him, "What are you doing?"

"What am I doing?" And then he said to Roland, Frank's cook, "Where are the mitts?

Give me them. Give me the oven mitts!"

Jilly took the mitts and headed for the oven. Because there were so many people there for dinner, Roland was cooking two turkeys. Jilly took both turkeys out of the oven, carried them out to the parking area, and put them in the backseat of his Cadillac.

As he got in the car, he said to me, "Tell Frank, if he wants his friends to eat, he can come around the corner and apologize to me." Then he roared out of the driveway with the aroma of roast turkey wafting from the backseat.

I went back inside and gestured to Frank to meet me outside by the pool. Once he got there, I said, "Look, Frank, Jilly's feelings are hurt. What you said embarrassed him. You need to go apologize, okay?"

Frank got my point. He told his guests, "Tony and I are going to check on dinner."

I drove Frank over to Jilly's house, and when we got there and walked in, we could see Jilly out back by the pool. Frank walked from the front door straight through the dining room and out the sliding glass door to the patio. I left them alone. I don't know what was said, but within minutes, they were both laughing. We left with the turkeys a little while later, and the three of us went back to Frank's house to celebrate Thanksgiving.

After a messy trial, it eventually became clear that Jilly had been a dupe, not a criminal. Three of the four others indicted with Jilly were given heavy fines and jail time. Jilly got a lower fine and a thousand hours of community service.

It's a miracle Jilly kept his temper with people as well as he did. Being in Frank's world wasn't always a picnic. In later years, I came to understand what it was like to live full-time in that vacuum called Frank Sinatra. He had a force that sucked in everyone and everything around him. Every time Jilly walked through a casino where Frank was playing, the loudspeaker would page him constantly. "Jilly Rizzo! Jilly Rizzo!" Jilly, Jilly, Jilly! Everybody wanted to get close to Frank, and they figured Jilly was their ticket. Frank used to get a kick out of watching people maneuvering for a position with him. He'd say, "Look at this! They're all jockeying to get close to what?"

Frank's relationship with Jilly had been solid for decades, but slowly and steadily, his wife, Barbara, started to change things. She was threatened by how close Frank and Jilly were. From the time of their marriage, one of the things that bothered her was Frank's assortment of misfit friends. Jilly was the worst in her eyes because his manners and way of speaking weren't sophisticated. Little by little, Barbara eroded the relationship between Frank and Jilly. Barbara got on Frank's back enough that it became an open sore, and she just kept pouring salt in it until Frank couldn't take it anymore. Finally, Barbara convinced Frank that he and Jilly should "take a break." It was supposed to be temporary, but Barbara hoped Jilly would never come back.

Frank didn't have the heart or the nerve to do it himself, so he called Mickey Rudin. Mickey was Frank's attorney, business partner, and to some extent, manager. When something unpleasant needed to be done, Mickey was only too happy to oblige. He took pleasure in being hurtful.

Mickey called Jilly and said, "Listen, this is not working out right now between you and Frank, and Frank thinks it would be wise for you two to take a breather."

At that point, Frank and Jilly had known each other for thirty-three years. This was like a divorce. Jilly was stunned and deeply hurt. He couldn't believe what he was hearing.

Ultimately, the numbness turned into anger.

Frank tried to play down what had happened, calling it a "spat." He used that word whenever he talked to me about it, but I wouldn't let him minimize the pain he'd caused Jilly. I told him it wasn't just a spat. Frank had deeply wounded Jilly. Once the reality of Jilly's absence began to set in for Frank, he painfully regretted his actions. Frank would be very emotional on the phone sometimes, trying to get Jilly to come back. Jilly wasn't having it. Who could blame him? Besides, Jilly wasn't sure he wanted to go back. He was suffering from the changes that had occurred since his club in New York had folded fifteen years earlier. He was living two blocks away from Frank, at Frank's constant beck and call. His time was no longer his own. Eighty percent of Jilly's time for three decades had been spent with Frank. Once he'd been "Jilly, owner of the coolest club on Fifty-Second Street." Now he was known as "Frank's guy." Jilly wanted his life back. In some ways, the separation from Frank was a relief for Jilly.

I stayed in touch with Frank, but my loyalty was to Jilly, and Frank knew and respected that. I knew that Frank wanted me around more, but I wasn't about to replace Jilly. I occasionally went with Frank on trips, but that was it. Frank and I would run into each other from time to time in Los Angeles, especially at Matteo's restaurant in LA. Every time, Frank would come over to my table or invite me to his for a cocktail.

He'd invariably ask me, "How's my buddy doing?"

I'd always say, "All right." But I wouldn't elaborate. Frank had enough class not to push it or say, "What's he up to?"

At dinner with Frank one night, I decided to mention that the next day, Jilly was going for an operation on his eye. A few days later, Frank asked me how Jilly was doing with the eye operation. I told him it had gone well, and he closed our conversation with something that would always prompt a predictable response from me.

"Thanks for taking such good care of my friend."

"No thanks necessary. He's my friend, too."

The rift lasted for almost two years. It was a strained situation. Jilly still lived just across the golf course from Frank, but he made a point of avoiding him. Despite appearances, I knew Frank cared a lot about Jilly and that he'd tried to make contact numerous times. Gradually, as time passed, Jilly began to soften. He and Frank both missed the stupid jokes, the energy, and the excitement. Mutual friends on both sides wanted to see them back together. Frank was trying to extend an apology to Jilly, but I knew that if Jilly rejected it, the breach could very well be permanent. When the time was right, I let them both know that if an approach was made, it would not be rebuffed.

Frank was on the Ultimate Event world tour with Sammy Davis and Liza Minnelli at the time. The next performance was scheduled at the Meadowlands Arena in New Jersey. I told Frank that I thought Jilly would be interested in going. Frank made the arrangements, and an invitation was issued and accepted. When Jilly arrived in New York, he headed straight for the Meadowlands and walked right into Frank's dressing room. As usual before a performance, Frank was having some Campbell's chicken noodle soup, watching television.

Jilly grabbed a bowl of soup, sat down next to him, and said, without preamble, "How you doing?"

Frank answered, "I'm fine. How you doing?" And that was it, like nothing had ever happened.

Barbara and Jilly seemed to make peace after that. Barbara had seen how painful Jilly's loss was to Frank and the extent to which Frank depended on him. Barbara and Jilly coexisted harmoniously for the most part. They'd never be close; they were too different. By the end, though, there was mutual respect and even affection between them.

To show his gratitude to Jilly for coming back, Frank had a surprise prepared. The trip included an entire tour of Italy. They'd be stopping in the region where Jilly's folks had come from, and this would be the first time Jilly had ever been there. Without Jilly's knowing, Frank had contacted Jilly's brothers and learned where their remaining relatives lived. It was in the province of Bari. Frank then sent all Jilly's relatives transportation so they could be at the airport when Frank's private jet touched down on the runway. When Jilly got off the plane, there were forty or fifty of his relatives waiting to greet him. Jilly was thrilled. It was a well-deserved welcome home for Ermenigildo Rizzo, a true son of Italy.

Three years later, on May 6, 1992, a big seventy-fifth-birthday celebration was planned for Jilly. I'd come out from my condo in LA to make the preparations. I'd be staying at Jilly's that week to help get ready and to clean up. The day before the party, Jilly and I were at his house cooking for the eighty-plus people coming the next day. To be more precise, I was cooking, and Jilly was helping. I made vats of red sauce, pasta, sausage, and marinated chicken. We'd had a lot of the food delivered to Frank's house because it wouldn't all fit in Jilly's refrigerator. That afternoon Jilly used one of Frank's staff station wagons to bring the food back to his place for me to prepare. Frank was just getting up and having his breakfast when Jilly picked up the food. They chatted briefly before Jilly headed back home. When Frank said goodbye, he didn't have the smallest premonition it would be the last time he'd see Jilly.

The party was going to be an old-fashioned backyard New York party. Jilly and I even strung a clothesline from the house to a palm tree in the backyard, where we were going to hang torn underwear as "decorations." Jilly was clearly excited. The two of us worked most of the day getting the food ready. Betty Jean, Jilly's girlfriend, came over for a while in the afternoon, but by dark, it was just me and Jilly.

Jilly said, "You know what? That sauce smells terrific."

"Well, good, 'cause we'll be having it."

"I don't want to wait till tomorrow. I want to taste it. Why don't we have some tonight?"

So we ate some sausage and some of the pasta with the red sauce on it. The radio station that we listened to in the desert, KWXY, went off the air at midnight, and its signing off triggered Jilly to leave. He had to get over to Betty Jean's house in the nearby Mission Hills complex. It was only three blocks away. I walked him out to the car. He was driving a Jaguar that a neighbor of Betty Jean's had offered to Jilly while the neighbor was out of town. The car had a Mission Hills resident's sticker on it, so Jilly could visit Betty Jean without having to stop at the guard gate every time.

Jilly gave me a hug and thanked me for everything I was doing. Since it was past midnight by then, I wished him a happy birthday. He climbed in the Jag, put on his seat belt, and pulled out of the driveway. I went back in the house and kept cooking until about two thirty. I finally shut everything down and went to bed about three, but I couldn't get to sleep.

At about four thirty, the phone rang on the private line. I thought, *It's either Jilly looking for me or Frank looking for Jilly.*

93

I picked up the phone and heard a male voice I didn't recognize say, "Is this the Jilly Rizzo residence?"

"Yeah, who's calling?"

"This is the Riverside Sheriff's Department. I'm investigating an accident."

"Okay." I thought, *Somebody stole the car and took it for a joyride and got into an accident.* It didn't occur to me that something might have happened to Jilly. Jilly was invincible, like a building. Besides, he'd only been going three blocks, and that was four hours ago.

The officer asked, "Do you know someone who was driving a white Jaguar earlier this evening?"

"Yeah, I know someone who was driving a white Jaguar. Why?"

"Well," he said, "there's been a terrible accident. Can you tell me what kind of jewelry your friend was wearing?"

"What kind of a question is that?"

"We're trying to identify the driver."

"He was wearing a gold watch with a black leather strap. He had his mother's plain wedding band on his pinky, and a heavy gold chain around his neck, with an eagle holding a diamond in each claw."

There was silence on the other end. I said to the officer a little impatiently, "It's

94

quarter to five in the morning. Are you still there?"

"Yeah," he said. "I think you'd better get dressed and come over." He gave me the intersection. It was only then that my wall of denial began to crumble, and I felt myself going numb.

I drove the three blocks to the intersection. What I saw, when I got there, was something I'll never forget in ten thousand years. A mangled, burned-out white Jaguar held what little was left of my best friend. I knew only one thing as people began arriving, and that was that nobody was going to get a photo of what I was looking at. The moment Jilly's identity got out, it would be plastered in every headline next to Frank's name. Jilly's children, his brothers, Frank — they could never see this.

Filled with shock-fueled adrenaline, I told the police, "Keep those guys away from here, because if they get one snapshot of this, there's going to be hell to pay. Do you have any idea who this man *was*?" They moved quickly to control the scene.

The officer in charge told me that Jilly had been hit by a 1991 Mercedes 300 sedan driven by a man named Jeff Perrotte, who was coming home after a night of drinking in a local bar. Perrotte had previously been involved in a DUI accident and had his driver's license revoked. He was currently under orders not to drink or drive. He'd run the intersection at eighty-five miles per hour, just as Jilly was about to pull up at the guard gate. Perrotte hit the saddlebag gas tank on the Jag's passenger side, bending the car's frame and sending the Jag spinning, with fuel spraying out of the damaged gas tank. When the Jag slammed into the curb, it ignited a spark that set the gas-spattered car on fire. The car door had jammed on impact, and Jilly had struggled to get out as the car began to burn. As the Jaguar burst into flames and Jilly screamed for help, Perrotte fled the scene. While the guard called 911, a passerby stopped and jumped out of his car with a fire extinguisher to try to help. By then, though, the car was fully engulfed, with Jilly trapped behind the torqued door. Jilly burned to death. I can't bear to imagine how much he must have suffered as he died. A few minutes later, Perrotte returned to the scene with his girlfriend, who told the cops *she'd* been driving the car.

The guard recognized the Jaguar and knew that Betty Jean was taking care of it while her neighbor was out of town. The police called her for information, which is how they got Jilly's private number and called me. I gave the officers the information they asked for and formally identified Jilly's remains from his jewelry before going straight to Betty Jean's house. She was distraught by then, and I did my best to comfort her after confirming her worst fears. Then I called Jilly's son Willie, nicknamed the Broom, and gave him the news. He knew the minute he heard my voice at that hour, before I had a chance to tell him. I could hear his convulsive sobs as the news of his father's death engulfed him. Willie completely disintegrated. I spared him as many details as I could, but there was no protecting him from the horror of what had just happened. He couldn't bear to tell his siblings, so I told him I'd do it. If he wanted, I'd take care of the funeral arrangements. The kids could tell me what they wanted, and I'd see that it was done. Willie was tearfully grateful.

Then, like an automaton, I went back to Jilly's house. I called the guard shack at Frank's compound at about seven o'clock.

I asked, "What time was it when any of you last saw Frank up and around?"

"Lights-out was about five thirty, maybe an hour and a half ago," the guard told me.

"Listen," I said, "do me a favor. *Listen*

*closely to me.* Shut off the phones going into the house, except for the kitchen line." I told him what had happened and said, "I'm going to take a shower and clear my head, and then I'm coming around the corner, and I'll deal with it when I get there." The guard soberly assured me he'd shut down the lines.

I showered and changed, then locked Jilly's house, took the key with me, and went around the corner to Frank's house. Roland the chef was up, preparing breakfast for Barbara, and Vine was with him. When he saw me, he asked, "What are you doing here?" I never came over that early.

When I told him, he fell apart. Vine began to sob and disappeared to her room, where she locked herself in. While they struggled to deal with their grief, I called Jilly's other two children, Joey and Abby, and broke the news as best I could. Then I called Frank's oldest daughter, Nancy Jr., in Los Angeles, to tell her what had happened. She told me she'd be there as quickly as possible. About three hours later, she pulled into the parking area. When I went out to meet her and saw that she was driving a Jaguar, it was like a punch in the gut.

Barbara, who always knew everybody's comings and goings, rang the kitchen at about eight thirty and, as surprised as Roland by my presence at that hour, said, "What's Tony doing here?"

I got on the phone and told her.

She cried out, "Oh, my God! I'll meet you in the den." She and Frank frequently slept in separate rooms because he never went to bed until dawn. I got a cup of coffee and sat in the den with her as she sobbed.

Finally, she said, "We have to tell Frank. *You* have to tell Frank. I can't do it."

I said, "He's only been asleep for three hours. God knows, after he hears what I have to tell him, when he's going to get another night's sleep. Let him sleep, and when he gets up, if I'm not still here, you call me, and I'll come back and tell him."

I made calls like crazy to everyone I could think of who needed to know. There were eighty people scheduled to come to Jilly's house for his birthday that day. Everyone had to be contacted and informed, including a doctor who was also a family friend. He took care of Frank and was also part of the clique that watched Monday Night Football at Frank's house. I wanted to hedge my bets because I didn't know how Frank would react when I told him that Jilly had been killed, much less how it had happened. I wanted the doctor there just as a precaution.

After an interminable wait, Frank finally got up in the middle of the afternoon. Barbara and I went to his bedroom. When I managed to tell Frank what had happened, he literally collapsed, dropping to his knees and sobbing uncontrollably.

When we got him back on his feet, he walked back and forth, saying over and over, "God, why? Why?" I didn't know if he was referring to Jilly's death or to the way he'd died.

Finally, I helped him back into bed and then sat with him for a couple of hours to make sure he was okay. Eventually, he stopped sobbing and just lay there, staring at the ceiling. I sat silently next to him, raw and mute.

Afterward, Barbara did one of the nicest things I'd ever seen her do. She told me, "You know, today is still Jilly's birthday, and I think we should celebrate it with the food that you guys have been cooking. Make a list of the closest of the close and call them, because I want them at this house tonight. I'll have Roland pick up the pieces of what you were doing, and we're going to eat some of the food you were making for Jilly's birthday dinner."

That night we gathered in Frank's dining

room for a very painful, very subdued dinner. It was a small gathering: me, Frank and Barbara, neighbors Danny and Natalie Schwartz, Nancy, Betty Jean, Frank's friends Harry Guardino and Jerry "the Crusher" Amanera, Jilly's cousin Pat Rizzo, and Jilly's son Willie, who'd driven down from Las Vegas. Nobody said much. Together, the twelve of us shared part of the meal Jilly and I had prepared less than twenty-four hours earlier. At one point, Barbara did what the rest of us couldn't do: she stood up, raised her glass, and asked us to join her in toasting Jilly and wishing him a happy birthday. The only things that got us through that dinner were each other and the knowledge that Jilly would have wanted it.

In many ways, Palm Springs is a small town, and everyone there knew Jilly Rizzo. Jilly was Frank's right hand, and Palm Springs was Frank's town. Besides, everyone who knew Frank knew Jilly. He was pictured with Frank in countless news articles, shown with Frank at every major event. He did cameos in Frank's films and showed up in Frank's lyrics. If you'd met Frank, you'd met Jilly. Jilly had friends among presidents, Hollywood royalty, and actual royalty in the persons of Princess Grace and Prince Rainier. Apart from his association with Frank, Jilly had also made a name for himself as a producer who'd discovered some of the industry's great music talents. Jilly's death made the papers nationwide, which is why I'd so fiercely protected the accident scene from photographers and onlookers. Jilly's funeral was a celebrity event.

The memorial service was a high mass held at St. Louis's church in nearby Cathedral City on Monday, May 11. Frank and Jilly went there occasionally. There is a small shrine to Frank's mother, Dolly Sinatra, in the church, where she regularly attended and supported church charities. The pallbearers were six close friends, Frank, and myself. The twelve honorary pallbearers consisted of ten friends, Jilly's cousin Pat, and Barbara's son, Bobby Marx. All of Jilly's brothers flew out from the East, and over 150 people attended. The list included everyone from neighbors and relatives to celebrities like Greg and Veronique Peck, Don and Barbara Rickles, Shirley MacLaine, Angie Dickinson, Keely Smith, Jerry Vale, Flip Wilson, Spiro Agnew, and, of course, Frank's daughters, Nancy and Tina. Jilly used to wonder aloud if he was a failure when he lost his club. I always reassured him that nobody thought that, but the truth became obvious at the end of Jilly's life. He wasn't just respected. He was beloved. It was a beautiful service. At the end, as Frank and I helped carry Jilly back down the aisle, we played Frank's "Put Your Dreams Away." It came on as we approached the exit so that Frank wouldn't have to hear the whole thing, which was torturous to him in that moment.

I rode in the hearse with Jilly to the cemetery because I desperately needed to be alone. I was beaten up emotionally from trauma and from postponing my own grief. The police escorted us as we drove past Jilly's house, in the traditional gesture, and then stayed with us all the way to the cemetery. It was a sign of their respect for Jilly. Some of the officers had been at the scene the night Jilly died, so they had their own feelings about his passing. Jilly was buried a few feet from Frank's parents, as befitted the man Frank considered his brother.

Only a very small number of us swung by the compound after the interment to have a cocktail and some light hors d'oeuvres. I didn't have anything but booze. We were only there an hour or so. At one point, Frank and I wandered out to the pool, where we could have a few minutes to ourselves.

Frank looked at me and said, "You know, you and I just lost the best friend we will probably ever know. I think it would be a good idea if we start spending a lot more time together because I'm going to need you, and you may need me. So I know you're doing a lot of things, but if you could see your way clear, I need you to be with me a lot more."

I was so overwhelmed with everything that was going on that his words hit me deeply on an emotional level. I was honored that he'd think of me like that. My nerves were in shreds from losing my best friend, and his kind words at that moment felt like the biggest bear hug I'd ever gotten in my life. I told him that I still had to do a lot to settle Jilly's estate, but once that was over, we'd talk about my joining him.

Feeling apologetic for voicing my opinion to Frank at such a time, I said, "I'm sorry if I'm out of line, but I think the best possible thing you could do for Jilly would be to go out there and entertain people, make them happy. Jilly would be upset if you canceled dates because of his passing."

Frank was due to leave on tour two days later, on the thirteenth. In the interval,

Frank's management team discussed who'd go on the road with him now that Jilly was gone. I later learned that Steve Lawrence and Eydie Gormé's manager, Frank's friend Judy Tannen, suggested I might be a good choice for Frank's road manager. She didn't realize Frank had already broached the idea with me. Tempting though the offer was, I had reservations. Frank and I talked about it privately later at his house. He told me he wanted to make our professional relationship official. I was silent for a long minute.

Finally, Frank said, "I'm sensing some apprehension."

I said, "With all due respect, it's been my experience that when you intermingle money and other people's jealousies with a relationship, sometimes things get derailed. And I value what we have far too much to jeopardize it."

After looking at me for a long minute, he said, "I hear ya, but here's my take on that. As far as I'm concerned, there are only two people in the world that can f★★★ up what we have, and that's you and me. And it's not going to be me."

I thought for a couple of seconds, then extended my hand and said, "Okay. If you're good, I'm good." We shook hands. The next day, the professional relationship was made official.

Frank knew I had to stay behind a few weeks to settle Jilly's estate, and he was supportive of that. We agreed I'd join him as soon as I could. Somehow, Frank found the wherewithal to pull himself together and leave on tour to Europe and Britain, returning home a month later. After a couple of weeks' respite, he started a Las Vegas engagement in late June.

Meanwhile, I got a call from the county coroner's office to go into San Bernardino and pick up what was left of Jilly's belongings. I protested that everything had been destroyed and should be thrown out, but they told me the belongings had to be relinquished to a family member, and the family had designated me. The police weren't allowed to dispose of it themselves. When I went to pick up Jilly's personal effects, the only thing that hadn't been completely destroyed in the fire was one credit card from Frank Sinatra Enterprises with Jilly's name on it. I put it in my pocket, where I've carried it ever since.

Closing out the estate took a while. In the weeks following the funeral, I helped Jilly's sons, Joey and Willie, clean out the house. One afternoon, I asked the boys to bring a ladder into the living room for me. I put the ladder under an air-conditioning duct in the ceiling and started loosening the screws. William and Joey looked at each other and then at me like I was nuts.

I took the vent off and removed the package that was hidden inside and handed it down to the kids. When they unwrapped it, they saw a big bundle of cash. The kids had no idea it was there. I knew it was there because Jilly had told me. Their jaws pretty much dropped at the sight of it. Then I climbed back down the ladder and told the kids to follow me into Jilly's bedroom. I opened the closet and took out several of Jilly's suits. I reached into one of the pockets and pulled out a gold ring. I kept reaching into suit pockets, pulling out a diamond ring, a bracelet, a brooch. I kept going, placing the jewelry in the boys' hands one piece at a time.

"Holy Christ," one of the boys said.

"Yeah," I said, "your father liked to hide stuff around." The jewelry the boys decided to sell went for over $100,000 at the subsequent estate sale.

Once Jilly's affairs were in order, I joined Frank at the Desert Inn in Las Vegas that June. We were both hurting, both wounded, both still standing. For travel purposes, I was now listed as Frank's road manager, a term that had sometimes been applied to Jilly in an organization that didn't believe in titles. I had no illusions that I could replace Jilly in Frank's life, any more than he could replace Jilly in mine. We both knew, though, that in a way neither of us could define, Jilly's passing had changed our relationship forever. The hours that slid by after midnight became the first of many Frank and I would spend alone together, drinking Jack Daniel's and reflecting on our lives. That first night, we shared stories about Jilly. Over the two thousand nights and mornings that followed, until the wee small hours, Francis Albert and I continued to talk. Conversation by conversation, story by story, he shared his life with me, because he needed someone to understand and to remember.

. . . .

# PART II
# IN THE WEE
# SMALL HOURS

. . . .

# CHAPTER 3
# LA FAMIGLIA
## FAMILY TIES

Frank was finishing up a series of concerts in the Philippines. He always put everything he had into his performances, and by the time he finished that night, he was exhausted. When it was time for him to "put it in the bag," Frank's term for going to bed, I could see that he was depleted to the point of weakness. I went to his room with him and helped him get into his pajamas. I was about to leave when I noticed that his night lunch wasn't on the bedside table. His girl Friday, Vine, always left a sandwich for him to eat if he woke up during the early morning hours. It was unusual for her to forget, but that night she'd been worn out, too. We all were. I told Frank I'd get his sandwich and went into the kitchen to fix it. When I carried it back to the door of his bedroom, I was surprised to see that he was no longer sitting on the bed. He was kneeling next to it, his hands folded, leaning against the top of the bed like it was an altar rail. I heard him speaking quietly. He was saying his prayers. Unwilling to disturb him or invade his privacy, I stopped in the doorway, afraid to move. He kept speaking.

"Lord, it's me, and as usual, I want to thank you for all you've given me. Not only financially, the success you've given me, but the family you've blessed me with and the friends that I have. And if I could implore you, Lord, please, if you can give me the wherewithal to continue taking care of the people who take care of me. Nancy Sr. Barbara. Nancy Jr. Tina. Frankie. A. J. Amanda. Vine. Tony." I felt my eyes smart when he said my name.

He continued, "And, Lord, I don't need to make a lot of money. I would be content making one more dollar, just one more dollar than what I need, to do what I need to do." Then he began to say the Our Father and blessed himself.

I waited, silent and unmoving, afraid to embarrass him if I betrayed my presence. He turned out the light and crawled wearily into bed. When his breathing had quieted, I tiptoed silently into his room. I put his sandwich on the nightstand and crept slowly out. The soft Manila night was warm and hushed except for the beat of the waves outside, rocking Frank's weary soul to sleep.

In the ways that were most important to Frank, my childhood was the one Frank wanted. I grew up surrounded by family with a stay-at-home mom, three siblings, an aunt and uncle just up the stairs, and Sundays filled with grandmothers and cousins. The loneliness I sometimes felt was rare and had more to do with me than those around me. Frank, in contrast, was the most profoundly lonely person I've ever known. Loneliness created his need for constant companionship, first with Jilly and then with me. That sense of aloneness had crawled under his skin and echoed in his voice, and though it became existential, it started the way most things start — in his childhood family.

To understand Frank Sinatra, you first have to understand his mother. Her name was Natalie Catherine Garavente, but everyone called her by her nickname, Dolly. I never had the privilege of meeting her. She died tragically the day we would have been introduced. Frank never got over losing her, and I spent many hours listening to Frank talk about her in later years.

When Frank talked about Dolly, he'd

often laugh because she was such a character. Dolly was a leader, domineering and sometimes aggressive. Physically, Dolly was small, but she dominated every room she entered. She was a ward boss for the Democratic Party during the years American women first got the right to vote. Dolly was such a political force in Hoboken, New Jersey, that she got a letter of commendation from Calvin Coolidge, congratulating her on her great work for the Democratic Party. She almost ran for mayor of Hoboken, but Frank's father, Marty, convinced her to decline the opportunity. Instead, she became a midwife who delivered many of the children in the neighborhood. She was incredibly tough, because Frank's birth would have killed a lesser woman. Ninety-pound Dolly, who stood less than five feet tall, gave birth to thirteen-and-a-half-pound Francis Albert at home, nearly bleeding to death in the process. The birth was so physically traumatic that she was never able to bear another child. For better or worse, she lavished all her maternal instincts on Frank.

Dolly had a mouth like a sailor. Her profanity was legendary. When her husband started suffering from what we now refer to as ED (erectile dysfunction), she nicknamed him Dry Balls. Her moniker for Jilly was

Fuck Face. She referred to her son as Cracker Ass because Frank didn't have a swimmer's muscular butt. Dolly said his ass was as flat as a saltine cracker. Frank adored his mother, but at the same time, he feared her. One year, his mother gave him a metal blackjack nightstick for a Christmas present. It had been his father's, and she told Frank he might need it sometime. Dolly and Marty were gone a lot, and she may have envisioned Frank's needing it when he was home alone. Because Frank's parents were often away from home, his grandmother frequently took care of him. When Grandma couldn't, he sometimes spent time with a Jewish neighbor named Mrs. Golden. She was very kind, and because of her, Frank felt a special affinity for Jews for the rest of his life.

Left to his own devices, Frank started to get into mischief. Most kids fear their father's wrath, but Frank was far more afraid of his mother. He told me that one winter when he was around ten, there was a three-foot snowfall in Hoboken. Frank and his pals were playing in the snow, grabbing on to the rear bumpers of cars and holding on while the cars went down the block at twenty, thirty, or forty miles an hour. It was basically like skateboarding with their feet.

Dolly saw what they were doing through the window, and she wasn't happy.

When Frank came in the house, she said to him, "What is wrong with you? Don't you realize that if you'd made just one slip, you could have gotten killed?" She followed up the reprimand with a slap to Frank's face with an open hand that knocked him across the room. She loved Frank fiercely, but when she thought it was warranted, she didn't hesitate to give him a hard smack or two. She also wasn't above grabbing him by the ear and dragging him home. By today's standards, some of it bordered on abuse — but at the time, it was pretty common. The only unusual thing was that it was Frank's mother, not his father, who dished out the corporal punishment.

Even when Frank grew up, his mother's attitude toward him never really changed. When Frank was getting his start singing in local clubs, Dolly went to see him one night. She'd bought him an amplifier and gotten him jobs in Italian clubs to boost his singing career, so she was anxious to hear how he sounded. Just as he was about to go on, she heard the announcer introduce "Frankie Trent!"

Dolly looked around like, *Who the hell is* that? And then Frank walked out.

After the show, she started lambasting him at the top of her lungs. "How dare you change your name?"

"But, Mom, 'Sinatra' might be too long."

"You either change your name back to Sinatra, or I'm taking the amplifier away from you!"

Frank told me, "I felt like I was twelve years old again. She did everything but grab me by the ear like she used to do when I was a kid."

There was a great television interview with Dolly many years later, while Frank was in Spain shooting a film, *The Pride and the Passion*. The interviewer asked Dolly if she wanted to send her son a message in Spain. Her message to her forty-two-year-old son?

"Frank, be a good boy. Be a good boy."

Dolly's hot and cold behavior with Frank shaped his sense of what was normal in a relationship with a woman. Sometimes Dolly smothered him; oftentimes, she left him on his own, and he felt abandoned. It was confusing.

Sharply contrasting with Dolly was Frank's father, Marty, a quiet man whom Frank revered. Marty was considered to be from a lower level of society than Dolly's family, and Dolly eloped with him to Jersey City against her parents' wishes. They started their lives in Hoboken, New Jersey, where Frank was born two years later.

Frank's father was a captain in the fire department. Marty also ran a local bar, Marty O'Brien's, named for his moniker as a boxer in earlier days. More times than not, when Frank got home from school, Dolly would be out, and his father would be at the bar. If Frank's grandmother and Mrs. Golden were busy, he'd go hang out in the bar and do his homework. Decades later, on his 1973 TV special, *Ol' Blue Eyes Is Back,* he had a set designed that mimicked his dad's bar. They even put out bowls of hardboiled eggs on the bar just the way his father used to. Is it any wonder Frank grew up to sing saloon songs?

The gin mill, as bars like Marty's were called in those days, had a player piano that started up when you put in a nickel. Patrons liked to have young Frankie sit on top of the piano and sing along with the music. They'd pick the song and have Frankie sing, and when he was finished, they'd give him a nickel. This was before microphones, so Frank would use a megaphone to be heard. The patrons would get drunk and start throwing coins in the megaphone, hoping the coins would go down Frank's throat when he opened his mouth to sing.

He told me, "I found out early on, the money came real quick when I sang. It was better than working for a living." One of the songs the guys in the bar liked him to sing was "Indian Summer" because it was their way of teasing him. They knew he had to scream to reach the high notes.

Even though Marty was a strong man, he was wise enough to pick his battles and let Dolly take the lead on a lot of things. Later in life, Frank did the same thing when he married Barbara. Marty spoke English very well, with no accent, when he could get a word in edgewise around Dolly, but Marty couldn't read or write. In fact, when Frank was around twelve, he finally taught his father how to write his name. Despite his lack of education, Marty was a shrewd businessman. Most important for the family, he loved Dolly.

Like his son, Marty was a romantic who could sing a good tune. While they were courting, Marty wrote a song for Dolly:

You remind me of a girl
Who went to school with me.
You remind me of a girl
I kissed beneath the tree.
Her hair all hanging down,
She wore a gingham gown.

You remind me of a girl
Who went to school with me.

He continued to sing it to her after they married, on their anniversary or in a special moment. Frank said that at one point, he wanted to record the song, but he never got around to it. Frank admired his father, and even in Frank's eighties, whenever we'd talk about his dad, Frank's eyes would well up with tears.

Few things better sum up the differing personalities of Frank's parents than the story of the monkey. Like all good tales, it begins, "One night a sailor walked into a bar . . ." — in this case, Marty's bar. The sailor had just gotten back from a trip to the Orient. He had a little monkey on a leash that he'd picked up in the East. It was relatively well behaved. That particular day, the sailor wasn't only drinking but playing cards for money. The guy ended up losing the monkey in a card game.

The monkey's new owner decided that he couldn't bring it home. He said, "What am I going to do with it? Does anybody want a pet?"

Marty was thinking that Frank was a somewhat lonely kid, so maybe he'd enjoy having a pet monkey. He brought the monkey home, and Frank was thrilled. He said it was almost like finally having a younger brother. He and the monkey got along really well. He kept the monkey in his bedroom and let it out to play when he got home from school.

Dolly and the monkey, on the other hand, didn't get along. She'd throw things at the monkey, and it would throw things back. Whenever Frank's mother would come in the room, the monkey would go crazy. It would jump up on the chandelier, unscrew the lightbulbs, and throw them at Dolly. This was not a stupid monkey, and it and Dolly shared a mutual contempt for each other. Inevitably, things came to a head. One morning when the rain finally let up after a three-day downpour, Dolly decided to do some laundry. She washed the clothes and hung them out on the clothesline to dry before going about her business. When Frank came home from school that afternoon, he let the monkey out of his room while he was making a snack. While Frank was busy, the monkey found its way outside and started running up and down the clothesline, pulling the clothespins off and dropping the clothes in the mud below. Frank was horrified when he saw what the monkey had done, and when Dolly came home, she was livid.

The next day, when Frank came home from school, no one was home. He opened his bedroom door. No monkey. Then he heard a faint whimpering. He followed the sound into the kitchen and saw one of the kitchen chairs wedged underneath the handle of the oven door. The whimpering was coming from inside the oven. Dolly had taken the racks out of the oven and put the monkey inside as though it were a cage. Frank let the monkey out, put it on its leash, walked down to Marty O'Brien's, and told his father what Dolly had done. They agreed things were just not working with the monkey and Dolly in the same house. They decided to give the monkey to the local zoo. Afterward, Frank never visited the monkey. He couldn't face it emotionally. What if the monkey wanted to come home with him? That would have been more than he could handle.

Despite his emotional intensity, Frank was a tough kid. He took a lot of abuse. He was bullied for being Italian, for the way he dressed, for being different. He was small for his age and skinny, but he learned boxing from his dad and fought under the name Young Marty O'Brien. Frank was a quick study and became a tough contender. He was no angel. His nickname among his school chums was "Angles" because he was always trying to get something cooking by working the angles. Frank was smart, and school came easy to him, so he was often bored. He liked to play hooky. His favorite place to avoid the truant officer was the Erie Lackawanna train yard in Hoboken. He and his friends would hide in the freight cars and sometimes pilfer a block of coal, which they sold for pool money. He also financed his time at the local pool hall with the church collection basket. On Sundays, he'd go to mass like a good boy. His mother always gave him money to put in the basket that they passed up and down the pews. Frank put the money in like he was supposed to, but then he'd take change. In other words, if his mother gave him a dollar, he'd put the dollar bill in, but he'd take two quarters back. He was very quick and never got caught. He'd use that money to shoot pool at Turk's Pool Hall with his buddies.

When he got older, Frank's nickname changed from "Angles" to "Slacksie." He attracted ridicule because he was always perfectly dressed. The guys used to tease him that they could cut their finger on the crease in his pants. Luckily, Frank's left hook kept the teasing to a minimum.

Like most Italian men, Frank's father rarely handed out compliments. He picked his moments with Frank, so when the words of approval came, they meant the world to him. In general, Marty held back on showing his son affection. That would mean showing his softer side, and fathers were supposed to be tough. The implicit message was, "You want a hug? Go to your mother." That was complicated for Frank. Going to Dolly for affection meant taking your life in your hands. You never knew if she was going to smack you or squeeze the breath out of you.

One story Frank loved to tell me because of his father's reaction at the time happened when Frank was fifteen. He was on his way home after shooting pool when he saw a man standing on the street corner not far from him, waiting for the light to change. The man had grabbed his dog by the leash, right near the collar. He was holding the dog off the ground with one hand and beating it with the other end of the leash. Frank walked over to the guy and tapped him on the shoulder. When the guy turned around, Frank coldcocked him with a left hook, knocking him to the ground. The guy quickly came to and called the police. The cops brought Frank, the man, and the dog into the police station and contacted Marty at work. Marty thought, *What in the hell did my son do now?* When he got to the station, Frank and his dad went before a magistrate. The dog's owner irately explained what had happened. Frank told me that it looked like the magistrate was amused by the story. He must have been impressed that Frank had decked the guy, given that Frank weighed less than ninety-eight pounds at the time. He admonished Frank and assigned Frank some community service.

After the dog's owner left the courtroom, the magistrate said to Frank, "Young man, please approach the bench."

Frank walked up, and the magistrate leaned over and shook his hand. He told Frank, "Please, in the future, think twice before you resort to fisticuffs. Having said that, I applaud your intentions." On the way out of the police station, instead of giving him a slap, Marty hugged him. Frank treasured that hug.

Frank was short-tempered and protective even then. He couldn't stand to see the helpless beaten up, and obviously, he never completely got over "resorting to fisticuffs." It was a reflex with him. He used to say to me, "I'm not the kind of guy who does a lot of brainwork about why or how. I get an idea — maybe I get sore about something. And when I get sore, I do something about it."

Although Frank could take care of himself, being the only child of two working parents made for a lonely, insecure childhood. Even when his parents were home, they didn't have much time for Frank. He grew up without the family closeness that most of his friends enjoyed in their traditional Italian families. Frank had buddies, but he wanted siblings.

He told me, "I never had any brothers or sisters. In my neighborhood, every family had twelve kids, and they fought constantly. But whenever there was a party, you never saw such closeness." It had a tremendous effect on him. In later years, that would impact how he dealt with friends and his own wife and children. There was a reason Frank called Jilly Rizzo his brother. Jilly filled a need from Frank's earliest years. When Jilly was gone, I was called on to fill the same need. Frank wanted me around all the time.

Even when his family was together for dinner, it was just Frank, Dolly, and Marty, and often one of his parents would have to leave. The phone would frequently ring in the middle of dinner. Frank said it got to the point that he hated the phone's ringing because he knew it would take one or both of his parents away from him. Sometimes the phone rang in the middle of the night. It would be either someone calling his father to a fire or someone summoning Dolly to help a woman giving birth. Dolly and Marty would come into Frank's room, give him a kiss, and say, "Okay, we're locking the door. You'll be fine. Mrs. Golden is across the hall if anything happens."

Once they left, Frank would be completely on his own until morning. He'd lie in bed wide awake, frightened that something would happen to his parents in the middle of the night — or to him while he was there alone. That's why so often in later years, especially on the road, every night was like New Year's Eve. Frank hated being alone at night. When we were on the road, especially at the Waldorf Towers, he didn't mind when the cleaning crew arrived in the morning. It was soothing for him to hear the hotel staff come in to clean the suite, vacuuming the living room and straightening up. Someone would say, "Don't do that! Mr. Sinatra's still sleeping," but I'd assure them it was all right. It meant that the world was now awake, and he was safe. Nothing bad could happen to him while the world was awake. He could finally go to sleep comfortably, knowing that the world went on around him. That feeling of vulnerability, of aloneness, followed him to the end of his life. You can hear it in his voice, in the lyrics of *A Man Alone.* He kept that part of himself private with most people. It only came out in his music. But his closest friends knew it because he let us see it.

By his teen years, Frank was expected to start contributing to the family income — and to Marty, that meant getting a conventional job. Frank got a summer job on Wall Street, working as a runner on the stock exchange floor. Another summer he worked for the local newspaper as a copy boy. He loaded trucks for a while. When he graduated from high school, his father got him a "real job," working full-time at Todd Shipyards as a rivet catcher. That didn't last long. Knowing that Frank had a pretty high IQ and was fascinated with geometric designs, Dolly wanted him to enroll in the Stevens Institute and become an architect. Frank, though, wasn't interested in either his mother's or his father's goals for him. He'd always known he was destined to be a singer.

The whole thing came to a head one night

over dinner with his parents. They were eating when his father said, "So, did you enroll in the Stevens Institute?"

Frank put his fork down and said, "Well, you know, Dad, I've given it a lot of thought. I really want to pursue the singing thing, and I believe that I could be as good as or better than Bing Crosby."

There was a silence. Finally, Marty replied, "Well, fine. If that's your final answer, that's your choice, but you're not going to do it on my dime. So pack your stuff and get out of here."

Frank told me, "The food stuck in my throat. My mother started to cry. I didn't even finish my meal. I went in my bedroom and packed a bag. Then I kissed them both, and I walked out. It was night already, and there I was, standing outside in the dark, thinking to myself, *Where the hell am I going? What am I doing?*" He had a little money on him, so he took the ferry across to New York and bunked in with his cousin Ray Sinatra. He slept on Ray's couch for a few months, and he never went home again.

What Frank's father did sounds coldhearted. But I understood it. I thought about my own father while Frank talked. Dad fought my going into show business every step of the way. But when I became successful in my chosen profession, my father couldn't have been prouder. Frank and I both went into show business about the same age. When you're twenty years old, you don't really understand that your parents have your best interests in mind. You only know that they don't support your dream. You resent it, and you feel guilty for letting them down.

Frank enjoyed success pretty quickly, first with Harry James and later with Tommy Dorsey's orchestra. But it wasn't until he began his run at the Paramount Theatre, in New York's Times Square, seven years later on New Year's Eve 1942, that his dream became a reality. That run is legendary. Girls in bobby socks, including my mother, Rose, lined up around the block for tickets. Even with his doing nine shows a day, they ran out of tickets. Frank was completely unprepared for what happened the first time he walked out on the Paramount stage. He was performing with Benny Goodman's orchestra. He said that when the orchestra played him on, he "was greeted by a deafening wall of applause and cheers," something he'd never experienced when he was with Dorsey. The audience noise was so loud that he could barely hear the orchestra that was right behind him. He was completely taken aback. Benny Goodman looked at Frank and said, "What the hell was that?" The wall of sound only got bigger as he began to sing his big hits "Night and Day" and "All or Nothing at All."

Frank was very flattered by the crowd's reaction, but he was also taken by surprise. It was unprecedented. This was long before the Beatles or Elvis Presley. It was a phenomenon that had never happened before. Mass hysteria. It was so unusual that a concerned citizen reported the deafening screams to the FBI as a brainwashing plot to create another Hitler. After that first night at the Paramount, the reaction became a regular thing whenever Frank performed. He wasn't caught flatfooted again like the first time. The pandemonium never inhibited his ability to perform, either. In fact, it pumped him up. It was the beginning of a lifetime love affair with his audiences. Frank's father came to one of those shows, and he brought Frank's uncle with him. The uncle complained that he couldn't hear Frank sing for all the screaming. By that point, Marty was finally realizing that Frank had made the right decision.

One of the questions that's asked about Frank is, "What drove him to be such a success and to continue striving for greater heights?" The answer is that he was hell-bent on proving to his father that he'd made the right decision. I have no doubt his father's misgivings weighed on Frank's mind when his career tanked in the early 1950s. He fought his way out of that slump, in part, to prove to himself *and* his father that he'd chosen the right path.

When you're Italian, taking care of your parents is in your DNA. Frank always took care of his parents. When Frank started making real money, he bought his parents a beautiful home in the Palisades in New Jersey, overlooking the Hudson River. Then when Frank was in his forties, his father got very ill. In addition to his heart problems, Marty had developed emphysema. Frank got the best doctors in the country to help, but it was clearly just a matter of time. Frank canceled everything to be by his father's side. He was with him for five difficult days, watching him fail. He held Marty's hand to the very end. Marty's death affected Frank like nothing before ever had. Millions might have praised Frank Sinatra, but his father's approval would always be more important.

After Marty's death, Frank tried to bring his mother out to California to live near him. Dolly refused to leave New Jersey because Marty was buried there, and she wouldn't leave him. So Frank got permission to have his father's body exhumed and moved to Desert Memorial Park in Palm Springs, where Marty was then reinterred. With Marty safely in California, Dolly finally agreed to move west. Frank bought Jack Benny's house for her, right next to his home. He knocked down the wall on that part of his property, so Dolly would have free access to his house, and he completely refurbished it for her. They were both happy to have her there, but she was still Dolly, overbearing and demanding. Worse yet, she and Barbara didn't get along. When Frank couldn't take the tension anymore, he'd call Jilly and beg him to come over and spend time with Dolly.

Most of the time, Jilly said, "Sure, Frank." Jilly loved Dolly, too. It didn't mean that she didn't get on his nerves now and again.

Dolly's passing was a shock Frank never recovered from. In January of 1977, disaster hit while Frank was flying to Vegas for a gig. At the last minute, Dolly refused to get on the plane because she didn't want to be on the same plane with Barbara. Frank arranged another flight for Dolly. That flight never arrived in Vegas. Those were still my performing years, and I was driving up to see the show that day. When I got to Vegas that Monday evening, something was clearly wrong. Jilly told me that Dolly's plane had disappeared into the fog and snow over the mountains near Palm Springs. It had been missing for several hours. Jilly and I watched as Frank somehow got through the first show. He was like a robot, doing the songs on remote control. The moment the show was over, he went straight out the door and flew back to Palm Springs. The remaining show that night was canceled. As soon as he got back, Frank went up in his helicopter to help with the search for the missing plane. It took three days for the authorities to find the crash site and recover the bodies. Frank was devastated.

For a long time, Frank blamed Barbara for Dolly's death. It wasn't her fault, of course, but Frank's grief-clouded view was that if it weren't for Barbara, Dolly would have been safely on the plane with him. The cause of the crash was eventually found to be pilot error, but Frank was never able to process what had happened. For years, whenever Frank talked to me about Dolly's death, he always ended with, "You know, I still don't know what the hell happened, how that happened."

Nearly twenty years later, in 1995, when

Frank and Barbara were moving to Los Angeles, he had me help him pack. Frank was very private, and he didn't want anyone else touching his personal things. I was packing some things in the bedroom when I found the FAA report about Dolly's crash in the back of one of the drawers. It explained the pilot error in detail. Frank had kept that report in his bedroom drawer for nearly twenty years. Either he hadn't read it, or he couldn't remember what was in it. He must have known what had happened to his mother all along. He just couldn't deal with it. Selective amnesia.

Dolly, with all her strengths and weaknesses, became the model for what Frank later experienced with his wives. When Frank married Nancy Barbato, he was marrying a homebody who'd finally give him the family he'd wanted as a child. Nancy was always a mother figure for Frank. He described her as the "quintessential Italian mama." She was an excellent cook and, once their first child was born, a devoted mother. Nancy Jr., named after her mother, was born in New Jersey in 1940. Four years later, Frankie Jr., named for Frank's idol Franklin D. Roosevelt, was born, shortly before Frank moved the family to Toluca Lake,

California. Frank was determined that their children would never experience the loneliness he had as a child. They had a stay-at-home mom and siblings. Maybe not the ten or twelve brothers and sisters Frank once dreamed of, but they weren't alone. In 1948, Christina (Tina) arrived. She was the only one born in California. After Tina's arrival, Frank bought a beautiful family home on Carolwood Drive in Holmby Hills. It was a fifteen-room house with a pool. Frank finally had his fantasy family, and with it, the internal conflict of his life. Be careful what you wish for.

The Nancy he'd married fit perfectly into the Hoboken neighborhood she and Frank had grown up in, but she was out of place in Hollywood. Frank adored Nancy Sr. (as she was called after little Nancy was born), and he was crazy about the children, but the traditional lifestyle at home suffocated him. He had a series of increasingly serious love affairs, which culminated in a crisis point when he became involved with Ava Gardner. For a long time, Nancy Sr. resisted divorce, but in February of 1950, when Tina was three, Nancy announced that she and Frank were splitting up. The pain for Nancy Sr. and their children was intense, and Frank never forgave himself.

In later years, Nancy Sr. told me that in spite of his serial infidelity, Frank was the best father he knew how to be. For many years after he left, he called the kids every day, no matter where he was in the world. She said he'd deprive himself of sleep to be there for the kids, rearranging his schedule to attend events in the children's lives, like graduations and birthdays. He was the same way years later, when I was with him full-time. Now he arranged his life around his grandchildren's events. He continued to call his children as often as he could, even though they were adults.

Frank always tried to go the extra mile for his kids. One year, because of contractual obligations, he was away for Christmas. Nancy Sr. and the kids got a ton of gifts, but he still felt terrible that he missed Christmas.

He told the kids, "I don't care what you're doing on June fifteenth. Everyone absolutely must be at my house on Bowmont Drive [his bachelor pad in the Hollywood Hills]. It's very important. Be there at eight o'clock at night."

He didn't breathe a word of what it was about. They tried to get it out of him, but no luck. He told them, "You just gotta be there."

When they showed up at the house that evening, manufactured snow was blown all over the property. The outside of the house was completely decorated with Christmas lights. Inside was a huge Christmas tree, with Christmas music playing, and piles of presents. He'd created Christmas for them all over again, to make up for not having been with them in December.

Frank could never completely let go of the little Italian dream family he'd walked away from, a reality that complicated life for them all. He'd go back to visit Nancy Sr. and the children and end up staying two or three days. Decades later, he was still tortured by the decision to leave Nancy and the kids. He'd talk to me about his guilt all the time. One night, on a flight to Germany, Frank was especially down on himself. We were sitting in the back of the plane. It was one of the few times we flew commercially, on a Lufthansa 747. He'd bought out the whole upstairs just for us. Everyone around us was asleep. Frank and I had been talking about many things when he stumbled onto recalling the time he'd taken Nancy Jr. and Frankie with him to the Academy Awards. He told me how, when his name was announced as Best Supporting Actor for *From Here to Eternity,* he'd run up to the stage and collected the statue. It was a big moment in his life. Afterward, he went back to Nancy Sr.'s house. She'd anticipated that he might win and put together a gathering at the house. He showed up, but for some reason, he didn't stay. Instead, he took the award, got in his car, and drove back to Beverly Hills.

He told me, "Like a schmuck, here I was, walking around Beverly Hills with the statue in my hand. I could see the pain on Nancy's face and the disappointment she felt when I decided not to stay."

He was in a lot of pain himself that night on the plane, beating himself up over it. I started to say something, but he cut me off, something that was rare with him. I realized that he wasn't looking for any kind of outside opinion. He just wanted to get this off his chest.

I fell silent, and after what seemed like an hour, he realized that I hadn't said anything.

He said, "You're awful quiet."

I said to him, "You know that you're a perfectionist in most things, but you're the best at this. You were really terrific."

"What?"

"I've never seen anybody beat themselves up as well as you can. It's really something."

"Well, I deserve it."

"Has it ever crossed your mind that just maybe, in the forty years that have passed since this incident, she has long since forgiven you and forgotten the whole thing?"

"Well, maybe that's the case, but I haven't. Either forgiven or forgotten. It was a lousy thing for me to do."

"Okay then, you're destined to be miserable about it."

Frank had a point, though. The demands of his career took a toll on his personal life. Like other career-driven fathers, he couldn't be in two places at the same time. His career and the divorce both took a toll on his children, and he knew it. It affected each one of his children, but it affected them all differently.

Frank was protective of all his children, but he was the most protective of his oldest, Nancy Jr. Nancy had a certain wide-eyed wonder and enthusiasm about her. She also had a lot of her mother's traits. There is a softness, a vulnerability to Nancy, a tendency to acquiesce, and a deep tenderness. Nancy had also inherited an innate musical ability from her father. Though Frank was proud of Nancy's musical talent, he purposely wouldn't do anything in the industry with her until she had some success of her own. It was only after she had a hit with her song "These Boots Are Made for Walkin'" that he did the duet of "Something Stupid" with her. It became another big hit for the Sinatras.

Nancy adored her daddy. She once called him "Don Quixote in a tuxedo." When the American Music Awards gave Frank their Award of Merit four months before his death, it was Nancy who accepted the award for her dad. Frank wasn't in good enough shape to attend, so he and I sat together in the den to watch the presentation on television. We watched as Nancy looked into the camera with tears welling up and thanked everyone for her father's honor.

She said, "When I left the house, Dad said to give all the fans a hug for me, because they made me possible." Then she looked directly into the camera and said to Frank, "And now, Daddy, I'd like to give you a few thanks. Thanks from me for being an inspiration to me and so many others, for setting so high a standard . . . I'm so proud to be your daughter."

That evening, a little while after the broadcast, Nancy came to the house. She walked into the den, told Frank, "I have something for you," and put the award in his lap. Then she put her arms around him, more like a mother than like a daughter, and told him how much he deserved the award. By then he was in tears, and she continued holding him. It was like role reversal, with her as the parent. For once, he not only allowed it, he welcomed it, which was a rare thing for him.

Nancy also had a natural propensity for motherhood, so it was no surprise that she gave Frank his first grandchildren, two girls whom Frank adored. Angela Jennifer (A. J.) was born in May of 1974, and for three brief years, until Dolly died, there were four generations of Sinatra women. When Amanda was born two years later, Frank was equally excited. Frank loved being a grandfather. Far from being vain about his age, he embraced being Grandpa. He spent a lot of time with the girls. Nancy Jr. would take them down and leave them at Frank's house for weeks at a time, just to be with Grandpa. The girls understood who their grandfather was. They knew he was FRANK SINATRA, world-famous celebrity. They'd go to his performances sometimes and watch from backstage, but, to Frank, showing them that side of his world wasn't the important thing. He just wanted to be their grandfather. They cherished the alone time that they had with him because they knew how valuable it was.

Both girls adored Frank. When he collapsed onstage in Richmond in 1994, A. J. was very worried about him. She and her boyfriend came down to Palm Springs when we got back, to spend some time with Grandpa and make sure he was okay.

After dinner the first night, Frank said to me, "Why don't you show the kids the property, and I'll make us a drink?" A. J.'s boyfriend had never been there before.

I figured Frank was tired and wanted a few minutes to rest. So I gave the two kids the tour of the compound (as Frank called his home) and got them settled in one of the guesthouses. As we walked back toward the main house a little while later, I looked ahead and froze. I could see Frank lying on the ground in the distance. I went into panic mode. Luckily, the kids hadn't noticed him, so I rushed them into Frank's paint studio a few yards away and said, "I'll be right back. A. J., you should, you know, show him Grandpa's paintings." It was the only thing I could think to say at that moment.

As soon as they were inside, I started running full speed toward where Frank lay. When I got closer to him, I saw that he was moving. Once I arrived, gasping for breath, I could see that he was fine. He was lying in the grass with a box of cheddar cheese Goldfish crackers, crumbling them on an anthill. I couldn't believe what I was seeing. Frank looked up at me and smiled.

I said, "Frank, what are you doing?"

"Hey, the ants got to eat too, Tony."

*That son of a bitch,* I thought, chuckling to myself. He scared the shit out of me.

Tina, the baby of the family, was a completely different personality from her older sister. If Nancy was like *her* mother, Tina was more like *Frank's* mother, Dolly. Tina would say she was like her dad. She was assertive. She was business savvy. If you hit her, she'd hit back. Tina was the one he felt needed the least protection because she could protect herself. Frank once summed up Tina this way: "Tina has her mother's charm and tenderness. At the same time, she inherited my bent for being a scrapper with a feisty short fuse."

Strong as she was and is, though, her parents' divorce was very hard on her. Tina was a toddler when her parents split up, too young to understand why her daddy just disappeared. Frank told me that leaving Tina was always the worst moment when he went to visit the kids after the divorce. When it was time for him to leave, Tina

144

would start crying and run upstairs to her room and close the door. She wouldn't let him in to say goodbye.

He said, "I could see her watching me pull out of the driveway from her room upstairs, and she'd be crying and waving to me at the same time." It tore his heart out.

Although Tina could sing, she never wanted to do it professionally. That was her older siblings' path. Instead, Tina turned to the business end of show business. She began producing and eventually took command of all the Sinatra business entities, including making decisions about how Frank's likeness could be used. It's interesting to me that all the images of Frank that Tina has approved since his death in 1998 are from the 1950s. The Sinatra stamp, for instance, shows Frank around 1954, with the trademark fedora. I've always thought that was, for her, more of an emotional decision than a business decision. The pictures she loves are the images of her father from when she was a young girl growing up. That's when she was missing her father the most, and those are the pictures she still carries in her heart. Until the day he died, she still called him Poppa.

The most complicated relationship Frank

had with his children was with Frankie Jr. Frankie was almost eight when his father left, an age when boys identify strongly with their fathers and need them at home. Frankie learned young to protect his emotions. It didn't help that, like his own father, Marty, Frank had great difficulty showing his feelings toward his son. Frank always felt that what really changed things with Frankie was when Frank and Nancy Sr. sent him away to boarding school. As Junior had grown into his teens, he'd begun to rebel. Frank Sr. talked it over with Nancy, and they decided boarding school was the best way to keep Frankie from getting hurt or ending up in jail. In Frankie's mind, though, it was, *Oh, they're shipping me off. They're not shipping Nancy or Tina off. They got their arms around them. Just me.* Frank told me that Frankie always had this feeling like, *Well, I'm his son, but only eighty percent.*

Boarding school served its purpose. Frankie *did* straighten up, but he also pulled farther into his protective shell and never really came out again.

Then on December 8, 1963, nineteen-year-old Frankie was kidnapped at gunpoint by two amateur kidnappers. Frank told me that when he first got the ransom call, he thought it was a prank and was stunned when it turned out to be real. Dolly was visiting Frank from the East Coast when Frankie was kidnapped because it was close to Frank's birthday. Dolly, always Frank's pillar of strength, fell apart in the face of the kidnapping.

Frank told me, "I couldn't get my mother up off her knees. She'd set up a little altar in her room and was praying eight to ten hours a day. It was devastating to see her like that."

Frank paid the ransom, and Frankie was safely returned, but the nightmare wasn't over. The capture of the kidnappers and resulting trial were a media circus, and when the defense claimed the kidnapping was a publicity stunt to boost Frankie Jr.'s career, it turned into a press feeding frenzy. The claim was a complete fabrication, as the kidnappers themselves later admitted, but it dogged Frankie for the rest of his life. When a priest wrote Frank Sr. from prison, asking for leniency for the kidnappers, Frank very politely told him what he could do with his request. The press jumped on that as well, condemning Frank for his unforgiving attitude. It was easy enough for them to judge. They didn't have to witness the lasting damage that had been done to his son.

Frank told me that after one of the kidnappers got out of jail, he wrote to Frank. When Frank didn't respond, the guy decided to confront him in person. One night, he just showed up. Frank was coming out of Chasen's after dinner to pick up his Jaguar from the valet. Just as Frank started to pull out of the parking lot, a man came up to the Jag and began motioning for him to roll the window down. Frank didn't recognize him at first.

When Frank rolled the window down, the man said, "Mr. Sinatra, I just wanted to apologize."

Frank told me that when it dawned on him who it was, he "completely lost it, and [he] told him, 'Just get the hell away from my car! I don't want to ever see your face again.'"

But the guy wouldn't leave. He kept going on and on, trying to apologize, while Frank kept getting angrier. Back in those days, Frank used to carry a piece, and he finally pulled the gun out from the glove box and pointed it at the kidnapper. The guy ran away.

Frank told me, "I never would've pulled the trigger, but I couldn't figure out how else to get this guy the hell out of my face. I couldn't listen to him for another minute. I

148

didn't want to ever relive that, even for two minutes." Frank rarely talked about the kidnapping. Even decades after it occurred, it was still too painful. The kidnapping brought father and son temporarily closer, but not enough to break through the invisible wall between them.

Living in his father's shadow, Frankie Jr. tended to be underestimated, his impressiveness not given its due. He had a highly organized mind and a very high IQ. Of Frank's three kids, musically, Frankie Jr. was the strongest. He was a hell of a singer, a piano player, a songwriter, and an arranger. Being Frank Sinatra Jr., of course, was both a blessing and a curse. He knew that a musical career was going to be a tough road, but he wanted to pursue music like his father had. To a great extent, Frank Jr.'s DNA, the chemistry Junior inherited, determined his life path. He couldn't help sounding like his father and using some of his father's mannerisms. When Frank Sr. retired briefly in the early seventies, Frank Jr.'s career skyrocketed. That's how I came to see him at the Rainbow Room the night I first met Frank. But then Frank Sr. returned to performing, and Frank Jr. was, once again, the second-best Frank Sinatra.

He joked about it sometimes. "You know,

actually, it's my own fault. I'm trying to sell antiques in a modern appliances store!"

When Frankie became his father's conductor and musical right-hand man in Frank's last decade of performing, it was good for both father and son. It was Nancy Sr.'s suggestion. Onstage, father and son were great together. As well as the arrangement worked out musically, though, it didn't have the effect on the relationship that Nancy Sr. had hoped for. Even right before Junior passed away, whenever he spoke publicly about his dad, he'd refer to him as "Frank Sinatra," not as "Dad." I know of only one time that Frankie openly expressed his love for his father in a public setting. It was the night Frank Sr. received the Will Rogers Memorial Award for his humanitarian work. I was back east that night, so I watched the ceremony on television. When Frankie took the stage, he looked at the audience and said, "It always seems to be difficult for one man to express love to another. I have a little impunity, I think, being a relative. Speaking on behalf of my sisters and I . . . this is for you, Dad." Looking at his father, he began to sing, "It's very clear . . . our love is here to stay . . ." As Frank listened, tears streamed down his face, and he looked down occasionally to wipe them away. When Frankie Jr. hit the last note, he told Frank, "From all of us, Dad, congratulations. We love you." I have no doubt that, for Frank, that moment was the evening's real award.

I was there on one of the rare occasions Frank Sr. was able to publicly express his affection for his son. It was December 8, 1993, the thirtieth anniversary of Frankie Jr.'s kidnapping. There was an article in the paper that day about a young producer who wanted to make a movie about the crime. Junior was telling his father about the article, and as I listened, I saw a flood of emotion overcome Frank. It was like all of a sudden somebody had flipped a switch, and he was reliving it.

Frank was doing a concert that night, and Junior was conducting. At a certain point in the show, Frank started introducing celebrities in the audience, as he did every night. He looked at the paper in his hand and introduced one celebrity after another. He never introduced Frankie or the members of the band until almost the end of the show. That night, though, he said, "There is a gentleman." He paused and made that characteristic fist with his index finger in the air and said, "I'll rephrase that. There is a gentleman, a gentle *man* in attendance

151

tonight, upon whom I cannot bestow enough accolades. He is a loyal soul, a stalwart supporter of his friends, and deeply devoted to his family. He's a brilliant . . . he has a . . . a brilliant intellect, [is] an accomplished musician, composer, and arranger. He's an extremely talented singer, but most importantly, a loving son. Ladies and gentlemen, say hello to my son, Frank Sinatra Jr."

And instead of making a joke, Frank turned upstage toward Frankie, put the microphone under his arm, and applauded as loudly as the audience.

Frank's children were his greatest joy, but they were also the source of his deepest conflict. Some of the conflict was self-inflicted, stirred up by the string of affairs he accumulated when he was young. Some of the conflict, however, resulted from the tug-of-war between his children and his wives. Ava resented the children primarily because when Frank went to visit them at their mother's, he sometimes stayed for days. Frank's marriage to Ava was ultimately short-lived. His marriage to Barbara, in contrast, which began after a long relationship, lasted for twenty years. The struggle between Barbara and his daughters over

Frank went well beyond a mere tug-of-war; it was more like he was being drawn and quartered. Separately, the three women could be lovely, but together, Barbara and the Sinatra daughters were like mixing bleach and ammonia. The result was toxic and occasionally dangerous, particularly for Frank.

I vividly remember a Father's Day about 1993 that illustrated the situation in stark tones. I'd been at the desert compound for a couple of weeks. By then, I was there 80 percent of the time, and Frank and Barbara would have preferred my being there 100 percent of the time. Barbara asked me to move in full-time twice. I was a buffer; I gave Frank companionship and Barbara freedom. For the sake of my sanity, though, I declined and kept my own place. The night before I was scheduled to go home to LA, the three of us — Barbara, Frank, and I — were having dinner. When Frank got up and left the table for a few minutes, Barbara said to me privately, "You know, he doesn't want to put any pressure on you."

"About what?"

"Sunday is Father's Day. He tentatively planned to go up to LA and spend it with his kids, but I know he doesn't want to go alone. He realizes that you've been here for a couple of weeks, though, and he doesn't want to twist your arm. I'd appreciate it if you'd go with him. I'm not comfortable with him going up there alone. They're going to manipulate him." The "they" was Frank's daughters. I forget exactly how she worded it, but she was implying that he'd be among a pack of wolves. Barbara was always afraid that his kids were going to talk him into doing something with his businesses that would jeopardize her interests.

When Frank came back to the table, I said to him, "I understand you're going up to LA on Sunday to see the kids."

"Well, yeah, that's the plan, but you know, I don't know . . ."

"Would you like me to go with you?"

"But you're going back to LA tomorrow."

"I can go back on Monday. How are you planning on going?"

"I don't want to drive up. We'll take the chopper or a jet."

"Hey, I'd love to go."

"Really?"

"Yeah, absolutely."

He suddenly brightened. "Great! That's terrific. Did you hear that, Barbara?"

That night, after Barbara went to bed, Frank wanted to talk with me in private. He kept checking on Barbara to make sure she was in a deep sleep. Finally, he said, "The drapes are moving. She's snoring loud, so I think she's asleep." We went out by the pool so he could have a smoke. He said, "I need your help with something else."

"Sure."

"Tomorrow when I get up, we'll go out into the painting studio. We'll go down in the hole because there are a couple more paintings there." The "hole" was what he called the downstairs of a separate building near the theater north of the main house, where he kept supplies.

I said, "Paintings for what?"

"I promised A. J. that I'd give her a painting for her new apartment. You can help me pick one out for her."

I said, "Okay," and told him I'd remind him when he got up the next afternoon. We went back inside, watched TV, and called it a night about four a.m.

The next day, Barbara had developed a cold, so she was spending most of the day in bed. When Frank got up for his breakfast, I got the usual call from Vine: "The gorilla's up."

Frank read the paper and said, "What's the plan today?" I reminded him of our conversation the night before, and we went out to the studio.

155

He looked at the paintings. It was clear he was in a quandary. He said, "I like that one because of the colors, but I'm not sure what color her apartment is. I like this one because I like the shapes." Frank did a lot of abstract geometric designs, and that painting was an abstract. He liked another one for another reason. Finally, he said, "Well, I'll tell you what. Why don't we take these and put them in the theater? Then we'll go down in the hole and see what's down there."

I said, "Okay." He was having fun with this and making it into a little event. I went down into the hole, and he stood at the top of the steps and told me which ones to bring up. Seeing them reminded him that he had one down in the hole that he hadn't finished, and he asked me to bring that one up and put it in my bungalow, in case he wanted to work on it again. Then he nodded at the finished paintings and said quietly, "You have to kind of smuggle these into the guard shack and put a tarp over them. Then we'll take the station wagon to the airport tomorrow. There are too many eyes around here."

"I get you. No problem." I followed Frank's instructions, putting the paintings in the guard shack and covering them. I took the unfinished one to my bungalow. A little later, when Frank went to lie down for a while, I took a break and went to my bungalow. As soon as I got in, the phone rang. It was Barbara on the kitchen line.

She said, "What are all those paintings doing in the guard shack?"

"Excuse me?"

"You know, the blue one, the orange one, the black one . . ." Not only did she know how many were there, she knew exactly which ones they were. "And why are you taking paintings into your bungalow?"

I interrupted her and said, "Wait a minute. That painting isn't staying in my bungalow. It's something that he hasn't finished, and he asked me to put it aside because he might work on it. As far as the other ones are concerned, he couldn't make up his mind about which one to give to his grand-daughter, so he said to take them all and let her choose."

Barbara replied, "Well, that's not going to happen. You pick out the one he was lean-ing toward the strongest and put all the other ones back."

What else could I say but "Fine"? I didn't want to start another battle, so I didn't say a word to Frank about it. Sunday morning — Father's Day — we walked out to the guard shack and brought the station wagon around. Frank said to me, "Are the paintings in the car?"

I told him, "The *painting* is in the car."

"What do you mean, the *painting*?" I told him that I'd been instructed to put the other ones back. He was noticeably upset.

"Will it ever stop? Come on. Let's just get the hell out of here." We drove to the airport, put the painting on the plane, and flew into LA. The limousine driver met us at Van Nuys Airport and drove us over the hill into Beverly Hills. When we got to Nancy Sr.'s house, we went inside and had a terrific time. We drank, laughed, ate food, laughed some more, and had more to drink. Frankie Jr. was on the road, but Nancy Jr. and Tina were there, and A. J. and Amanda. Frank's close friend and business manager, Sonny Golden, was there with his wife. And of course, Nancy Sr. She'd cooked all of Frank's favorite foods, including her signature eggplant Parmesan. Frank gave the painting to A. J. It was a wonderful afternoon.

About a half hour before we were getting ready to leave, Frank's mood started turning somber. He kissed his girls goodbye. Afterward, we walked out to the car, and Nancy Sr. came out and gave him a kiss.

They embraced for quite a while. When he finally let go of her, we got in the limo. As we pulled down the driveway, Frank looked back at his family. I wondered if he was remembering three-year-old Tina, looking through her bedroom window, sobbing and watching him drive away. Frank didn't say a word as we drove back to the Van Nuys airport. He just looked out the window. After the plane took off, Frank turned to me and said, "Want something to drink? I could use a Jack and water. I'm sure you could, too."

I said, "Sure."

The flight attendant brought us a drink, and I said to Frank, "So that was a nice afternoon."

"Yeah." Silence.

"Is everything okay?"

He took a deep breath, then sighed and said, "Yeah, well, I just had a glimpse of what my life could have been. You do realize it's going to take me months to get over it now?"

"What do you mean?"

"You see, this is what I wrestle with. As many laughs as we had there, and as many warm emotions as we all felt, it's going to take me a long time to get over it." Then he added, "I built it this way. I have to live with it."

"Frank, it doesn't have to be this way."

"Yeah, it does." He was very quiet during the entire trip back to the desert.

Frank Sinatra was an imperfect man, an imperfect father, and certainly an imperfect husband to Nancy Sr. He knew that better than anyone, and the deepest wish of his heart was to make things right. But as occurs with all of us, the patterns established in his childhood became a blueprint for everything that followed. He remained the fearful, lonely child who longed for attention and validation and had no idea how to soothe the ache inside him. He didn't know how to make peace between the loving Italian home he longed for and the adventure he craved. He never learned how to stand up to a domineering woman in a healthy way. The result was the pain of recognizing his own failures and living in an abyss between his wife and his flesh-and-blood family. It was an abyss that would stretch all the way to his deathbed.

Even at eight years old, the hat, eyes, and snappy clothes make Frank easily recognizable. He'd already acquired the nickname "Slacksey" because he loved to be well-dressed.

Me at thirteen (*right*), circa 1965, with my big brother, Pete (*left*), both of us on guitar, and my buddy Gary Berzolla on drums, in our backyard in Franklin Square, Long Island. It was my first "trio." (Photo courtesy of the author)

When Frank walked onstage at the Paramount Theater for the first time in 1943, the audience's deafening roar shocked him. It was the beginning of a love affair with his fans that would last a lifetime. (Photograph by John T. Burns for the Associated Press)

I was twenty-one in 1972 when I met Frank Sinatra. It took me months to work up the nerve to ask him to have this picture taken of us together. The photo was taken in front of Jilly's with my friend Les Stanco (*center*), who happened to be with me that night. (Photo courtesy of the author)

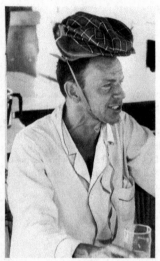

Frank lovingly referred to this photograph as the "afternoon after." He loved to clown around and chose this moment to jokingly wear an ice bag on his head, pretending to nurse a hangover. (Photo courtesy of the author)

Frank's marriage to Barbara Blakeley was his last and longest. Their relationship was complicated, but they loved each other and made it work for twenty-two years. (Photo courtesy of the author)

In acknowledgment of my contributions to the *Duets I* and *II* albums, the executives at Capitol Records awarded me a triple platinum record for *I* as well as a gold and platinum record for *II*. Framed with beautiful cover art by LeRoy Neiman, this award hangs proudly in my den. (Photo courtesy of the author)

My best friend Jilly Rizzo, whom Frank considered his brother, ended up without a single souvenir from his Manhattan jazz club. Luckily, I'd held onto memorabilia from the old club. For Jilly's birthday, I presented it to him in a big shadow box. (Photo courtesy of the author)

Frank and Barbara's twentieth wedding anniversary renewal and celebration at their Malibu beach house was a wonderful event. I had a ball singing "Nice 'n' Easy" at the reception. Despite all of the singers in attendance, Frank wanted only Steve Lawrence and me to perform. (Photo courtesy of the author)

# CHAPTER 4
# VENDETTA
## FRANK AND THE MOB

In May 1947, New York *Daily Mirror* reporter Lee Mortimer sat down for a chat with FBI agent Clyde Tolson, J. Edgar Hoover's right-hand man and reported life partner. What did Mortimer want to talk about? Frank Sinatra. Mortimer was about to publish another piece on Sinatra and wanted help from the FBI in collecting dirt on Frank. The newsman handed Tolson a picture of Frank with a man whom Mortimer thought looked like a gangster and said he'd also heard a rumor that Frank's godfather, underboss Willie Moretti, had originally backed Sinatra's career. Mortimer then mentioned hearing allegations of a "sex arrest" of Sinatra in 1938. This was just the kind of stuff Hoover was looking for. The FBI was only too happy to give Mortimer what he wanted. The deal was done to the satisfaction of all parties, and Mr. Hoover

161

could be assured of Mr. Mortimer's understanding the terms.

So continued the long, sordid history of the
cooperation between our federal government and muckraking journalism, carefully
recorded in an FBI file titled "Francis Albert Sinatra." The allegations made the
careers of dozens of journalists and, in their
endless spin-offs, created a legend that
destroyed the reputation of an American
citizen. From the day Lee Mortimer published his first article on Sinatra and the
Mafia, until Frank died fifty years later, the
top secret FBI file was supposed to be the
smoking gun proving Frank's role in the
Mob. Lurid biographies made vague refer-
ences to it whenever they wanted to smear
Frank. When the file was finally released a
few months after Frank's death, showing no
evidence of Mob ties (or sex crimes) had
ever been found, it made no difference.
Nobody wanted to read a dull thirteen-
hundred-page file debunking stories the
public was already in love with. The FBI
"sources" often turned out to be the gossip
columnists themselves, but the press didn't
exactly rush forward to clear Frank's name
when the file was published. Frank loved to
joke that the initials *FBI* stood for "Forever

Bothering Italians." No kidding. What did Frank say the FBI called three Italians talking on a street corner? An indictment.

For months in 1947, Mortimer had been circulating rumors that Frank had ties to the Mob. When the two men accidentally encountered each other in the entrance of Ciro's restaurant a month before Mortimer visited the FBI, Mortimer murmured "Dago" as he passed Frank. For Italians in the forties, *dago* was the equivalent of the "n-word" for African-Americans. Italians might call one another "dago" affectionately, as Frank and Dean Martin did. But coming from a non-Italian, the word was a reason for fisticuffs. Frank decked Mortimer with a left hook and paid the resulting fine with no regrets. In fact, when he found out how low the fine was, Frank joked he should have hit him again. Frank liked to tell me that someday he was going to do an oil painting depicting his point of view of the night he punched Mortimer. He said the majority of the painting would be a view of the soles of Mortimer's shoes as he flew down the steps at Ciro's. I really wish he'd done that painting.

To understand Frank Sinatra's relationship with mobsters — and the FBI's interest in him — you have to understand what it meant to be Italian when Frank was growing up. Frank was the son of Sicilian immigrants. His father, Anthony Martin Sinatra, was born in Sicily in 1892, the same year eleven randomly chosen Italian-Americans were lynched by vigilantes. The *New York Times* referred to these Italians not as victims, but as "sly, coward Sicilians, descendants of bandits and murderers . . . parasites, rattlesnakes." When Frank was born in New Jersey in 1915, he joined a nation whose view of Italians hadn't changed much since the lynchings twenty-three years earlier. "Ol' Blue Eyes" was a "black Italian" in the eyes of neighborhood gangs, and he was bullied for it. Immigration laws throughout Frank's life kept most Italians from coming to the United States, referring to them as a "criminal element." When America entered World War II, thousands of Italian-Americans (along with Japanese Americans) were sent to internment camps or required to carry special IDs like the Jews in Nazi Europe. When *The Godfather* was released three decades later, it included a character supposedly "based on" Frank and made mafiosi the hottest thing in Hollywood. For the public, Frank's heritage made him dangerously attractive, but for Frank, the assumptions he was forced to battle were hell.

So what *was* Frank's relationship with the Mob? Did he know mobsters? Sure. Some were his friends. That's true of most Italian-Americans born into a less affluent Eastern neighborhood in the last century. It's true of my family. It was true of Frank's. In the blue-collar Italian neighborhoods of Frank's youth, everyone knew mobsters. The Mob had a foot, or at least a pinky finger, in pretty much every business in town, from pastry shops to bars. They were part of the scenery. Italian people are very clannish, and many people in the neighborhood were connected to someone in the Mob. Sometimes those connections were a button man or a soldier; sometimes they were captains, underbosses, or even capos. Most were small-time criminals with sticky fingers and large fists who had big-time friends with big guns. In that respect, it wasn't much different from being part of the labor union, or even the local constabulary.

If you were descended from Sicilians, like Frank and me, it wasn't unusual to be related by blood or marriage to a member of the Mob. It was a simple matter of DNA and the laws of probability. Nancy Sr. had a cousin who became a soldier for a Mob guy named Willie Moretti, who was chosen by

Marty as Frank's godfather at his baptism. Neither Nancy nor Frank got involved in Willie's "business." Years later, though, when the press found out that Frank was Willie's godson, they pounced on it. "Young Sinatra's Career Financed by Mobster." Tipped off by the press, the FBI later added a note in Frank's surveillance file that the Mob (again in the person of Willie Moretti) was "forcing" Frank to leave Ava Gardner and go back to Nancy. Our tax dollars at work.

Did Frank Sinatra associate with the Mob? Absolutely — by necessity. He learned young that when you met a mobster, you were polite, showed respect, shook hands if a hand was offered, and asked no questions.

Frank said a thousand times, "I was raised in a society that when you're introduced to someone, you shake his hand before you ask him how he comes by the money that's in his pocket." Even if you knew, you weren't rude or stupid enough to turn your back on the guy.

The fact that Frank was an entertainer sealed his fate where the Mob was concerned. He was in the entertainment business, and the Mob owned the business. Most of the really great clubs, even if ownership was two corporations deep, were Mob owned. Sam Giancana, who took over as the boss of Chicago in the years after Capone, was one of the owners of a club called the Black Orchid. Frank played there. All the big guys played there, including Don Rickles, Danny Thomas, and Bing Crosby. Since their last names didn't end with a vowel, however, no one cared.

Frank used to get frustrated and say to me, "The joints weren't exactly owned by Cardinal Spellman! I didn't know any bishops, cardinals, or monsignors who owned nightclubs. Otherwise, I would have ended up rubbing elbows with *them*!"

Clubs were highly attractive to Mob guys. They provided an environment that fit the mobster's day-to-day lifestyle, where they never knew if there was going to be a tomorrow.

Frank made a parody out of it and used to say to me, "Live each day as though it's your last, and one day you'll be right." (He also used to joke, "Anyone who's dumb enough to take a nap in the trunk of a Cadillac deserves to be shot in the head"!)

The bobby-soxers hadn't cared who Frank spent time with, but everything changed when Lee Mortimer wrote an article about Frank's trip to Havana in 1946. Frank had been performing at the Fontainebleau nightclub in Miami, the premier place to work at the time, owned by the usual Mob connections. Wiseguy Joe Fischetti came down from Chicago regularly to check on the business. Joe was an easygoing guy, and he and Frank would hang out and share a drink after the show when Frank was performing there. One night, Frank was complaining to Joe that he needed a vacation, and he was thinking about going to Cuba for a break. He'd heard that the Havana nightlife was hot, and so were the women.

Joe said to him, "You know, I'm going down there myself this weekend. So why don't we go together?"

In the ultimate example of "It sounded like a good idea at the time," Frank agreed. He threw enough clothes for a couple of days into his small travel bag. They hopped on a plane and flew to Havana. Then he and Fischetti went to a club to have some food and a couple drinks with some friends of Joe's. One of the people in the group was the notorious mobster Lucky Luciano. Frank acted like himself, partying all night and performing for Joe's friends. He signed a lot of autographs and posed for pictures. This went on for a few days. Then Frank went home. The rest of what happened in

Havana is history, or in Mortimer's version, fiction.

Frank told me he had no idea until afterward that a Mob convention was being held while he was there. The story Mortimer told was way more interesting, though. According to him, Frank had gone to Havana as a bagman for the Florida Mob. The suitcase Frank was holding in a picture of him getting off the plane contained $2 million in small bills. The story caught on big. It's been reprinted millions of times, right up to today. Once it came out, Frank fell down the rabbit hole of innuendo and could never climb out.

Is it true? It isn't difficult to figure out. Frank was supposedly carrying the money in the travel bag shown in the picture. Let's say the small bills were all twenties (though it's more likely they would have been a mixture of twenties, tens, and fives). The sum of $2 million in $20 bills weighs 220 pounds — almost twice as much as Frank weighed at the time — and has a volume of four cubic feet. The suitcase would have to have been two feet by two feet square and a foot deep. The bag Frank's holding in the picture is much smaller than that. Even if Frank hadn't packed anything else, like underwear or a toothbrush, there's no way

$2 million could have fit in it. But people believed Mortimer because it made a great story. Frank came home from his trip to Havana to a changed world. Mortimer's article was ground zero for all the garbage that followed. Mortimer and another Hearst writer, Westbrook Pegler, wrote a whole series of articles about Frank's activities as a so-called Mob courier. Because journalists copy from each other, the stories spread like wildfire. No protests or threats of legal action on Frank's part fazed the press. Frank was angry and increasingly desperate to stop the stories from spreading further.

So far, much of this story is pretty well-known. What happened next is something only I know. I'd never heard the tale until Frank told it to me in vivid detail. It's the story of the day Frank Sinatra met newspaper tycoon William Randolph Hearst, the inspiration for the iconic film *Citizen Kane.* The whole experience was like something out of a movie.

The meeting with Hearst came about because of Nancy Sr. Nancy was good friends with gossip columnist Louella Parsons. Parsons, in turn, was old friends with silent-film star Marion Davies. Marion Davies was the live-in mistress of William Randolph Hearst, whose newspaper empire was the biggest in the world. Mortimer and Pegler were both Hearst writers. Louella contacted Marion Davies for Nancy Sr., and a one-on-one private sit-down between Frank and Hearst was arranged. The face-to-face was to take place at Hearst Castle in San Simeon, California, under the strictest secrecy. Frank, Nancy Sr., and Louella Parsons drove north to San Simeon together for the meeting.

For anyone who has ever seen it, the first sight of Hearst Castle, an art deco masterpiece, is spectacular. This was Frank's first sighting. He told me he was awestruck by the sheer beauty of the place, astonished by its size. When he, Nancy, and Louella parked and got out of the car, the front door they approached looked like the entrance to a fortress. They rang the bell and waited for a staff member to admit them. They were very surprised when Marion Davies herself opened the front door to welcome them. In the towering entrance hall, Miss Davies spoke briefly with Nancy Sr. and Louella, then guided Frank down the hall to the library. She showed him to a seat and then left.

Of all the magnificent rooms in Hearst Castle, the library is the largest and most beautiful. A series of wooden archways with elaborate frescoes supports the high coffered ceiling from end to end of the eighty-foot room. Tall glass shelves lining the sides hold over four thousand books and hundreds of artifacts, some as much as two thousand years old. The room is filled with well-stuffed sofas, beautifully upholstered in gold tones. A few mahogany tables are scattered among the sofas. Windows line the walls above the shelves on either side, for the length of the room. Despite the high ceilings and heavy furnishings, the room is well lit, the sunlight falling on the furniture from above and creating a golden glow. It is a genuinely magical place. No wonder it made such an impression on an artist like Frank. Frank described it in such vivid detail that I felt like I'd been there.

Frank was very nervous as he waited for Hearst that afternoon, mentally rehearsing what he was going to say. After a few minutes, the big door to the library opened, and Hearst was pushed into the room in a wheelchair. Physically, he looked frail, but his face revealed a mind and will that were still strong. His attendant parked him across the table from Frank and then left the room.

Without preliminaries, Hearst said to Frank, "What do you have to say to me?"

Frank pleaded his case with all the passion he possessed. He told the eighty-three-year-old Hearst that Mortimer and other Hearst journalists were creating an elaborate lie about him. He said that he wasn't a Communist or anti-American or affiliated with the Mob, except as a performer in their clubs. He told him about the problems the articles were creating in his career, and the personal anguish it was causing him and his family. He supported his points with logic and passion. Eventually, Frank ran out of things to say and sat back to wait for a response. After an excruciating silence, Mr. Hearst picked up the phone next to him and put a call through to his headquarters.

In a surprisingly strong voice, Hearst said, "From now on, any articles written about Frank Sinatra will be in glowing terms. Anybody who does anything different will have to answer to me." Then he hung up the phone and, without further comment, called for his attendant to wheel him out of the room. Frank sat there for a while pondering what had just happened, until Marion Davies came in to guide him back to Nancy.

For a few months, Hearst's ultimatum was respected. The result was a brief moratorium on Frank in the Hearst press. But not long afterward, Hearst left San Simeon to seek medical care for what would be his final illness. His sons took over the running of the papers, and editorial policies shifted. Frank's reprieve was a short one. Frank used to say about the press, "All day long, they lie in the sun. And after the sun goes down, they lie some more."

Even if William R. Hearst had lived longer, you can't un-ring a bell. The damage to Frank's reputation was done. Once Mortimer opened that door, the word was out that the feds wanted dirt on Sinatra. Unnamed informants flocked to the FBI to describe favors Frank did for the Mob, mentioning things like getting wiseguys concert tickets and signing autographs. Informants volunteered information on Frank in hopes of avoiding prosecution themselves. J. Edgar Hoover lapped it up.

Journalists continued to meet with FBI agents. In 1957, journalist Bill Davidson asked the FBI for derogatory information on Frank that he could use in what became a three-part series he was writing for *Look* magazine. Here's what Davidson asked the FBI:

Was Frank Sinatra charged with rape in the 1930s?
Was Frank Sinatra "arrested and convicted

of criminal assault" in the 1930s?

Was Frank Sinatra's mother arrested 6 or 7 times for operating an abortion mill in Hoboken between 1930 and 1950 and convicted once?

Were two of Frank Sinatra's uncles, Champ and Lawrence Garavente, "arrested and convicted of bootlegging in Hoboken" in the 1920s and 1930s?

Here are the answers the FBI found for Davidson in their record search:

No, Sinatra was never charged with rape. He was charged with seduction and adultery in the 1930s (when such laws were still on the books), but all charges against him were thrown out of court.

No, there is no record that Sinatra was ever charged with criminal assault.

A police card showed that Dolly Sinatra, a midwife, was arrested once on an accusation of performing an abortion but was never charged or tried.

No, there is no record of arrests for either Champ or Lawrence Garavente.

Did that information exonerate Frank in Davidson's eyes? Of course not. He was too invested in gathering dirt on Frank. The drip, drip, drip of rumors and allegations eventually led the government to formally subpoena Frank about his Mob affiliations. The IRS questioned Frank under oath. Part of the transcript from that affidavit is almost funny. If you knew Frank, you not only know he was telling the truth but that he was thinking, *This again, guys?*

IRS: Are you acquainted with a Mr. Sam Giancana?

Frank: I am.

IRS: Have you ever had any business dealings with Mr. Giancana?

Frank: None.

IRS: Has this relationship been strictly social?

Frank: Yes.

IRS: Mr. Sinatra, in regard to the interview . . . of November 6, 1959 . . . you said that your relationship with Mr. Giancana was strictly friendly . . . that you possess no knowledge of Mr. Giancana's business activities; that you were never approached by Mr. Giancana with a financial proposition . . . Do you have any way of knowing how Mr. Giancana would have come into possession of your unpublished home phone number?

Frank: I gave it to him.

Neither the IRS nor the FBI believed him. The government's suspicions became a problem whenever Frank wanted to invest in something. Being business savvy, Frank had always dreamed of owning his own club. Las Vegas, where he headlined starting in the fifties, seemed the obvious place. The Flamingo was a lucrative possibility, but Frank told me he didn't want to be at the Flamingo because that had been out-and-out owned by mobster Benjamin "Bugsy" Siegel. When Frank started appearing at the Sands, that seemed more like the kind of place he'd like to be involved with. Like all Las Vegas casinos at the time, there were Mob connections, but it wasn't owned outright by the Mob the way the Flamingo was. To explore the possibility, in 1954, Frank talked to the Sands owners about investing and was able to buy two points in the casino for $54,000. The press jumped on the purchase, and it was widely reported that it was a Mob deal, something the FBI repeatedly tried and failed to find evidence for.

Frank's businesses kept expanding. In 1960, he invested in the Cal-Neva Lodge, a hotel and gambling establishment favored by celebrities that was on the border between California and Nevada. I appeared there in my performing days. It was called Cal-Neva because the California-Nevada state line ran right through the center of the property. There was even a line through the swimming pool. One side of the line was California. If you crossed the line, you were in Nevada. In the middle of the lobby, within six inches of the state border, there was a slot machine on the Nevada side. The Cal-Neva deal was put together with Frank's own group of guys. Dean Martin and Sammy Davis each had a small piece. Cal-Neva had a whole series of bungalows down by the Lake Tahoe beach, removed from the main hotel. It was a private area for guests who wanted to keep a low profile. Frank told me Joe Kennedy met with Mob boss Sam Giancana there a few months before the 1960 presidential election. The old man wanted Giancana's help to elect his son John to the presidency. Frank put Sam and Joe together, but from then on, whatever happened was between them. Frank never asked. That was rule number one when dealing with mobsters: Don't ask, because you don't want to know.

In 1963, three years after Frank invested in the place, Giancana went to Cal-Neva to see his girlfriend, singer Phyllis McGuire of the McGuire Sisters, who was appearing there. Giancana wasn't allowed in Nevada by order of the Nevada Gaming Commission, so he had to stay in California. The bungalows were on the California side of the property, so the commission could legally do nothing about who stayed there. Once government spies informed the commission that Giancana was at Cal-Neva, however, it was all over for Frank. The commission pounced, claiming Frank was conspiring with gangsters, and revoked his gaming license. It was a mushroom cloud of insinuation and manufactured Mob involvement that just kept getting bigger and bigger in the press. There were not-so-veiled threats from the government. Interestingly, nobody accused Sammy or Dean or anyone else involved in the ownership and running of Cal-Neva with wrongdoing. Just Frank. Frank went ballistic. He sent back a telegram that said, "You keep messing with my business, and you're in for a big fat f***ing surprise!" It wasn't intended as a threat, but Frank didn't always choose his words wisely when he lost his temper. The commission added making criminal threats to the charges against Frank. By then, he felt surrounded, so he pulled the plug on one of his dreams and decided to get the hell out. He worried that the gaming commission might next go after his license to perform in casinos, and he figured he should cut his losses.

I asked Frank once why he didn't fight it more. He said there was no point. By that time, everyone from the federal government to the major newspapers was deeply invested in the fiction that Sinatra was a major player in the Mob. Frank was in the position of having to prove that something had never happened. He told me you can't prove a negative. The fact that the government had no evidence to support their story didn't slow the vendetta. It only made them more determined to find dirt on Frank, the way crooked cops pick a suspect first and manufacture evidence later. As for the press, they'd spun a fascinating tale that enthralled their readers. Why would they want to give that up? It made great copy. The romanticized version of Frank's life was so much more intriguing than the reality.

There was one funny moment in the middle of all the misery. An editorial entitled "That Old Gang of Mine" appeared in the *Chicago Tribune* in October, at the same time the newspapers announced Frank was losing his gaming license. It reads in part:

We put it flatly: Will Frankie's principal

patron stand up and be counted? We refer, of course, to JFK, who has been entertained by the gambler at Las Vegas and who permitted Frankie and Pack to take over provision of the entertainment at the Kennedy Inauguration Ball in Washington.

The writer goes on to suggest that maybe Kennedy should arrange for Frank to be given the "gaming concession" at the State Department! Bobby Kennedy must really have enjoyed that.

So many writers talk about Frank's fascination with the Mob, but in reality, it was the other way around. The Mob, like the rest of the world, was fascinated by Frank. He possessed incredible charisma. Everyone wanted to bask in it, including mobsters. The Mob guys especially admired Frank because they recognized that he'd pulled himself up by his bootstraps — with his charm, sometimes with his fists, but most of the time with his voice and innate talent. He did it on his own — *his* way — not with Mafia money.

Something else you have to understand about the mobsters Frank knew: they were loyal to him when few others were. In the early 1950s, Frank became a pariah in the entertainment world. The articles about his

Mob affiliations, divorce from Nancy, and affair with Ava Gardner, and the damage done to his throat by a broken blood vessel — all these things combined to destroy his career virtually overnight. His agent, his record company, the movie studio, the producers of his show, all dropped him like a hot potato. Only the Mob-owned clubs continued to give him work. Frank was offered jobs there even when he couldn't put any butts in the seats, but the club owners paid him anyway. It wasn't a quid pro quo on their part, at least not in the usual sense. Frank was never asked to do anything but show up and perform. It's that Sicilian loyalty. Later, when his popularity soared again, Frank continued to work for those clubs, even though they couldn't afford to pay the fees he once again drew. Frank's continued presence attracted other headliners the clubs could never have secured otherwise. As Frank said, those guys fixed it so he could take care of his kids. Loyalty. That was Frank's idea of a quid pro quo.

During the last years of Frank Sinatra's life, I was the guy who acted as a buffer between Frank and the thousands all over the country who wanted his attention. I handled the calls and the requests. Some were from wiseguys wanting to hang out and pal around. But by then, Frank was trying his best to avoid any association with them. He used to say to me, "Tell so-and-so, if he wants to do me a favor, don't do me any favors."

But he had a hard time being rude.

A wiseguy would reach out to Frank and ask if he'd pose for a picture with him and his cousin. What was Frank going to say? Sometimes he'd have me make excuses for him. Most of the time, he ended up saying, "Okay."

Sometimes the guys didn't want to take "no" for an answer. A classic example was Mob boss John Gotti. To say that Frank's relationship with Gotti was contentious is an understatement. Gotti acquired the nickname the Dapper Don for his image as a flashy dresser and man about town. Most mobsters avoided the limelight, preferring to operate in the shadows. Not Gotti. He loved the idea of being a celebrity, so naturally he wanted to be a Sinatra insider. He wanted to be seen around town with Frank and get his picture in the paper. Unfortunately for Gotti — and Frank — that was the last thing Frank wanted.

Jilly didn't tell me about it at the time, but during Frank's last Carnegie Hall performances in 1987, Gotti used his connections to get seats in Frank's block for one of the concerts. He told everyone Frank had sent him the tickets (something Frank never would have done) and assumed that because he would be sitting in the reserved area, he'd be socializing with Frank after the concert. This was news to Frank. When he got word backstage after the concert that Gotti was expecting to go to dinner with him, he sent word that he wasn't feeling well and politely begged off dinner. Unfortunately, the story didn't end there.

Frank and Jilly went to dinner together after the concert at the Savoy Grill, which wasn't one of his favorite haunts, to keep a low profile. I don't know who was there that night, but word apparently got to Gotti that Frank was not only healthy but was happily having dinner with friends. To Gotti, this was a mortal insult. He sent one of his guys, Joe Watts, to threaten Frank at the dinner table that night, telling Frank and Jilly that if Frank ever insulted Gotti like that again, Joe's was the last face they'd ever see alive.

A little over three years later, I was in New York City to support Jilly, who was dealing with some legal problems. Frank was there too, about to start the Diamond Jubilee tour with Steve Lawrence and Eydie Gormé. Frank always flew in two or three days before the concert to settle in before rehearsal. One evening, Frank wanted to go to dinner at one of his favorite restaurants, owned by a guy named Vinnie Panetta. He wanted Jilly and me to go with him, but Jilly couldn't go because he had to update his brothers that night on what was going on with the lawyers. While Jilly was with his brothers, I went with Frank and some other friends. I called the restaurant ahead and told Vinnie we'd be in about 8:00 or 8:30 that evening. Frank had known Vinnie for years; in fact, I have a photo of Vinnie attending Marty Sinatra's funeral in 1969. When we pulled up to the building that night, Vinnie was waiting for us downstairs, something that never happened.

I told Frank, "Let me go talk to him and see what's going on." I got out of the car and said to Vinnie, "What's up?"

Vinnie told me, "I wanted to give you a heads-up before you go into the joint. Your regular table is occupied. I thought they'd be gone by now, but they're not. I'm going to have to put you at a table on the opposite side of the room. It's a similar set-up, with the entrance to the kitchen in between. I don't want Frank to be surprised when I don't seat him in the usual place."

I said, "Okay, no problem," but it seemed

a little strange that an old friend like Vinnie met us at the curb just to tell us that.

As Vinnie walked us into the room a few minutes later, I looked over to see who was at our regular table. Sitting there with a couple of his guys was the Dapper Don himself, John Gotti.

We sat down and ordered drinks and appetizers. Ten or fifteen minutes later, I saw one of Gotti's crew get up from the table and head in our direction. I excused myself to Frank and went to meet him.

Once there, I introduced myself and said, "How can I help you?"

He replied, "Mr. Gotti was wondering if Mr. Sinatra would come over to the table and say 'hello.'"

I said, "Unfortunately, that's probably not going to happen. I don't think it would be a good idea for either Mr. Gotti or Mr. Sinatra to meet publicly because there are too many people, too many eyes."

The guy said, "My boss is not going to be too happy when I tell him this."

I said, "Listen, if you'd like to come, Frank's going to be doing a concert at the Meadowlands. I can guarantee you'll have great seats because they'll be from Mr. Sinatra's personal block in the first three to five rows. You can use your contacts to get a hold of Jilly Rizzo." I didn't say anything to Frank when I went back to the table. I didn't know at the time how risky my refusal was.

Later that night, I told Jilly what had happened. He told me he'd take care of it. The next day, I flew back to California to prepare for a gala I was producing for Bob Hope in a couple of weeks.

Jilly told me later that Gotti bought six seats out of the block for the concert. Frank's friend producer George Schlatter was there filming concert footage for the seventy-fifth-birthday special he was producing on Frank. When George found out where Gotti and his crew would be sitting, he wasn't happy. Gotti would be sitting where Barbara Sinatra and George's wife, Jolene, had been sitting the night before, when George was filming them as part of the crowd reactions. He'd planned to seat them in the same place that night so he could maintain continuity.

George was worried for nothing. Gotti never showed up. Barbara and Jolene were seated in the same place, and George got his footage. There was no word from Gotti. At the time, Jilly thought it was his way of giving Frank the finger. As we found out when the headlines hit the next day, though, it turned out Gotti had an unexpected alternate engagement. Two hours before the show started, fifteen feds showed up at his social club and arrested him. He spent the rest of his life in prison.

Frank knew better than anyone that there was a downside to being loved by mobsters. For one thing, you can't control them. They're prone to doing favors you don't want, without telling you, that you find out about the hard way when it's too late. One example in Frank's life involved comedian Jackie Mason. When Frank married actress Mia Farrow in 1966, he became the butt of a lot of jokes because of the thirty-year age difference. Jackie Mason was one of the most vocal. He used to talk about Frank's buying Mia a box of crayons for her birthday, or Frank's being asked to leave a bar because Mia's rattle was making too much noise. It started to get to Frank, so after a while, he sent a note to Jackie, asking him to please do him a favor and lay off. Instead of responding like a gentleman, Jackie made his jokes worse. Some guys from the Chicago Mob apparently heard about what Mason was doing and sent some people to "have a conversation with Jackie." The conversation didn't go well, so one of the Mob guys took out a blackjack and broke

Jackie Mason's nose. Frank was never sure exactly what went down, but whatever it was, he didn't know about it until it was done, and the story started making the rounds. Naturally, everyone assumed Frank had planned the whole thing.

Frank never wanted the Mob to do anything violent on his behalf. If Frank wanted to punch somebody, he did it himself. He never went further than that. In fact, on a few occasions, Frank got wind of threats against people he knew and did what he could to head off trouble. One time, the Mob got angry with actor/producer Desi Arnaz of *I Love Lucy* fame for dropping some mobster names in dialogue on *The Untouchables,* a television show produced by Desilu, Desi and Lucille Ball's company. Word got to Frank that a hit had gone out on Desi. While Frank tried to talk down the guys who'd been offended, he hid Desi in an apartment in Del Mar to keep him safe. Out of gratitude for Frank's saving his life, Desi created a show for Frank about a singer who works as an informant in Mob-owned clubs. Frank thanked him but declined the part. He needed that kind of role like a hole in the head, and expected he'd get exactly that if he followed through.

Frank was proud of his Sicilian ancestry.

There's one thing you have to understand about Sicilian-Americans, though. As a group, we're as patriotic and law-abiding as they come. But we're not stupid. We know that it can be a gray area between the government and the Mob, and those who end up in the middle are in double jeopardy. That's what happened to Frank's friend Marilyn Monroe.

Frank and Marilyn were close, and he idolized her. She was beautiful and funny and charismatic and radiated sexuality. She was also as fragile as a troubled child, always looking for a man to take care of her and make her feel safe. Frank knew her for years, and they'd had a romance of sorts. Contrary to widespread belief, however, Frank never slept with her. He told me he badly wanted to, that he was terribly attracted to her, but he always stopped short. Marilyn was more than willing, but Frank felt she was too troubled, too fragile, for him to sleep with and then walk away. He just couldn't get rid of the feeling that sex with her would be taking advantage of a woman who'd already been used by so many men. They were close, though, and Frank was her confidante right up to the end of her life.

Things got ugly for Marilyn when the

Mob and the Kennedys both got involved with her, and she found herself in the middle. By 1962, Marilyn was in turmoil about the Kennedys, and she would pour her heart out to Frank about her affairs with Jack and Bobby. The affairs had ended by then, and she was struggling with their treatment of her in the aftermath. They'd cut her off abruptly and without explanation, and she no longer had access to either brother. When she called Jack and Bobby using their private phone numbers, she found they were no longer in service. Marilyn told Frank she didn't understand why they'd shut her out of their worlds so completely once she stopped having sex with them. She told Frank that she was disappointed in both brothers.

The weekend before her death, Marilyn came up to Cal-Neva Lodge to stay in one of the bungalows and figure out the next step in her life. Publicly, she hung out with Frank and his friends. Privately, she was there to spend time with Joe DiMaggio. Joe had never gotten over Marilyn, and in her usual fashion, she looked to a man, a father figure, to fix her life for her. She decided Joe was the refuge she needed. Marilyn spent most of the weekend holed up in private with Joe as they planned their next step. She decided to make a press announcement the following week, saying they were officially back together. Once the press conference was announced, however, the rumor started that she was going to publicly rat out the Kennedys and maybe even Giancana. In reality, Marilyn had no intention of going public with what she knew about any of them. Frank said she'd never have spilled her guts to the press about the Kennedys because she still had feelings for John Kennedy.

Frank said he thought at the time that the situation with Jack, Bobby, and Giancana could have been handled discreetly if Joe Kennedy had talked to his sons. He thought it was strange that the old man apparently hadn't given Bobby a heads-up about the Mob when Bobby went after them as attorney general. Frank was surprised that Joe hadn't called Bobby in and told him how much the Kennedys owed Sam Giancana and the Mob in his brother's election. Bobby only learned about that later, from the Giancana wiretaps his own office had ordered. According to Frank, Joe should have told him, "Don't be a schmuck."

Frank was also furious with Peter Lawford. As Bobby's brother-in-law, Peter knew what was going on between the brothers and Marilyn. When the Kennedy brothers began to worry she was a threat to them, Frank thought Peter should have intervened, should have told Bobby, "Let me see what I can do." Frank believed Peter could have found out if Marilyn planned to say anything about Jack or Bobby publicly. If she had, Frank said Peter could have talked her down if he thought she posed a threat. Frank told me it was Marilyn's death that was the final nail in the coffin between him and Peter. When everything spiraled down with Marilyn, Lawford did nothing to help her. As Frank saw it, Peter could take care of himself, but Marilyn couldn't. Frank thought Lawford could have — should have — protected her.

No one living knows the truth about the death of Marilyn Monroe. But Frank believed he did, and the knowledge was a burden to him to the end of his life. Within days of her death, Frank's friend and attorney Mickey Rudin, who was told of Marilyn's death six hours before the police were, told Frank that Marilyn had been murdered. The same rumor was circulating among Sam Giancana's men, some of whom claimed involvement. Journalist James Bacon, Marilyn's close friend and former lover, told Frank the same thing shortly after Marilyn's passing. All three of Frank's sources told the same story: she'd been murdered with a Nembutal suppository, and Robert Kennedy or the Mob was involved.

Is it true? Conspiracy theories abound, and I can't lay them to rest. I didn't know Marilyn; I was ten years old when she died. What matters to me is that Frank believed she was murdered by people she trusted, and he never got over it. Whatever Peter Lawford said to him about Marilyn's death obliterated what was left of their relationship. Frank found it unbearable that such a damaged, vulnerable, helpless human being had lost her life because some powerful men feared what she might say. The assassination of Jack Kennedy a year later compounded Frank's sense of grief and loss. He never got over losing either to premature and unnatural deaths.

Thirty years after JFK's death, on November 22, 1993, Frank and I stopped over in Palm Springs for a brief hiatus in a heavily booked two-month tour. We got in at one a.m., drove to the compound, and slept for a few hours. That night, as usual, Frank and I watched the eleven o'clock news on the Palm Springs CBS affiliate. The reporter was doing a piece on the thirtieth anniversary of John Kennedy's assassination. We watched soberly, each lost in our own thoughts. When the news went off, Frank and I went outside so he could have a cigarette. It was a warm evening, and the tip of Frank's cigarette was a small glow in the dark desert air. A short while later, we went back into the house and settled down in our usual place in the small den by the bar. Frank started talking to me, reminiscing about Jack Kennedy. Gradually, the conversation drifted to Marilyn Monroe. In the hours before dawn, in the vast silence of the desert, Frank talked to me about his friends Marilyn and John. His words rose and fell in a soft rhythm I can only describe as a lament. Three decades later, his pain and anger at their passing still haunted him.

# CHAPTER 5
## ONCE UPON A TIME
### THE WOMEN

It had been a long night at the Desert Inn. Two performances the night before, and at least six hours of Jack Daniel's and talking afterward. The sun was now up, but Frank was still in his tuxedo from the night before. It was seven a.m. by the time I finally convinced him it was a respectable hour to go to bed. We took the elevator up to Frank's suite in the Wimbledon Tower, I unlocked the door, and we went in quietly. Everyone was sound asleep, Barbara locked in the inner sanctum. Frank was exhausted and a little the worse for wear after too little sleep and too much whiskey. He needed help getting ready for bed. I helped him get undressed, then brought the baby-blue, custom-made pajamas he liked. By that time, he was completely naked, and as I knelt on the floor to put the first pants leg on, I noticed he was staring down at his manhood.

He mumbled, *"Maronn'!* [Italian slang for the Holy Mother, aka, Madonna] If you could only tell my friend where you've been."

Worn out from the long night, I concentrated on maneuvering the pajama leg and said, "You know, Frank, it's seven thirty in the morning, and I'm really tired. Perhaps it would be a shorter list if he told me where he *hasn't* been."

Frank chuckled, and so did I. Unfortunately, the statement was as sad as it was funny. It had been far too many places, and both Frank and the women in his life had paid a price for his inability to control it.

Frank once told me he'd never met a man who could give another man advice about women. "I'm supposed to have a PhD on the subject, but I've flunked out more often than not. I'm very fond of women; I admire them. But, like all men, I don't understand them. Sex? There's not enough quantity, and certainly not enough quality." I also love women, though I've never married. I've come close twice, but my life hasn't exactly lent itself to happily ever after. I've been on the road most of the time since I was in my twenties, and what woman wants a husband who drops by every couple of months with his dirty laundry? As the song so aptly says, "Darn it, baby, that's love!"

Frank couldn't walk down the block without three women throwing themselves at him. His effect on women defied explanation. In his young days, when tall, muscular men were the masculine ideal, girls went nuts for the skinny kid who barely showed up on an X-ray. My mother was one of the Frankie fans at the Paramount. Maybe it was the hair that flopped over his forehead. Maybe it was the blue eyes. Whatever it was, women couldn't resist it, and men couldn't comprehend it. When he was at the Paramount, the lucky females who scored seats to his performances were afraid to leave them because the moment one moved, another girl would nab their seat. Instead of going to the restroom, girls were just squatting in front of their seats, pulling their panties down, and urinating. By the middle of the performance, small rivers of urine would run down and form a pool at the base of the stage. Frank said that by the fourth show, he learned not to go anywhere near the edge of the stage. Not exactly romantic.

There's no question that Frank Sinatra loved women, sometimes two at a time when he was young. He used to tell me, "If I was fatigued, I'd tell the girls, 'You start, and I'll catch up to you.' " He enjoyed women, but he also had a lot of respect for the fairer sex, something he learned from his mother. Frank loved the ritual of courtship and seduction. He liked to pamper a woman, buy her gifts, make her feel like a queen. Frank knew what he wanted sexually, and he seemed to know what they wanted, too. But he'd rarely jump into bed upon first meeting someone. He was never a *Wham, bam, thank you, ma'am* kind of guy. He was surprisingly protective of a woman's reputation. He'd drive a woman home after a date and see her to the door. Women never had to do the walk of shame with Frank. Some of Frank's love affairs started as friendships and went from there. Many of his romances ended as lifetime friendships, including with the women he married and eventually divorced.

One of the results of his weakness for women was that Frank became the victim of his own reputation. He's gotten a lot of press based on the assumption that any attractive woman he was close to, he slept with. That was never the case. Frank said to the press, "If I'd had as many affairs as you fellas claim, I'd be speaking to you today from a jar in the Smithsonian." Frank's sexual morals might have been pretty loose, especially in his bachelor days, but he *did* have boundaries. He might say yes in a New York minute to a good-looking girl looking for love, but he put the brakes on if sex would be damaging to her.

As I've said, Marilyn was a woman Frank considered off-limits for ethical reasons. Another widely publicized example is Natalie Wood. Books about Frank nearly always state that Frank had an affair with Natalie Wood when she was a fifteen-year-old starlet, and he was nearly forty. It sounds sleazy, and it would be if it were true, but it isn't. Frank was involved with Natalie when she was older, in between her two marriages to Robert Wagner, but never when she was a young teen.

I talked about the allegation recently with my friend R. J. (Robert) Wagner, who was appalled by the story. He told me in pretty colorful language that it was absolutely untrue. He and Natalie had been close friends with Frank and discussed him many times. R. J. felt certain that she'd had a romantic relationship with Frank later in her life, but never as a kid. R. J. echoed what I already knew: Frank would never have done that. If he had, R. J. and Natalie's conversations about Frank would have been very different.

Another true story about women Frank never slept with is iconic jazz singer Keely Smith. Keely and Frank struck up a friendship early on, and Frank asked her to duet with him on a couple of tunes for Capitol Records. Her husband, Louis Prima, decided Keely should spend some time with Frank so they could work on their music. So he drove Keely down to the desert and left her at the compound. This was in Frank's bachelor days, and apparently, Louis was wondering what might happen while she was staying there. Keely, who was a good friend of mine, told me the story.

She said that when Louis dropped her off, he told her, "Hey, if one thing leads to another, fine, don't worry. It'd be good for your career." Keely didn't know quite how to take that. She wasn't sure whether he was encouraging her or warning her off in a left-handed way. He was definitely planting a seed.

At the time, she wasn't a drinker (though years later, I got her drinking Manhattans). One night while she was staying with Frank, she had a little bit too much to drink, and they ended up in bed together. She said they were both very nervous. They got into bed and then just lay there on their backs, staring up at the ceiling in silence. Finally, he turned onto his side and looked at her, and she turned onto her side and looked back at him. And before she knew it, the two of them were just laughing like, *What the hell are we doing?*

Frank had a long list of women who were platonic with him. People find it hard to believe he could actually have just been a pal when temptation beckoned, but it's true. Silken-voiced Peggy Lee ruefully acknowledged it at the Ella Awards, given by the Society of Singers to honor their own. She had a crush on Frank for years, and they were close, but always as pals. The Italian bombshell Sophia Loren was another friend. She'd come over occasionally to see Frank when she was in town. In other cases, what began as a romance for Frank turned into a platonic relationship. He was close to former flame Angie Dickinson from the time they made a movie together, but the romance became a friendship. He also remained close friends with Princess Grace after their affair. For a long time after Grace married Prince Rainier, Frank would go to Monaco and do a charity ball for her every year. He had a lot of respect for Rainier, which kept his relationship with Princess Grace at the friendship stage once she married. Like I said, Frank did have boundaries, and one rule was that you didn't sleep with your buddy's wife. Contrary to rumor, he didn't sleep with Lauren Bacall, either, until after Bogie had passed away.

Another famous example is Jackie Kennedy Onassis. There was obvious chemistry between her and Frank. They were close friends, but I'm fairly certain it never came to fruition. I remember meeting her at Jilly's club when I first became friends with Frank. It was November of 1974, and I was sitting in with the band that night. It knocked me out when Frank walked in with Jackie Onassis on his arm. She was beautifully dressed, that understated look that costs a fortune to pull off. She was wearing a very well-tailored pearl-gray pantsuit and just the right amount of jewelry, rich but not ostentatious. Very pretty, very classy. Frank introduced me and invited me to sit down at their table, and I joined them, eager to make a good impression. Mrs. Onassis was very polite, very attentive, very personable. She had a readily summoned smile and a good sense of humor. About twenty minutes after I sat down, I was startled again when Aristotle Onassis walked in. He was very gentlemanly, also very classy, and shook everyone's hand before he sat down. That's when I opted to make an exit to rejoin the band.

It was about four thirty in the morning when they left. Jilly was walking them out, and I was walking behind them because we were all leaving at the same time. When we got outside, Onassis said good night to everyone and told his wife, "I'll meet you in the car." He left her to say her own goodbye to Frank. She and Frank shared a tender hug and a kiss on the cheek. There was clearly chemistry between them, a combination of attraction and affection, but that's where it stopped. Twenty years later, on May 19, 1994, Frank and I were at Foxwoods Resort Casino when we got word that Jackie had passed away. Frank couldn't bring himself to perform that entire weekend. Frankie Jr. took over for him and did all the shows. Frank and I spent a lot of hours together that weekend, but there wasn't a lot of conversation. Frank just wanted me there for company.

Frank was impulsive when it came to women. He might work weeks on music to perfect it, but when it came to women, quick decisions were the rule. The pattern first became apparent with second wife Ava Gardner and continued until his hasty decision to marry his last wife, Barbara. Nowhere was it more obvious, though, than in his third marriage, to Mia Farrow. In a flawed search for youth and renewal, he discovered Mia, a fragile-looking blonde thirty years younger than himself, and married her on July 19, 1966. A little over a year later, they separated, and another year later, they divorced. Frank told me he suspected it wouldn't work, but he thought he'd enjoy it while it lasted. In spite of the love they felt for each other, they were incompatible on many levels. The age difference was insurmountable — Mia became good friends with Tina and Nancy Jr., and together they looked more like three sisters than Frank's daughters and wife. Nowhere was the age gap more obvious than in their differing interests. Frank was an old-fashioned man's man, set in his ways. He might have put on love beads in an attempt to fit in with the times, but he wasn't fooling anybody. Frank was still Frank. Mia, on the other hand, was the quintessential flower child. When she took off for India to sit at the feet of the Maharishi Mahesh Yogi with the Beatles, Frank couldn't believe it. His idea of a yogi was Yogi Berra.

The public ridicule Frank got for the age difference didn't help. But the deal breaker was their divergent expectations of married life. Mia was beginning to attract serious attention as an actress, coming to national prominence with her starring role in *Rosemary's Baby*. Frank didn't want a working wife; he wanted a wife who'd make a home for him, travel with him. He insisted that Mia agree to making no more than one film a year. He also wanted a say in her choice of roles, and even created a part for her in one of his film projects, *The Detective.* It wasn't so much that he was a male chauvinist who didn't want his wife to work. It was more about what had happened with Ava. Ava's career had driven an emotional wedge between them, something she used as a weapon. He didn't want to relive those feelings. He admitted that to me sheepishly when he said, "I guess maybe that's why I was hoping that Mia would give up her acting career or only act in projects that we were going to do together."

It was Mia's breakout role in *Rosemary's Baby* that was the tipping point in a relationship that was already strained. The film was supposed to wrap in time for Mia to shoot *The Detective,* but it ran late, and Mia had to pull out of Frank's film. Frank was furious. When the inevitable split came, Frank didn't handle it well. As always with people he loved, he ran away from confrontation.

He had Mia served with divorce papers on the set of *Rosemary's Baby*. Mia was devastated, and for a while, Frank was miserable, too. Eventually, when the initial pain passed, she and Frank salvaged a friendship out of the disaster of their marriage. They remained in touch, and when the news of Woody Allen's sexual involvement with his stepdaughter hit the news, Frank immediately reached out to Mia to offer his support, whether it be financial assistance or a sympathetic ear.

One evening in 1992, when Frank was in New York performing at Radio City Music Hall with Shirley MacLaine, Mia came to see Frank backstage in the green room. They only had a brief time to chat while Shirley was onstage, so they agreed that I'd set up a time for them to meet at Frank's residence in the Waldorf Towers. I chose a day Barbara would be at lunch with her girlfriends to avoid complications. It took even more finesse to get Mia to Frank's rooms without being stopped by Frank's security, who would certainly have told Barbara. I knew it would just be a visit between old friends, but Barbara might not see it that way.

On the agreed afternoon, Mia took the elevator up to the floor below Frank's and called me when she arrived. Meanwhile, I'd arranged a diversion that sent the security guard on an errand. The security station was right by the elevators, so to be doubly safe, I used the stairwell to bring Mia up. I showed her into Frank's living room, where he waited in his pajamas and robe, having woken up midafternoon as usual. He sat in his armchair, and she made herself comfortable on the end of the couch across from him. They were talking earnestly when I left, and when I returned later at the prescribed time, they were in the same places, still talking. We repeated the process with the security guard, using a different diversion this time, and I saw Mia safely out.

A scene in a hotel room, however innocent looking, naturally begs the question: What was Frank and Mia's relationship at that point? Had they continued seeing each other after the 1968 divorce? Were they romantically involved in 1987, when Mia's blue-eyed son, Ronan Farrow, was conceived? Over the years, there's been a lot of gossip about Frank's possibly being Ronan's biological father — rumors that I believe I'm in a position to tamp down, if not put to rest.

Ronan Farrow, born December 19, 1987, would have had to be conceived between

March and early April of 1987. In late 1986, Frank had emergency diverticulitis surgery at Eisenhower Medical Center in Rancho Mirage. When he came out of the hospital, he had to wear a colostomy bag until he fully recovered. In early February of '87, he was in Hawaii shooting *Magnum, P.I.* When he returned home to the desert afterward, he had to be hospitalized again, and a new colostomy bag was inserted. He spent the following weeks recovering at home. Except for a one-night gig in LA, he was at home in Rancho Mirage with Barbara throughout March, healing from the second surgery. From April 3 to 6, he performed at the Golden Nugget in Las Vegas, then came home again to Rancho Mirage for the charity concert for Barbara Sinatra's children's center. He remained in the desert until his tour started on April 21, taking him to Chicago, Boston, and Atlantic City. Barbara went with him. That was the only time he was on the East Coast in April, and if he'd rendezvoused with Mia then, Ronan would have been over a month premature — which he wasn't. Throughout this time, Frank had to continue wearing the colostomy bag. As for Mia, throughout March and April of 1987, she was shooting a movie called *September* that Woody was directing on location at their home in Connecticut.

There are only two ways that Frank could have fathered Ronan, both different shades of absurd. Either Mia made a secret trip to shack up with Frank in his California home with Barbara present, or Frank, wearing his always romantic colostomy bag, made a quick secret trip to Connecticut between his Atlantic City performances to rendezvous with Mia.

As for Ronan's blue eyes — have you seen Mia's eyes? For that matter, have you seen photos of Mia when she was young? Ronan looks like her twin. And one final observation to end the speculation, though it isn't something I can prove. If Ronan had been Frank's son, Frank would have acknowledged him. There's no way he would have denied Ronan if there'd been any possibility Ronan was his. Frank adored his children, all of them.

As everyone knows, Frank was still married to Nancy Sr. when he met Ava Gardner. Ava was the total opposite of Nancy Sr., which was part of the attraction. If Nancy was the angel on one of Frank's shoulders, Ava was the devil on the other. Nancy was the devoted Italian wife and mother, every inch a "good girl." Ava was a two-fisted drinker, and like his mother, Dolly, Ava had a mouth as bad as Frank's. Frank told me, "When Ava was relaxed, she could have a mouth like a truck driver. She drank as well as I did or better." Ava was also stunningly beautiful, the Angelina Jolie of her day.

Frank wanted to marry Ava, but it was a long struggle to get Nancy Sr. to agree to a divorce. He'd also battled his own emotions. *Do I go back to Nancy? Am I mistaking friendship with Nancy for love?* Even after Nancy gave him a divorce, he and Ava argued constantly about the time Frank still spent with Nancy and the kids. He told me it drove a wedge between him and Ava. As gorgeous as Ava was, she was threatened by the situation. When Frank came home to Palm Springs after a visit to the kids, Ava would give him the cold shoulder. Sometimes he could tolerate it until she softened. Other times, it would lead to an argument, and she'd get in his face about it.

"Make up your mind! You're going to be with me, or you're going to be with her."

"Well, you know, I'm going there because I want to see my children."

And she'd reply, "Yeah, yeah. Sure."

The problems in Frank's career added more pressure. He was at an all-time low professionally. Nobody would hire Frank, partly because of the bad publicity he'd gotten by leaving Nancy for Ava. He told me about one night during that time when he was walking in Times Square, not far from the old Paramount Theatre, where fans had rioted to see him a few years before. It was evening, and he was walking all by himself, with his collar turned up and wearing a hat. Most people didn't recognize him. Even when they did seem to recognize him, they wouldn't acknowledge it. He said it was like he had the plague.

When Ava went to shoot a film in Spain and got romantically involved with a bullfighter, reporters would ask her, "What about Mr. Sinatra?"

She'd answer, "Oh, you mean Mr. Sinnada." In Spanish, it literally translates to "Mr. Without Nothing." It was a cruel nickname she'd concocted for Frank.

Frank told me, "I felt I was a bit overshadowed by her. And it was an uncomfortable position that I'd never found myself in before." He felt like his manhood was being threatened. When things switched back to the other way around, and he got his Academy Award for *From Here to Eternity,* it affected the marriage. Even though Ava had worked hard to get him a shot at the role, the return of his success was a problem.

Frank admitted to me, "I can't fault Ava for being . . . not exactly resentful, but a bit threatened when my career enjoyed the resurgence. I was back on top of the world again, and she felt a little uncomfortable, despite the fact that she was still a major player in the film industry. She viewed my new confidence as a lack of humility, and it would cause fights between us."

There were other problems between them. When she left filming in Africa to fly to London, Ava told Frank she was ill. She later told Frank she had a miscarriage while she was there. It was the second one she'd told him about. In reality, as she later admitted to the world, she'd had two abortions. Frank mourned the "miscarriages" of the children he wanted to have with her. She must have known that telling Frank about the abortions would have been pushing him too far. If he heard about the abortions later, he was in denial about it. He told me with great sadness about how Ava had lost the babies.

Frank and Ava's relationship was like fire and ice, either burning hot or ice cold. When their relationship was hot, it worked for a while, but when it cooled off, it was freezing, and Frank would be miserable. Their arguments were legendary. Frank said

they were too much alike in all the wrong
ways. She was a ball of fire with a red-hot
temper like his. Paradoxically, the things
that he found attractive in her were the
same things that he found repulsive. The
fire that attracted him was the same fire that
pushed him away. Everything between them
was always to an extreme degree, either a
positive or a negative. Whenever we talked
about Ava, he summed it up the same way:
"Anything that burns that hot is bound to
burn out."

I had my own encounter with Ava almost
twenty years after she and Frank split up
for good. I hadn't known Frank for long at
the time. One night, when I was sitting in
with the band at Jilly's club, Ava walked in.
Jilly immediately went to greet her and
made sure she was treated like a queen. He
seated her in Frank's booth, and the waiters
fawned on her like she was royalty. It was
instantly obvious why Frank had been so
crazy about her. She had the same magnetic
aura about her that Frank did, a very com-
manding, very compelling persona. You
couldn't help being drawn to her. At fifty-
two, she was still a very beautiful lady. She
took good care of herself. Her appearance
was impeccable. She was wearing a dark,
relatively low-cut, beautiful wrap dress that

accentuated her curves. It was very complimentary to her physique. It draped around her hips to her knees, and it was tied to the side rather than sewn, so you could see flashes of her legs when she walked. Her hair was dark and glossy and fell just so. She was still every inch a movie star.

When my first break came, Jilly pulled me over to Frank's table and introduced me to her. I was invited to sit down at the table and be a part of the conversation. We talked a bit. She was pleasant and very funny. I joined her again on my second break, and then it was time for her to leave. I was about to head downstairs to use the men's room before I started my next set. She was getting up to leave at the same time, so Jilly and I walked her out. We paused at the doorway with the plywood cutout of Frank. Ava leaned over and planted a kiss on "Frank's" mouth and said to Jilly, "Take care of my man."

I was still very young then, so I had the nerve and the stupidity to ask her a completely inappropriate question that I'd been curious about since Frank had married Mia. Knowing I'd probably never see Ava again, I said, "Miss Gardner, I never thought I'd get an opportunity to ask you a question like this or take the liberty to ask you."

She said, "Yeah, what?"

Her tone was very disarming, so I said, "Given your relationship with Frank, what was your take when he took up with Mia?"

She laughed. Then she said, "Well, you know, I surmise you grew up in a similar fashion to the way Frank grew up. I'm guessing your only interaction with girls would be that it was either someone's mother, or a relative, or it was someone that you were hoping to score with on a date. Otherwise, most of the time you spent hanging out with your pals. It's a man's world, and you guys were hanging out with the guys, and no one ever thought that there was anything else going on with that. You just were enjoying the kinship of your male friends."

I said, "Yeah."

"So when Frank took up with Mia, I figured, you know what? He finally found something that he's been looking for his whole life. A boy with a c**t." Jilly and I looked at each other like, *Well, okay then.* Neither of us could believe what she'd just said, and we had no idea what to say in reply. I was shocked.

I finally said, "Okay . . . . Well, it's been an absolute pleasure. And I hope to see you again one of these days. But I need to,

216

uh . . ." She leaned over and kissed me on the cheek. I went downstairs to the bathroom, shaking my head in disbelief. I didn't know if she'd said it just to see what kind of a reaction she'd get from me, or if that was really the way she felt, or if she was trying to be funny. To this day, I'm not sure. I do know that Frank got one thing right. She was a firecracker.

It's been printed over and over that Frank pined for Ava the rest of his life, that he never got over her. That wasn't the case. He always had a special place in his heart for her, but he rarely talked about her, and he had no desire to renew the relationship. It took him a long time to get over her, but he did. The fire burned itself out. He always loved her, and when she passed away, he mourned her as he did all those who'd been close to him. In the long run, though, he was better off as her friend than her lover, and he knew it.

Frank's longest marriage, though not his longest relationship, was with his fourth and last wife, Barbara. In the late forties, Barbara Blakeley had married her first husband, Robert Oliver, an executive with the Miss Universe pageant. The marriage produced Barbara's only child, Robert Jr. After her

217

divorce from Oliver, she left Bobby with his father for a while and went to Vegas to seek her fortune. Tall, blonde, and beautiful, she got a job as a showgirl, one of those statuesque beauties who pose onstage in a giant headdress. That was how she met and eventually married Zeppo Marx, the least-known brother of the Marx Brothers comedy team. She and Bobby moved to Zeppo's home in Rancho Mirage after the marriage. When Bobby was about eighteen, she had him take Zeppo's name, and he became Robert Marx. Barbara wanted a man who'd pay attention to her. Zeppo was more interested in gambling than he was in Barbara. Barbara and Zeppo lived on the fringe of the Tamarisk Country Club golf course, just across the fairway from Frank's compound. I don't know if meeting Frank was calculated, kismet, or just propinquity.

Frank and Barbara met at the club. Since Zeppo was too old to play tennis, Frank invited Barbara to play doubles with him. Soon Frank was asking Zeppo's permission to "borrow" his wife to serve as the hostess at Frank's cocktail parties. Zeppo didn't seem to care one way or the other, so Barbara became more and more of a fixture at Frank's side. She divorced Zeppo in 1973, the year after I met Frank. By 1974, the year

I met her, she was living as something of a camp follower, sometimes traveling with Frank. They dated, but not exclusively. He dated other women, too. I don't know how seriously he took her at that point, but Barbara already had her eye on the prize. They married in July 1976.

I could understand why Frank married Barbara. For starters, she was absolutely drop-dead gorgeous. Even in her later years, she was a very pretty lady. She could also be kind and thoughtful. She had a great sense of humor. She'd be flirtatious with Frank in a playful way, teasing him to bring a smile to his face. Sometimes she did little things to make him happy.

One time down in the desert, when the chef was off, she told me, "I'd like to cook. Why don't we cook together?" Barbara never cooked. The running joke was that Barbara thought *cook* was a noun, not a verb. That evening, though, we made dinner together. She took great pleasure in it.

When Frank complimented the food, Barbara said, "Thank you, sweetheart."

He looked at her, and then he looked at me, and I said, "Yeah, she made it this time."

He said, "This is delicious!"

Barbara beamed. She'd do little things like that to try to please him. Sometimes, though, she'd do things to please him that weren't well thought out and ended up backfiring.

After dinner one night at the beach house, she said, "Come on, sweetheart. Come on, Tony. I want to show you guys something."

So we walked outside and were facing the pool, on the north side of the property. There was a narrow walkway eighteen inches wide on the left side of the pool, in between the edge of the pool and the wall. Barbara had planted some vegetables in pots along the walkway. They were growing well, and she was very proud of her vegetables. Barbara was wearing one of her caftans that evening. It was long, down to her ankles, with wide legs that floated when she walked. As she bent down to one of the pots to show Frank a tomato, she caught her foot on the flowing hem of her caftan and toppled over into the pool. She went completely underwater. When she came up, her hair was hanging down all over her face. She was splashing like crazy with her arms, trying to stay afloat because the caftan was heavy from the water it had soaked up. She was struggling to get to the side of the pool. I stood there looking at her, wondering if I needed to take my shoes off and jump in after her.

Frank said to her, "Oh, for Christ's sake, get out of there. What the hell are you doing in there?" You would have thought she'd dived in on purpose! I had to kneel down and extend my arm for her to grab on, to get her out of the pool.

In those moments, she could be a regular girl, not Mrs. Frank Sinatra. I could see the little girl inside her, the cute little girl who was still there. I understood what Frank meant when he said, "Inside her, there's still a frightened little girl, and sometimes that's why she does the kinds of things she does. And I can't fault her. She acts first and thinks later."

Barbara could be thoughtful, too. She wrote little love notes to Frank all the time. On their sixteenth anniversary, she scrawled on a small notepad:

Sweetheart, ♡ I am the happiest lady in the world. Because I have you. You're the best. Happy Anniversary. I love you. Always, forever. 16 years is just the beginning. Love, Love, Love, from U Wife ats a me

The somewhat cryptic signoff was Barbara comically trying to imitate an Italian accent. She was saying: *Love from your wife, that's me!*

She was frequently sentimental. As their twentieth wedding anniversary approached, she began to think about a special way to celebrate it. One spring evening, as the three of us sat at dinner, Barbara began to tell Frank how happy and proud she was to be the woman who'd been his wife longer than anyone else. Frank was clearly touched. She wanted them to renew their vows at church, with all their friends in attendance, and have an alfresco dinner afterward at the beach house. Frank was happy to agree. They had two months to bring Barbara's vision to life.

The ceremony was held on July 11, 1996. It was a perfect Malibu day, with blue skies and a light salty breeze carrying the scent of the ocean. Barbara wore a beautiful, filmy light pink pantsuit with legs billowing down to her ankles. She glowed with excitement. Frank was wearing a charcoal sports jacket and light gray pants with a white shirt, a red tie with two white diamonds in the middle, and a matching red pocket square. I don't know whether Barbara chose the jacket or Frank did, but he asked me to pick out the tie. I knew he wanted to look just right because his picture that day was going to be in papers all over the world. He asked me to knot the tie for him because at that point, he sometimes had trouble doing it properly. He told me, "You knot it better than I do. You knot it just like I used to."

The ceremony was at Our Lady of Malibu Catholic Church, a small jewel tucked under the hillside below Malibu Canyon. The Spanish-style structure, with its adobe roof and ceiling of golden wooden arches leading to the altar, is both beautiful and peaceful. It is a small church, accommodating about two hundred people at most, so it provided an intimate setting for Barbara's romantic vision. That day, it was filled with the Hollywood elite, along with old friends from the desert. Afterward, we returned to the beach house for the reception, held outdoors on the ocean side. It was an area between the glass doors leading into the house and the back boundary of the property. The glass doors at that end of the house all slid back so that the indoors actually became part of the outdoors. The ocean was only a heartbeat away, its waves a gentle cadence like ambient music. The ocean view was stunning as the great orange ball of the sun slowly sank into the waves. The interior of the house was sleek and open, large rooms furnished with clean white furniture, glass, and chrome. It looked like a luxury hotel. That day, there were cocktails and hors d'oeuvres inside the house when we got back after church, and afterward, dinner was served in the backyard. The ocean breeze rose in the evening, riffling unattended napkins. A bandstand with a microphone was set up inside the sliding glass doors, across from the glass-topped bar.

There were many singers there that day, including Peggy Lee and Jerry Vale, but Frank didn't want any singers performing except me and Steve Lawrence. I had a blast performing again. I was so thrilled to be in the company of those people, all of whom I knew well. I sang "Nice 'n' Easy," and Steve, if memory serves, sang "Where or When." Afterward, Barbara asked people to get up, and she got R. J. Wagner to say a few words. Then Don Rickles got up and "insulted" Frank and Barbara until people were in stitches. Barbara was thrilled with the day, and Frank had a very good time.

Later that evening, after everyone left, when Barbara went to bed, Frank took his tie off, held it up, and looked at it admiringly, saying, "This is a really beautiful tie. Jeez, I'm glad you chose this one." I didn't say anything. I just smiled.

He said, "Okay, let me have it. What's so funny?"

"It was a Christmas present last year from

Mrs. Nancy."

He cracked up and said, "You son of a bitch! There's going to be photographs of me wearing this tie circulated all over the world on my twentieth wedding anniversary with Barbara."

"I know. It's just between you and me." He found it very funny.

The next day, Barbara and I still hadn't heard from Frank by four o'clock in the afternoon. Barbara asked me to check on him, so I went upstairs. When I pushed his bedroom door open and peeked in, he was lying on top of the covers, staring up at the ceiling. I knocked on the door, and he said, "Hey, T, come in. What's going on in the world?"

"Same stuff. How you doing?"

"I got a question for you. What the hell did I do yesterday?"

"Frank, you *did* it twenty years ago. You just *redid* it yesterday." He started to laugh, and then we went downstairs, and he had his breakfast.

Despite their love for each other, there were strains in Frank and Barbara's marriage from the beginning. They had different ideas about money. Frank spent freely on people and causes he believed in. Barbara, in contrast, guarded every dollar, as though constantly afraid someone would take it away from her. All of her self-esteem was tied up in her status as Frank Sinatra's wife. Her beauty was all she felt she had, and she'd worked hard to parlay her looks into the lifestyle she'd dreamed of. As gorgeous as she was, Barbara seemed to be afraid she could lose it all and be right back where she started if she wasn't careful. Underneath the blonde sheen, she was insecure. Her insecurity extended to her son. She was always worried that Bobby wouldn't get his fair share. Her biggest rivals, in her mind, were Frank's children. She even tried to get Frank to adopt Bobby, who was already an adult, so that Bobby would be on equal legal footing with Frank's children. That idea put pressure on Frank, who ultimately refused, and it infuriated Frank's children. It also reinforced Barbara's fear that Frank's children would get more than Bobby did. It was like she was always shadowboxing.

Barbara was single-minded when she wanted something, and sometimes this caused problems. She wasn't very good at seeing the consequences of her actions from other people's point of view. For example, Barbara wanted a proper church wedding, with a priest performing the service. Because Frank was Catholic and divorced, he hadn't been able to marry Barbara in the Church. Barbara was Protestant by birth, but she'd converted to Catholicism when she married Frank. Early in the marriage, she asked Frank to annul his marriage to Nancy Sr. so that she and Frank could have a "proper" Catholic wedding. The request wasn't intended to be hurtful. I don't think Barbara ever said to herself, *How would I feel if someone were trying to erase my marriage? How would Frank's kids feel if an annulment made them illegitimate?* An annulment was just a formality to Barbara, a way to remove the roadblock to her dream. Whatever her reasoning, the consequences were devastating for Frank's family. Barbara's friend Father Rooney persuaded the Church to grant Frank an annulment in return for a sizable contribution. Nancy Sr. was heartbroken, humiliated, and deeply disillusioned about the church she'd always loved. She never attended mass again. The annulment, of course, made Frank's children technically illegitimate. It was the nail in the coffin of Barbara's relationship with them.

Over the years, the dynamic between Frank and Barbara gradually changed. When I first met her, she was completely submissive. She was very cognizant back then of not getting in Frank's way. Early on, she worried that he might lose interest in her like he had with many others. As Frank aged, however, he gradually relinquished more control to Barbara. I really became aware of this dynamic in the last decade of Frank's life. As the years passed, she began keeping track of Frank's possessions.

Frank had a lot of watches. He loved timepieces, as he called them. One of his watches was a Piaget that Barbara had given him for Christmas the first year they were married. One night, like a mischievous little kid, he took the watch out of the drawer and hid it. He wanted to see if Barbara would notice.

Sure enough, she asked him, "Sweetheart, where's that watch I gave you?"

He said very innocently, "I don't know, sweetheart." Then he smiled to himself. We sat in the den, listening to her going through drawers.

She came back a few minutes later with a fistful of watches, saying, "It's not here."

He held up the Piaget, smiled innocently, and said, "Oh, is this the one you're looking for, sweetheart?"

Frank and I used to joke about the amount

of jewelry he bought for Barbara. One night, sitting up with me as usual, he looked at me and said, "It's always just you and me. When did I stop spending my nights with a beautiful woman?"

"Yeah, I've been meaning to talk to you about that."

"About what?"

"About you and me. But then I realized you don't have any jewelry left. You gave everything to Barbara."

"You crazy SOB!"

At times, it was hard for me to understand Frank's relationship with Barbara. I knew that he often gave in to her against his wishes. Sometimes it was because he was chivalrous. When he was trying to please her, he'd say things like, "Yeah, sweetheart. Yes, dear, whatever you want. It's okay. Sure, sweetheart." He wanted to make her happy at that moment. But afterward, when he reconsidered what he'd just done, he'd get angry with himself. He'd ask me, "What the hell did I do?"

I'd say, "Well, you said it right. What did *you* do?"

At the end of the day, Frank was afraid of what might happen if he said no to Barbara. When he did say no to something she desperately wanted, she'd pull out the most effective tool in her arsenal, withdrawing her company. She wouldn't talk to him or even see him for days at a time. It was Frank's worst nightmare. When he was a kid, he was terrified every time his parents left him alone all night, frightened they'd never come back. He'd grown up fearing Dolly's disapproval. As an adult, he had trouble coping with any strong-willed woman he loved. The thought that Barbara might leave him was more than he could face.

My own relationship with Barbara was complex. It wasn't always an easy one, but I had real affection for her. I used to call her every year to wish her a happy birthday. When she'd pick up the phone in Palm Springs, I wouldn't even say hello. I'd just start to sing "Happy Birthday." Twice she thought it was Steve Lawrence singing, and I was very flattered. Even after Frank was gone, Barbara and I remained friends.

Barbara Sinatra was Frank's longest-lasting marriage, and I have no doubt that Ava Gardner was Frank's grand passion. But Nancy Barbato Sinatra was his great love. I knew Nancy well. I've always believed that Nancy Sr. was the woman Frank was meant to be with from the beginning to the end of

230

his life. She was his best friend for over six decades, and in the truest sense of the words, she was the love of his life.

Frank met Nancy Rose Barbato in the summer of 1934. She was seventeen, and he was nineteen. They met on her porch in Long Branch on the Jersey Shore. She was a dark Italian beauty, a sweet girl from a traditional family. Frank brought over his ukulele and sang to her. What teenage girl could resist young Frank Sinatra, singing to her on her front porch? Definitely not Nancy. Her father wasn't thrilled with young Frank. He would have preferred someone steadier, but a teenage girl in love isn't going to be held back by a skeptical father. The following year, Frank took Nancy to see Bing Crosby perform at Loew's Journal Square, a former vaudeville theater in Jersey City. He told me it was there that he turned to her and said, "You know what? I'm going to be a professional singer. Someday, that's gonna be me up there. Like I told you earlier, I'm going places."

It was a bold thing to say, but Nancy never doubted him. She told him, "I'll never get in your way." It was a prophetic and ironic response.

In 1939, Frank and Nancy got married.

He was twenty-four, and she was twenty-two. Her parents gave them a brand-new black Chrysler as a wedding present, and they drove to North Carolina for a four-day honeymoon. When they came back, they took a three-room, third-floor apartment in Jersey City. It was a working-class neighborhood, with Nancy's relatives and the occasional small-time mobster (in some cases, also a relative) living around the corner. When they had a party, it was a New York backyard party, the kind where if you needed a sandwich, someone would throw it to you across the yard. Nancy worked as a secretary, earning $25 a week, while Frank made $15 a week singing. At a combined $40 a week, they thought they were living the high life. Early in their marriage, Nancy got a $15 advance on her salary so Frank could get some publicity photographs made. They were hoping Frank could get the attention of orchestra leader Harry James. He did.

Frank signed with James at $75 a week and hit the road. At first, Nancy traveled with him some of the time. Nancy was with him when they were playing a gig in Chicago at the Palmer House. Frank told me that was where Nancy Jr. was conceived. Once Nancy Jr. was born, Nancy Sr. stayed home with her in New Jersey. Frank sent money home, but sometimes money was tight. Nancy sewed his gloves and bow ties to save cash, and sometimes Frank would find money sewn into the fingers of his gloves when he went back on the road. Nancy saved every penny to make sure he'd be all right.

Frank was soon touring with Tommy Dorsey and making good money, but the constant touring took a toll on the marriage. Frank and Nancy were now living very different lives. Things only got worse when they left New Jersey to move to California. Nancy didn't fit into Frank's new, glamorous existence. Nancy Sr. became a very elegant and sophisticated lady in later years, but when they first came to Hollywood, she remained that Jersey girl from the neighborhood. Besides, of course, there were the other women. That had started on the road, during those long nights traveling with the band. It was a no-strings-attached atmosphere, and from the beginning, women threw themselves at Frank. With unlimited access to beautiful and willing women, he gave in to his desires and did what many men wish they could do. It only got worse when he got to Hollywood, where there was much more temptation and much more serious consequences. Frank had romantic opportunities others would die for, and he turned few down. He did things he'd bitterly regret one day, and the more he did them, the easier it became to do them again. It soon became a well-worn groove. Although he seldom suffered immediate consequences, his chronic wrongdoing diminished his opinion of himself. In later years, when I became close friends with Nancy Sr., she and I talked about those years with Frank.

One day I asked her, "Why did you put up with his shenanigans for so long?"

She said, "I never would have stopped putting up with his shenanigans because that was a physical thing he was going through. I knew he adored me, and he adored his children, and he adored our home — not our house, our home. And he adored that part of his Italian self that he could get nowhere else. He always came home to me, no matter who he was with, no matter how long- or short-lived it was. He always came back to me, so I knew where his heart was. Other pieces of his anatomy are a different story altogether."

She said the only reason she finally gave him a divorce so he could marry Ava Gardner was that the publicity was hurting him professionally. The relationship was so public, so torrid, and so on-going that it was having a negative effect on Frank's public image. His popularity was beginning to falter as a result. Nancy agreed to give him the divorce he so desperately sought, primarily because she knew that the bad publicity was destroying his career. As much as she was suffering herself, she based her decision on what was best for him.

I told her, "It's no surprise he fell in love with you and cared deeply for you until the day he died." What a remarkable woman she was.

Despite his many affairs, Frank never stopped meeting with Nancy, even long after the divorce. She was, of course, the mother of his children, but it was more than that. As late as 1974, when Barbara was already in the picture but not yet married to Frank, he'd still have Nancy Sr. meet him at places on the road. Once he flew the family up to Lake Tahoe and had a romantic weekend with Nancy there. That kind of thing stopped when he married Barbara, but the love didn't. Nancy remained in his life until he died. He trusted her completely because she'd always been there for him, even when he had nothing, even when he didn't deserve her.

When Frank moved permanently to Los Angeles in the nineties, I'd have lunch with Nancy Sr. once or twice a month. She loved the pizza from Barone's in Toluca Lake. It was a throwback to when she and Frank lived in New Jersey. When I visited her, I'd bring her four or five of those pizzas to put in her freezer. In return, she'd give me "care packages" of Italian food wrapped in aluminum foil, reminiscent of when she and Frank were married. I'd take them to Frank. When I'd get to Frank's house and walk into his bedroom with a foil package, he'd look at me and say, "What have you got there?" I'd start to unwrap it, and he'd say, "You had lunch with her again, huh?"

"Yeah."

"Why do you do that?"

I'd smile at him smugly and say, "Because you can't." He'd laugh, though always with an undercurrent of melancholy. He loved every bite she cooked, especially when she'd make eggplant Parmesan. That was like giving him the Taj Mahal.

One small incident comes back to me whenever I think about Frank and Nancy. It was Christmas Eve 1996, a year after Dean Martin died, and Frank's health wasn't quite up to par. For once, both parts of the family had been able to assemble peacefully together at Thanksgiving, and in a moment of generosity, Barbara had invited Nancy Sr. to come for their Christmas Eve party, along with the kids. I don't think Barbara expected Nancy to take her up on it, but she did. Frank wasn't feeling well that night, so he told me he wasn't going to get dressed up. As we walked together down the hallway from the den, Frank got a glimpse of the guests in the living room ahead. He stopped and grabbed my arm. "Is that who I think it is?"

"Yeah, that's her." Nancy Sr. was standing there, but she hadn't noticed us yet.

"I'm not going to let her see me like this!"

We went back to his room, and it was only when Frank was dressed in classic Sinatra style that we went to the living room. After seven decades, Frank still cared what Nancy Sr. thought.

Frank used to tell me, "She'll always be there, the mother of my children." Unfortunately, that was part of the problem. Nancy was the mama; she represented traditional Italian family life and all the expectations that go with it. There are some aspects of Italian home life that are heavily demanding, traditions that need observance. In Frank's mind, it was easier to just dip the ladle in the Italian stew once in a while, take a sip, and deal with a controlled amount instead of being immersed in it. He could walk away from it all if it got unbearable. He'd seen the amount of control Dolly exercised over his father. He didn't know how to have a relationship with Nancy that wouldn't become stifling at some point. Ironically, of course, in choosing a very different marriage to a woman who was the farthest thing from Italian — who was, in fact, a WASP — he became entangled in different tentacles.

One time, when Frank was bellyaching to me about something between him and Barbara, I reminded him of how Nancy Sr. felt about him. After I went through the litany, he broke down and said, "What the hell am I doing?"

I told him, "I don't know, buddy. All I know is, there's a lady who doesn't live too far from here who'd sleep on the floor next to your bed just to be near you."

One day, I asked Nancy Sr. why she never remarried. She told me, "After you're married to Frank Sinatra, where are you going to go? And I never wanted the kids to have any question in their mind who their father was, so I didn't want to introduce another man into their world." I believe she also had a third, unspoken reason. From our conversations, I came to the conclusion that up until the day Frank passed away, in her heart of hearts, she believed that at some point in time, there'd be a Hollywood movie ending where he came back to her. On the surface that looked like self-delusion, but in reality, she was very nearly right. He did almost go back to her, more than once. I know, because I took him.

Frank asked me over and over what he should do about Nancy. Should he go back to her, or should he stay with Barbara and leave things as they were? I always told him it was his decision, one I couldn't make for him. Whatever he decided, I would support. One day, after a long conversation about Nancy Sr., Frank said to me, "I want to go over there" (meaning Nancy's place). Nancy had a house in the Tamarisk Villas, just down the block from the compound. She stayed in the desert quite often.

I said, "Let's take my Cadillac."

He said, "Okay. Good idea. I'll be right back." He went to his room, came back, and got in my car. We left through the gate of his compound, drove down the block, and pulled into the parking area inside Nancy's gated community. When I turned off the ignition, I could tell that Frank's breathing had changed. He was having an anxiety attack.

He said, "Ah, you know what, this is not . . . This is a mistake. I can't do this. I've got to go back."

I gently reminded him, "Frank, you've been talking about this for I don't know how long. You're sure this isn't what you want to do?"

"No, I can't do it. You've got to get me out of here. This is going to hurt too many people." I started the car, and we pulled away. As far as I know, Nancy Sr. never saw us.

The same scenario happened more than once, but the result was always the same. I'd drive Frank to her house, he'd panic, and we'd go home again. Frank never stopped loving Nancy, but he couldn't bring himself to go through that door. It was a complicated situation. We both knew that getting back together with Nancy Sr. could have made things worse. It could have invited increased tugging from his children, which already made him very uncomfortable. Not to mention the guilt he would have felt for leaving Barbara. If he stayed with Barbara, at least he'd be dealing with familiar problems. And he did love Barbara. He didn't want to hurt her, and he still wanted to please her. His ambivalence wasn't fair to either woman, and it wasn't fair to him. There was no good way out of the dilemma, and knowing that he was the one who'd created it only made it worse for Frank. He didn't really believe he deserved a happily-ever-after, even if he'd known how to find it. If his marriage to Barbara was a struggle, he thought it was no more than he deserved. He'd created the situation himself.

For most of their lives, Frank and Nancy's relationship was an exquisitely painful thing for them both, yet there was beauty in the heartache because he adored her. I wrote her a letter after Frank passed away. I told her that he never stopped loving her. She deserved to hear that. Her love for him was unconditional, no matter what problems he might have had. If he'd come back to her completely broken, financially and physically, the door would always have been wide open. If necessary, she would have walked out to the car to pick him up and carry him inside. Their story was like a Shakespearian tragedy. The potential for happiness was so close, and at the same time, so infinitely far away.

# CHAPTER 6
## YOU WILL BE MY MUSIC
### THE MUSICIAN

Frank's music had me hooked from the day I bought that first album at Woolworth's, when I was thirteen years old. I still remember sitting in the basement of our house when I got home and listening to "The Nearness of You." It was the first Sinatra song that knocked me off my feet. The very first thing I heard on that record was just a voice a cappella, a very rich, very deep baritone with a little bit of a buzz in it, singing, "It's not the *pale* moon that excites me . . ." Right as the voice sang *pale,* Bill Miller on piano came in, and it was piano and voice as Frank sang, "It's just the nearness of *you.*" Finally, eight bars in, the orchestra came in with that beautiful arrangement by Nelson Riddle. The richness of it reverberated through my body. I was captivated.

"Civilians" (a.k.a. non-musicians) sometimes think that successful singers are naturally talented, so when performance time comes, they just have to open their mouths, and golden sounds will pour out. It doesn't work that way. Good singers work as hard as good athletes to get and stay in shape vocally. When I first discovered Frank and went through my father's 78s from the Big Band days, the earlier Frank had a thinner voice that didn't sound quite as rich or as appealing as the Frank I discovered. This growth in Frank's vocal skills didn't happen by osmosis. Frank worked very hard at his craft. He studied voice technique very early in his performing career. After the scare of temporarily losing his voice in 1951, Frank took no chances. He was careful with his vocal exercises.

Frank had the utmost respect for opera, and whenever he had any kind of a vocal problem or question, he'd always call on opera singers. Frank admired the great opera star Luciano Pavarotti. At dinner with Pavarotti one night, Frank asked if he had any suggestions on how to improve his *diminuendo* (fading out a note).

Pavarotti answered, "Thatsa simple! You justa close-uppa-you-mouth!"

Afterward, Frank jokingly told me, "I'll never ask that guy a question again."

He also asked advice from the diva Maria

Callas. One night at Jilly's, I was sitting with Frank and his friends, including Maria, when Frank asked her, "How do you warm up your throat before a show?"

She kidded that one of her favorite techniques was to "deep-throat" a good-looking guy in the chorus. She said it relaxed all her throat muscles. I nearly fell out of my chair. In his best *Amos 'n' Andy* impersonation, Frank laughed and said, "Well, ah, I won't be doin' *that* any time soon."

Sometimes Frank would go for a high note, and if you were a singer, you could literally hear and see him planning to attack it. One night when we were at dinner, he discussed it with Keely Smith. Frank was a big fan of hers musically.

That night she was telling us, "Now that I'm getting older, some of those notes that I used to hit when I was younger are getting harder to hit. They're still within my grasp, but I've got to prep even more now to hit them. On some nights, I'm really scared that I'm not going to make it."

Frank said, "Well, use what they call the insurance clench."

Keely said, "What?"

"The insurance clench. You've never done that?"

"What's the insurance clench?"

244

"Prepare as best you can with your stomach, to get as much air in as possible. Then as you're going for the note, clench your ass cheeks. It'll push you right up over the top."

Clench your ass cheeks. Words of wisdom from the Chairman of the Board.

Frank was famous for his breath control. He never took a breath in the middle of a line. I still cringe every time I hear a singer do it. It was hard work, he'd tell me in our singer-to-singer discussions. The first thing he needed was extraordinary breath control, which he didn't have when he was starting out. He began swimming every chance he got in public pools, taking laps underwater and running lyrics to himself in tempo as he swam. He continued the practice until the end of his performing career. I'd watch him swim at the compound, and later at the beach house, when he was in his late seventies. Swimming developed his lung capacity and helped create his unique style. He said, "Instead of singing only two or four bars of music at a time, like most of the other guys, I was able to sing up to eight bars without taking a visible or audible breath. This gave the melody a flowing, unbroken quality, and that, if anything, was what made me sound different."

Frank and I talked ad infinitum about

vocalizing and how this talent was all about expressing a complete thought without a break. He'd tell me, "In normal conversation, you don't run out of air until you've completed your thought, even though you don't know what you're going to say until a split second before it comes out of your mouth. Why wouldn't you do the same thing in singing?"

Frank's detailed study of the normal use of breath enabled him to sing the way people talk. That simple idea made him sound like he was speaking to the audience personally. Frank also liked to tell me that every singer should approach the lyrics of a song as though they were a script. This meant that for Frank, a strong lyric was crucial. Frank approached his songs like an actor, putting himself in character. Like he did in his films, he tapped into an experience that he knew would help him lend depth to the lyric.

Frank was a consummate artist. All the elements of a song mattered to him. Choosing his favorite song was like choosing his favorite child for Frank, but if I had to pick for him, I'd say it was "Laura." Both the melody and the lyrics are not only beautiful but haunting. Frank loved that song. It captured the nostalgia, the beauty, and the regret he carried with him all his life for the loves he'd known and lost. The images in the lyrics lived in his mind: Laura's "face in the misty light . . . the laugh that floats on a summer night." Like so many of his greatest songs, the images evoked both his great love, Nancy, and his great passion, Ava, both lost to him, in part because of his own failures, as he well knew.

If you want to understand Frank Sinatra, listen to his music. It's his life — the love, the passion, the pain, the loss, and the jubilation. Audiences knew it. That's what drew them. All his secrets are hidden in plain sight. The real man reveals himself: his strengths, his weaknesses, his loves, his regrets, and his humor, all in his music. Frank was an autobiographical singer. He would draw personally on his own experiences.

Sometimes the biographical connections were very direct. There were many allusions to Nancy Sr., beginning with "Night and Day," which Frank was already performing when he and Nancy were dating. He had a strong affinity with the song because the title was his and Nancy's nickname. When they were first together, Nancy was working as a secretary during the day, and Frank was performing at night. Her father, Mr.

Barbato, would be sitting on the porch as they came up the walk after a date and say in Italian, *"Adesso vene notte e giorno"* (Here come night and day).

He said to Nancy, with love in his heart, "I don't see how this is going to work. You work all day and sleep all night, and he sleeps all day and works all night." Frank recorded that song several times over the course of his career, always for Nancy.

Frank knew he was a fool to leave Nancy for Ava Gardner, and nothing makes that clearer than one of the rare songs he co-wrote in 1951, the year he married Ava. It was called "I'm a Fool to Want You." He knew he was a fool to want Ava, "But right or wrong, I can't get along / Without you." Frank told me he called his arranger, Nelson Riddle, a day or so before the recording session and told him, "Listen, do me a favor. Make sure you run that chart as many times as you feel you need to, because I'm not sure that I've got more than one take of that song in me. It affects me too much." He went into the studio and did one take of that song, one take that has stood over time. The depth and emotion of the recording speak for themselves. When Frank's close friends Steve Lawrence and Eydie Gormé sang the song to him the night he received an Ella Award, Frank visibly shrank into himself, his face a mask of misery, on the verge of tears.

Another deeply personal song about both Nancy and Ava is "Forget to Remember." It was supposed to be included on the *My Way* album in 1969. Frank did record it, but he purposely left it off the *My Way* album and performed it only once, on a television special. I asked him why he'd never published it, because I loved the song.

Frank said, "I purposely didn't put it on the album. This sounds strange, but I was afraid it might become a hit, and I'd be forced to sing it in concert, night after night after night. And I didn't have the wherewithal emotionally to do that." He connected some lines from the song with Nancy. Others he connected with Ava. And for both women, "But don't remember, refuse to remember / Forget to remember love."

The song was finally released in 1995 as part of *The Complete Reprise Studio Recordings,* a twenty-CD set gathered from the Reprise vault without Frank's participation. Comparatively few listeners have ever heard it, but it's worth the search through the long collection it's housed in.

Frank went on to record songs referencing his third wife, Mia ("The Man in the Looking Glass," from *September of My Years,* 1966), and later his last wife, Barbara, both the self-titled "Barbara" and the tongue-in-cheek "I Love My Wife." He recorded "How Do You Keep the Music Playing?" with Quincy Jones in 1984, looking back at his relationships with Nancy and Ava, and briefly with Mia. The most powerful connections, however, were with his first great loves. Those songs capture the quintessential combination of joyousness and painful regret that was Frank Sinatra until the end of his days.

Whenever Frank talked about his work, he'd always give credit where credit was due. He looked at his career as a collaboration, working with other great artists to create something none could have created separately. This included the songwriters and musicians. If I had to pick the musician that Frank relied on the most, I'd have to say it was Bill Miller. Musically, Bill and Frank were like a hand and a glove. Bill once said to me, "The secret to us being a good musical fit is that I'm every place he's not, and where he is, I'm not." Bill also paid attention to the lyric the same way Frank did. For example, on "Send in the Clowns," as Frank sang the words, Bill would make the music follow. The lyric goes, "One who keeps tearing around / One who can't move." At that point, Bill would lay the chord out and just hold on it. *He* wouldn't move. There was a period of silence. Then he'd take his hands off the keyboard and wait for Frank to continue singing.

That's an artist who's thinking about the music and allowing the vocalist to do what he does best.

No matter how great the songwriter or the musicians, however, a song doesn't work without a great arranger. Arrangers can make or break a piece of music. They create the charts that guide both the singer and the musicians. A chart is like a musical map, telling them where the song is going. An arranger looks at the lyric and the melody barebones, with nothing. Then he creates a frame for the song like an artist creates a frame for a picture that highlights key elements for the viewer. The same song can be arranged a variety of ways. Frank used to tell me, "Any song that is constructed well musically can lend itself to any number of approaches. I can do the same song as a ballad. I can swing it. I can do it as a bossa nova. I can do it as a waltz. You'd be surprised. If a song is constructed properly, it lends itself to a whole rainbow of treatments."

Maybe the best example I can give you of what an arranger does comes from a story Frank told me. One afternoon, Frank was on his way to a recording session with Gordon Jenkins, who arranged many of Frank's ballads and themed albums. In the car on the way to the session, Frank heard a twangy song by a folk group called the Brothers Four. It caught his attention, for as he often did, he tuned out the delivery and just concentrated on the melody and the lyric. When Frank got to the session, he pulled Gordon aside and said, "I just heard a song by the Brothers Four on the car radio. It's done very country with banjos, but the lyric and the melody have far more depth than that treatment, and I want you to look it up and write a chart that would fit me." The song was "It Was a Very Good Year."

The man who wrote that song was Ervin Drake. He composed hundreds of songs in his career. None of his other work came close, however, to equaling Frank's version of "It Was a Very Good Year." Ervin lived well into his nineties. In later years, after Frank was gone, I finally met him. He came to see Don Rickles at a performance in

Westbury, Long Island. After the show, he was introduced to me since I was Rickles's manager by then. He knew nothing about my connection to Frank.

As we shook hands, I said, "It's a pleasure to meet you. I love your work. And that was an absolutely gorgeous letter that you wrote to Frank. Frank was grinning ear to ear when I read it to him."

Ervin said, "Letter?"

"Yeah, you wrote Frank a letter on his eightieth birthday about how he found the depth of that song that even you hadn't envisioned, and you thanked him for putting your kids through college based on his version of that song."

"Oh, my God. So you read that? Geez, I got to get in touch with Nancy Jr. and see if I can get a copy."

"You don't need to do that. I still have it. When I get back to California, I'll make you a copy and mail it to you." And I did. He then proceeded to write me a beautiful letter thanking *me.*

Frank worked with many brilliant arrangers over his long career, but his greatest collaboration was with Nelson Riddle. Nelson was a genius in his own right. He saw his job this way: "As an arranger, you have to stay out of the vocalist's way. You have to understand that it's not the vocal accompanying the orchestra. It's the orchestra accompanying the vocal." Nelson became an integral part of Frank's world and distinctive sound. Initially, he didn't vary too far from patterns that Frank was accustomed to, but from the start, he offered a unique and fresh approach. For a long time, Nelson and Frank were magic together.

Frank once told me a very funny story about doing an album with Nelson. Back then, albums always had twelve songs. Frank was working on an album, but he only had eleven songs in the can. He wanted to finish the album at the next recording session because he was leaving to go on a trip, but the missing twelfth song didn't have a chart. So he called Nelson Riddle at home the night before the recording session and said, "We're one song short. Write me an arrangement of 'I've Got You Under My Skin' for tomorrow night." It was a ridiculously short time to write a chart. Nelson started writing it immediately, but when it was time to leave for the session the next day, he hadn't finished it. Desperate, he had someone drive him to the studio in his station wagon while he sat in the back with a piece of plywood across the backseat to use as a table. He wrote the arrangement for

"I've Got You Under My Skin" in the car on the way to Capitol Records from his beach house in Malibu!

Despite Frank's working with so many great arrangers, every now and then an arrangement would go horribly wrong and still end up on a record. It usually happened when Frank didn't have the lead time he needed for a piece of music. Frank liked to live with material for as long as a year ahead of going into a studio, trying it out on the road and modifying it based on performance experience. Frank said that recording a song was like carving it in granite. If something went wrong, it would haunt him afterward, looping back to bite him on the ass. We'd be in a club somewhere, and a song that he hadn't done the best job on would come over the speakers. He'd do everything short of putting his fingers in his ears and would try to talk over it: "Oh, here it comes. I don't want to hear that. Oh my God, what the hell was I *thinking*?" A classic example is "Some Enchanted Evening," the gorgeous song sung by Giorgio Tozzi on the *South Pacific* soundtrack. God knows why, but instead of the usual strings accompanying the singer, the arranger for Frank's version decided to go with brass. Loud brass. It went like this: *Frank's voice:* "Some enchanted *evening*" / *the full horn section blast-ing a deafening echo:* Da-da-da-da-*da*-da / *Silence* / *Repeat.* The result is so jarring, it's comical.

After the 1984 release of the album *LA Is My Lady,* with Quincy Jones, Frank took a break from recording. A long break. He continued to travel and perform in concerts, but for the greater part of a decade, he wasn't sure he wanted to go back into a studio. During those years off from record-ing, he liked to watch the late-night talk shows. Talk-show hosts like Johnny Carson or Dave Letterman were always asking performers, "Who was influential in your career? Who did you listen to?"

He'd hear performer after performer say-ing, "Well, Sinatra was the quintessential singer, and this particular song, it's one of my favorites . . ." So Frank kept hearing performers say how they were fans of his and talk about their favorite Sinatra songs. Eventually, he started asking himself, *What if I paired with so-and-so on their favorite song?* The initial idea of doing the *Duets* albums came from Frank himself. Duetting on an album would give Frank a chance to do one of his favorite things: perform with another singer. By then, though, Frank was in his late seventies, and he wasn't sure

Reprise would be interested in doing another album with him. The last album he'd done for Reprise was *Trilogy* in 1980.

Frank told Jilly one night, "This whole duet thing I've been thinking about, I like the idea. I'm liking the way it sounds. But the prospect of doing another album for Reprise, the way they've been handling my stuff, I'm not so sure." He left it at that. What he didn't say was that this would probably be the last thing he was ever going to record, and he wanted it to be good.

After decades with Frank, Jilly knew how to interpret Frank's meaning when he said something. The unspoken words Jilly heard were, *Why don't you look into it for me, because I don't want to make a formal inquiry and then put myself in a position of being embarrassed by what I hear back.* Frank wanted to find out how Mo Ostin, the head of Reprise, would feel about Frank's going in and doing another record, and he wanted Jilly to test the waters. So Jilly made an appointment with Mo, and I took him over to Warner Bros., because at that point Warner had already bought a portion of Reprise. When Jilly came out of the meeting, he didn't say anything about what went down, and I didn't ask, but he clearly had something on his mind.

We were driving back down the hill to my condo when Jilly said, "I can't believe the attitude that Mo just gave me."

"What do you mean?"

Jilly told me that Ostin had said, "I think the world of Frank. I appreciate everything he's done for me, but I think Frank's recording years are behind him."

Neither I nor Jilly told Frank what had happened. Shortly after that meeting, Jilly passed away, and I sure didn't have the heart to tell Frank about the meeting with Mo. Fortunately, Charles Koppelman, the head of Capitol Records and EMI was already interested in re-signing Frank with Capitol. Koppelman presented him with a picture that was very appealing. Frank said Charles told him, "Well, you pretty much started your career at Capitol. What better way to close out your career than coming back home to Capitol?" So Frank made the transition and signed a very sweet deal with Capitol, with a blue-chip royalty fee and substantial back-end payments if the record was successful.

When the announcement that Frank was going back to Capitol Records was made in the press, he got a telegram from Mo Ostin, saying, "I'm very disappointed you never even inquired about doing this at Reprise.

And I'm very disappointed personally." Frank felt terrible. We were in the desert when the telegram came. It was late, and Barbara had gone to bed hours earlier, but Frank and I were still up. After listening to Frank beat himself up over it for a while, I couldn't take it anymore.

I said, "I got something I need to tell you. Jilly couldn't bring himself to tell you because he didn't want to piss you off, and he didn't want you to be hurt. But now that I'm hearing this, I have to tell you. Jilly went to see Mo about a possible deal for you on this duets thing. Jilly said that Mo basically told him that your recording years are behind you."

Frank looked at me. "Oh, really? Oh, *really*?" That did it. Frank did a complete turnaround and never looked back. Reprise's loss was Capitol's gain.

So *Duets* was a go. But when they started to look into the whole thing, it became clear that Frank wouldn't be able to do the album the way he'd envisioned. We were in Vegas with Hank Cattaneo, Frank's production manager, at Frank's suite in the Desert Inn. Hank was one of the producers on the record, and he told Frank that because of scheduling conflicts with other artists, it wasn't possible to put Frank in the studio recording live with the other singers. Frank would likely be in the studio by himself, laying down his tracks. Then the duet portion would be put together in post-production.

Frank balked. He told Hank, "It's not going to come out right. You cannot duplicate the energy you get between artists when you do something right there in the moment, live. That's why I recorded live with a studio orchestra, and I'm in the middle of it on every single record I've ever done." He was starting to get really worked up.

Finally, I looked over at Hank and said, "Let me jump in here." Then I turned to Frank and said, "I understand what you're feeling, Frank, but let me tell you the way most performers record these days. Very few record live with the band there. These performers are accustomed to doing records in pieces. They go in, and they record the rhythm section, and then they go in two weeks later and do the brass and the woodwinds, and eventually, they stand in an isolation booth and lay down the vocals. That's the way most artists are accustomed to recording these days. So picture this: You're asking these people to come into the legendary Studio A of Capitol Records with a live fifty-plus-piece orchestra and then look across the room and see *your* face. You know what you're going to get? Dust." He looked at me a second, and I could see a smile kind of creep over his face. So I continued, "What Hank's telling you is extremely possible."

"I don't know, T."

"Frank, you remember when we were in the desert a couple of weeks ago, we were sitting out by the pool, and we were listening to the radio? And that gorgeous recording came on, 'Unforgettable,' with Natalie Cole?"

"Oh yeah, what a great record."

"What year is this?"

"Don't be funny."

"How long has Nat King Cole been dead?"

"Holy shit, that's right. If they could put her voice with a dead guy . . ."

"Exactly. It can be done."

Frank thought for a moment and then said, "Okay, you made your point." He still wasn't crazy about the idea, but I convinced him it was possible.

Once Frank was on board, the people who were involved came up with a tentative list of singers they wanted to have on the album with Frank. Frank had only limited control over the singers he duetted with. He would have loved to record with the people he'd sung with over the years. Frank wanted to do "Mack the Knife" with Ella Fitzgerald. At the time we were doing *Duets,* though, Ella had just had her leg amputated because of her diabetes. She lived only a few blocks away from Frank. I told producer Phil Ramone, "People are recording their portions all over the world, and she's right down the street. There's nothing wrong with her throat, and there's nothing wrong with her voice. I think this actually might be a major plus for her, given what she's going through." He agreed with me that Ella would be ideal, but he thought her health was too fragile to risk it. The executives wanted more current performers, people who'd be a draw for younger audiences. They lined up Jimmy Buffett to do "Mack" with Frank. No disrespect to the man — Jimmy Buffett is good at what he does — but "Mack the Knife" isn't really his style.

Thirteen people were eventually signed to duet with Frank on the first album. Capitol had no trouble finding people eager to sing with Frank. Once performers were approached as potential duet artists, they'd submit a list of their favorite Sinatra songs. The songs were then cross-referenced, and that's how the producers figured out who'd do what. Frank would lay down his tracks first. Then Frank's voice would be removed, and the duet voice plugged in, and the couple paired.

The first night we were due to record was a disaster. It was a Monday. I drove Frank to the studio, along with one of the executive producers, Eliot Weisman. As we walked down the hall of Studio A, Frank's tension was obvious. When we got to the studio, we saw that the orchestra was in one part of the studio, and an isolation booth was set up for Frank in another part.

Frank said hello to everybody, then said, "Where do you have me?" They pointed to the isolation booth, and Frank said, "Wrong."

Several of us huddled together, and I said, "Listen, he's not comfortable unless he's in the room with the band."

Then Frank turned around and looked at me and motioned with his index finger. "Let's go." And we left. The producers were panicked. The evening had cost them a load of money, with a full complement of musicians and engineers who had to be paid, whether Frank sang or not.

The next night, I drove Frank to the studio again. I didn't know what to expect. They had made some changes to the layout overnight. They now had Frank set up in a semi-isolation booth off to the side of the room. They'd put up baffles (padded portable walls with sound insulation), creating a four-by-eight soundproof structure. In the middle of it was a window that Frank could look through and see the orchestra. Frank still wasn't happy. He came back to where I was waiting in his dressing room and started getting himself all worked up.

I said, "Listen, relax. But you know what, Frank? The guys have been here rehearsing, and we didn't do anything last night. I think it would help the musicians to phrase what's written if they know where you're going to put your voice. Then if you really want to split, we'll get out of here." I knew Frank had a soft spot for his musicians. Most were guys who had recorded with Frank from the late fifties on.

Frank finally said, "Okay."

At that point, I'd started to wonder whether the problem was really all about the isolation booth. Frank hadn't recorded anything of substance in almost eight years, and I knew how he felt about things that were laid down for eternity. Knowing that this was probably the last recording he was ever going to make, he didn't want it to be embarrassing. What crossed my mind was,

*He's afraid he can't do it anymore.* So I figured, okay, if he can hear what he sounds like, maybe he'll be all right.

I went out and said to one of the sound guys on the sly, "Listen, I only got him to do one or two scratch vocals, and I need you to do me a favor. Plug something into the board so that I can have a recording of it. And don't tell anybody." He nodded.

Frank came out and ran through a few tunes with the orchestra, and then he wanted to leave.

He said, "Okay, we'll see you soon, fellas." Once again, people in the control booth were looking like at us like, *Holy shit. Oh, my God, he's leaving again, and we've got nothing.*

As we were walking out, I saw the guy I'd talked to in the control booth. He glanced around, then handed me a cassette he'd made on a Dictaphone. I murmured, "I'll meet up with you later. I don't want anyone to have any evidence of this, and I don't want to get you in trouble."

The next day, Wednesday, there was no recording session. The producers tried to figure out what to do next. That afternoon at lunch, Frank and I were sitting by the pool, and as usual, we had the little portable boom box (radio/cassette player) that we used to take outside with us. We were listening to music on KMPC when Frank went in the house to get a cigarette. As soon as he left, I stuck the cassette of the scratch recording in the boom box and cranked the volume down a little bit. When Frank came out, I hit "Play." He lit his cigarette and sat down again next to the boom box. I waited. I knew I was taking a big risk. Frank might be really angry about what I'd done, something that had never happened with us before.

He took a drag and all of a sudden got this weird look on his face. "What the hell is that?" Then, "Turn that up."

I turned it up, and he said, "When the hell did I record this?"

"More important, do you like the way you sound?"

"Well, yeah, it sounds pretty good. Why?"

"Well . . ."

"You did that?" Then it dawned on him. He smiled and shook his head. "You son of a bitch."

I said, "Frank, do you like the way it sounds? It's raw, not mixed, and no effects, but I think you still sound pretty damn good."

"Roll it back to the top." I ran the thing back and played it for him in its entirety.

He looked at me with this big smile on his face. "When's the next recording session?"

"Tomorrow night if you want."

"They better be ready. Because if I get mine, they better get theirs." Ol' Blue Eyes was back.

Thursday night, I drove him to the studio again. We went in, Frank said his hellos, and we looked at the new arrangement of Studio A. They had reconfigured his isolation booth again, and he was as close to being in the middle of the band as possible without the band's bare stuff bleeding into his microphone. It was as close to what he was used to as he was going to get. Frank was okay with it. You could practically hear the collective sigh of relief in the room. We started shortly after eight o'clock, and in an hour and a half, we recorded nine songs. *Nine.* When he finished, Frank was jubilant. We were in the control room listening to the playback, and I looked over at him and said very quietly, "Too bad Mo can't hear this."

Frank grinned. He turned to producer Phil Ramone and said, "Crank that shit up. I want them to hear it over the hill at Reprise."

There were several more nights of recording while Frank laid down the remaining vocals. But some of the tunes, like "One for My Baby," were one take. The sessions were giving me goose bumps. I stood there one night thinking, *This is the same studio, the same exact studio where thirty-five, almost forty years ago, the same musicians were in this same place, recording this same tune for the first time.*

With Frank's vocals down, the other performers could go to work. Some of the performers were not even in this country when they laid down their tracks. There were people sitting at Capitol in Hollywood and people on other continents. Bono was in Ireland. Charles Aznavour was in Paris. It was the first time an album had ever been done that way. The process was done with a technology called Avnet. Basically, they were playing the original recording in Hollywood over a secured line, and the other singers were listening to it and laying down their tracks in an isolation booth at a remote location. Then it was put together in post-production.

Overall, it went very well, but we did have one little hiccup. We got a call from Phil Ramone one night, saying that Barbra Streisand had finished the recording, and it had come out phenomenal. However, she'd decided to personalize the tune, and she'd sung, "Oh, you make me blush, Francis," without telling anybody she was going to do it. So now the producers felt the need to have Frank personalize it back. At first, Frank didn't want to have anything to do with it. We were in Connecticut at Foxwoods casino, not in a recording studio. He didn't really want to personalize a song for someone besides his wife, anyway.

I pulled him aside and said, "Frank, what's your wife's name?"

"Barbara."

"Well, don't sing to Streisand. Sing to your wife."

He thought a second and shrugged. "That would work." We brought a Nagra recorder into Frank's inner dressing room, and Frank told the crew, "Keep it down. We're doing something really special." Frank recorded that one line, "I have got a crush, my Barbara, on you," on the road, in a dressing room, in a casino in Connecticut. That's show business.

That year Capitol Records created an award called the Tower of Achievement Award, after the Capitol tower in Los Angeles. It was the first award of its kind, and they gave it to Frank as part of the *Duets* celebration. Frank was ecstatic. One of my favorite memories is when Frank found out

*Duets* had knocked Pearl Jam out of first place in the music charts. Frank was absolutely thrilled that he could do something like that at his age.

"Eighty years old, and I just knocked out Pearl Jam!"

When it came time to do *Duets II,* Frank was very much looking forward to it, and once again, people were lining up to do it. He was very excited about duetting with Frank Jr. on "My Kind of Town." He felt Frankie deserved a place on the album. A few of the song selections had to be adjusted when they started recording. Someone decided Willie Nelson should be paired with Frank for "My Way." Willie didn't seem very comfortable with the song. I talked to Frank about it, and he said, "Let's pick another song to do with Willie." They ended up doing "A Foggy Day" together, and it was great.

Frank and I were talking one night when Frank asked me what I thought about his doing another album. "What would you suggest I do?" Of course, I'd already given plenty of thought to that.

"I think you should do an album of ballads that can swing. Ballads like 'The Second Time Around' and 'I Hadn't Anyone Till You,' things that can lend themselves to swing." I sang a little to show him what I meant.

He loved the idea. He said, "Jesus, why didn't I ever think of this?"

It never happened, of course. When the subject of doing a third album came up, the powers that be decided to put out a Sinatra live album. They ended up extracting songs from different concerts and covered the segues with applause and audience reactions. However, they did take my suggestion on one thing and included "Maybe This Time" on that album. It's a poignant ballad from *Cabaret*. It was one of the best arrangements Costa ever did, and one of the best songs Frank did in concert, but he'd never recorded it in a studio. It was good to see it preserved for posterity.

If you look at the *Duets* albums, you won't see me credited, even in the thank-yous. That's show business. That's politics. The people who mattered most, though, were very gracious in their acknowledgments. Capitol Records Vice President Michael Frondelli and other executives at Capitol recognized my contribution, awarding me a triple platinum for *Duets I* and a platinum and gold for *Duets II*. I have both framed with their cover art. They knew the integral part I'd played in keeping the project afloat.

Both framed copies are hanging on the wall in my den. I don't know how, maybe Frank made him aware of it, but LeRoy Neiman found out about the role I played in making that project happen. He sent me a copy of the album cover art, which he drew. It's a gorgeous copy, and written across the artwork are the words "Tony, Bravo, LeRoy Neiman, '93." He sent it to me in 1998, the year Frank passed away. Most important, *Frank* knew what I'd contributed. At the end of the day, that's what really mattered.

Music has been my best friend from the very beginning. It was Frank's, too. I don't think he and I would ever have gotten so close if we hadn't shared that. We spent hundreds of hours talking about music and the art of singing. They'd fascinated us both from childhood. From the time I was a little boy, whenever life felt overwhelming, I'd sit down alone in the basement and play music. Frank understood how I felt. He used to joke with me about his album *Only the Lonely,* the "Pagliacci" album with the picture of Frank as a clown on the cover, a tear rolling down his cheek. The music is beautiful, haunting. Frank liked to tell me, "That recording should be available to the general public by prescription only." He said it was tantamount to a drug, one that would help the listener. You'd be listening to this poor bastard and what he was going through, and it kind of made your problems disappear. I still listen to that album, and it still makes my problems disappear. Except for one: missing Frank. That's something even his music can't fix.

# CHAPTER 7
# THE HOUSE I LIVE IN
## THE MAN BEHIND THE MYTH

It was dim in the banquet room, crowded with round tables. A breathtaking array of musicians was there in formal clothing, the women's bejeweled dresses glimmering in the half-light. The grand ladies of the Big Band era had just finished serenading Frank Sinatra. The applause died down, and then, without preamble, a spotlight picked out a glittering figure in the second tier of tables. Her white-blonde hair shone in the darkness, and her black sequined dress twinkled like raindrops under the moon. The tabletop hid her wheelchair from the cameras. She was a little older, a little heavier, but still beautiful, still undeniably Peggy Lee. When she began to sing "The Man I Love," the familiar voice slid through the darkness like cool silk. Seated behind Frank and his family, Jilly and I could see where the spot picked her out of the darkness.

As Henry Mancini led the orchestra in the

opening bars, Peggy smiled at Frank across the room and sang the lyrics she'd written especially for that night. At first they were playful, funny, a little flirtatious. But when she reached the last verse, the tone changed:

> But when I needed you,
> Oh, what a guy,
> You sent your plane for me,
> So I could fly.
> You brought me home, my friend,
> You made me try.
> That's why you are the man I love . . .

Most of the audience had no idea what she was singing about that night, but Frank, Jilly, and I did. We were all in tears. As she sang the last note in that sultry voice that defined her, she gripped the sides of the wheelchair and painfully forced herself to a standing position.

Then she beamed at Frank and said, "I'm standing!" It was her way of giving Frank a standing ovation.

The evening was December 3, 1990, nine days before Frank's seventy-fifth birthday, the night the Society of Singers gave him their coveted Ella Award. The best musicians, old and new, had come to honor Frank. They all knew the singer. Unlike

Peggy, few knew the depths of generosity in the man.

In the decade between his marriages to Ava and Mia, Frank lived on Bowmont Drive in the Hollywood Hills, near the fabled "Lovers' Lane" known to every local teenager. The view at night is stunning, the lights of LA like diamonds scattered across black velvet. It was the perfect location for a swinger's bachelor pad. Peggy lived two doors down from Frank, on another of the small hilltops that populate the drive. She liked to joke that she could no longer go to sleep without the sound of Frank setting off cherry bombs at night because it meant that he was home and well. Peggy had begun to struggle with some chronic health problems by then, but she was still one of the great ladies of music. She and Frank became close friends, good neighbors.

Peggy wasn't in the best of health one morning when she had to fly out to New York on business. Things only got worse after her arrival, and she was soon hospitalized, gravely ill. Frank kept tabs on her from LA. He'd been worried about her making the trip when her health was so fragile. When he found out she was in the hospital, he talked to her doctor directly.

"So what's the deal?" Frank asked him.

The doctor told him, "Well, I'm worried about her state of mind. She's very depressed because she's not home in her familiar environment."

The doctor explained that Peggy was in a bad way — in strange surroundings, away from her loved ones, seriously ill, and desperately homesick. Frank offered to fly her home on his plane, but the doctor said she wouldn't survive the trip.

"We've discussed that, but I've explained to her that it isn't safe. She has to be in a hospital environment right now."

Frank said, "Okay."

He made a few calls, and within twenty-four hours, he'd had his private plane completely reconfigured as a hospital plane, including the necessary equipment and medical personnel. He contacted Peggy's medical team and sent the plane to New York. An ambulance took Peggy from the hospital to Teterboro Airport. There, they put her on Frank's jet with a doctor and a couple of nurses and flew her home. Meanwhile, Frank had her home set up like a hospital room and made arrangements for 24/7 medical care. When the plane landed in LA, it was met with an ambulance and nurses, who brought Peggy home. It must have cost a small fortune, but Frank brushed away any mention of the money. The world didn't know about it, but Peggy and her doctor knew that Frank had saved her life.

That was the Frank Sinatra I knew. The one the world seldom saw.

Frank's emotional life was intense and complicated. Whether he was two or eighty-two, the child from Hoboken was still alive and well inside him. He'd been alternately smothered and abandoned as he grew up. He learned early that screaming was the best way to get his parents' attention. If he screamed loud enough, he'd get what he wanted. It was an approach to life that he used until he died. Surviving much of the time on his own when he was young, he developed both impressive skills and quirky idiosyncrasies in dealing with other people. Sometimes he was the perfect friend. Other times, he could be your worst enemy. Sometimes he was the tough guy, the immovable force, living up to the name Chairman of the Board. There was another side, though — the man who avoided conflict with family and close friends. He had a terror of standing up to those he truly loved for fear they'd abandon him. His heart was deep and tender, and at his core, he was a big softie. But the other side of him ran as deep.

If he felt injured, or if he thought that someone he cared about had been wronged, then as generous as he could be, that's how angry he could get. Frank was never quite sure why or how he found success, and that made him insecure. He couldn't quite comprehend the magnitude of his own popularity. Nobody gives you a handbook on how to navigate the kind of mega success he achieved. Sometimes, it was overwhelming for him.

When he was in his twenties and thirties, he'd frequently revert to the street skills he'd learned in Hoboken. If he got angry and thought a guy deserved it, he'd deck him. On several occasions, his anger was aimed at the press, though he very rarely got physical with them. Lee Mortimer was a notable exception. If Frank felt somebody had something coming to him, he could be cruel. If someone was nasty to him, you can bet that he was going to be nasty back. He was unrepentant about hitting Mortimer. He figured the guy had more than earned it for the smear campaign Mortimer mounted against him. It had all started because Frank had brushed aside Mortimer's songwriting attempts. Not long before the press campaign began, Mortimer had sent Frank a song he'd written, asking for Frank's opinion. The song was terrible. Frank told him so. Shortly afterward, the negative articles began to appear.

It was a similar situation with Kitty Kelley, who wrote a best-selling book about Frank titled *His Way,* with a very "creative" and derogatory version of Frank's life. People still believe all kinds of allegations in that book, like Frank's being involved in Mob hits. If people read the actual transcripts of the Mob wiretaps that have since been released, they'd see Sam Giancana complaining because Frank *wouldn't* play ball. Why, then, the character assassination from Kelley? Frank told me Kelley had been furious when she'd hit on him many years earlier and he'd turned her down. That was long before the book. Frank didn't pull any punches when he was angry.

He told me, "You know, Tony, I wouldn't have f***** that broad with your d*** if you'd lent it to me!" Frank was never one to mince words.

Frank had a very Sicilian temper. When he was angry, you'd hear about it. He'd yell. When he used that formidable lung power to scream at someone, it was impressive. Like his mother, he also had a very colorful vocabulary. If someone did something that made no sense to him, he'd shout, "Oh, for

280

Christ's sake, what the hell were you thinking? What is wrong with you?"

I was lucky. Frank never once raised his voice to me. Never swore at me. He'd share his anger and frustration about things or other people, but he never once said, "Goddamn it, Tony!" Not in all the years I knew him. I don't know how many people can say that. I'm very proud to be one.

It's true that he sometimes referred to himself as a twenty-four-karat manic depressive. Late in his life, he told me that he thought he'd be referred to as bipolar. As far as I know, that was never a clinical diagnosis, but it was how Frank explained his moods to himself. When he was exhausted or ill or under pressure, he had a short fuse. Sometimes, he'd explode.

One night he told me, "I've done my best to level the playing field in that regard. When I was young and stupid, I could be a hothead. My quote-unquote 'celebrity' sometimes went to my head. Afterward, I'd realize I'd done something foolish or stupid, and I'd end up beating myself up over it. I knew I was wrong, that I shouldn't have done it. But you can't un-ring a bell."

Frank struggled with impulse control from the time he was young, and he didn't always understand why. Why couldn't he control his temper? Why couldn't he say no in his younger years to any attractive woman who made herself available to him? He didn't understand the cards he'd been dealt at birth any more than the public did. Frank's birth was physically very traumatic. He'd been a thirteen-and-a-half-pound baby emerging from a ninety-pound woman in a home birth where he was pulled out with forceps. Not only did it nearly kill his mother, it nearly killed Frank. They thought he was dead and put him in a sink while they cared for Dolly. He didn't breathe for the first few minutes after birth. If his grandmother hadn't held him upside down in the sink and run cold water over him until he gasped, he would never have drawn breath. When they did revive him, it was clear that he'd suffered significant damage to the left side of his head. Part of his earlobe and the skin covering the left side of his skull had been ripped off. He had scar tissue there for much of his life, until Barbara insisted he have plastic surgery. His eardrum was punctured. More significant, he'd suffered a kind of brain damage that wasn't understood at the time. The combination of oxygen deprivation and brain trauma profoundly affects things like impulse control and emotional stability. He spent his life dealing with surging emotions and the impulse to strike out. When I consider what Frank had to deal with, I'd say he did pretty damn well.

Contrary to rumor, Frank didn't harbor many personal grudges, because if he did have trouble with someone, he'd usually just write them off. If people crossed him, he might nurse a hurt quietly for a while if it was someone he cared about. But if you stepped over a line that couldn't be uncrossed, the effect was often permanent. When he was done with you, he was done with you, and you might as well be six feet under at Forest Lawn cemetery.

I remember one particular time when he felt that someone had abused his friendship. They'd had several confrontations over it. Frank finally realized the relationship was a one-way street. He felt like he was being used. So after their last confrontation, Frank stopped talking to the guy.

About a year or so later, we happened to run into this guy at a restaurant, and he walked up to Frank and said, "Hello."

Frank said, "Hi, how you doing?"

The guy said, "Oh, my God."

"What?"

"You're talking to me."

"Yeah."

"So, you're not angry with me anymore?"

"No, you're misunderstanding. Anger is an emotion I save for people I care about. So don't misinterpret it when I say I'm not angry with you anymore. I don't give a f*** about you. I'm not going to waste my emotions on someone I don't care about. So no, I'm not angry with you anymore. What do you want?"

He didn't treat most people like that. Only when he thought they'd earned it.

Most of the time, he was very generous with his fans, because, in his parlance, these were the people who'd paid the freight to get him where he was. He felt obligated to pay it forward. If we were in a restaurant, sometimes a fan would either send a note by way of a waiter or stand there and wait politely to be acknowledged.

Either Frank or I would say, "Can I help you?"

They'd typically say something like, "Mr. Sinatra, I'm such a fan. I'm sitting over there with my family. We're visiting from [wherever]. We'd love to be able to say a quick hello."

Frank would respond, "Okay, I'll be over in a minute."

Usually, he'd have a waiter take their drink order or send them a dessert. When we finished our course, he'd go over to the fans and often sit down, let them take pictures, and talk for a few minutes.

Frank could be extraordinarily generous with his fans. A memory comes to mind of our being at Waldorf Towers after a performance. Frank had been playing at Radio City Music Hall with Shirley MacLaine. He liked to unwind after performances in the back section of Sir Harry's, which he lovingly called Sir Herpes because the hookers who gathered there sometimes came over and hung on me. Sir Harry's closed at four a.m., so afterward, we moved over to Peacock Alley. If you've ever seen the Waldorf-Astoria NYC, you'll know the gorgeous signature clock that forms the centerpiece of the golden-arched lobby. Peacock Alley is on one side of the clock, opposite the registration desk and near the elevators. I left Frank a couple of times that night, once to do an errand for him and again to go to the restroom. The second time I walked through the lobby, I noticed two women in the vestibule that led to the elevators to the towers. They'd been there when Frank and I had walked into Peacock Alley, and they were still there past five in the morning.

So I walked over to them and said, "Hi, is everything okay?"

One of the women said, "Oh, my God! You work for Mr. Sinatra."

I wasn't sure how she knew that, but I said, "Yes. How can I help you? My name is Tony."

"Well, we were just hoping to say hello to him. We know that he's there."

We chatted briefly, and I found out they'd come into the city hoping to get tickets to Frank's concert. Even the nosebleed seats were sold out, and they hadn't been able to get in. So they thought maybe they could at least get a glimpse of him. They knew he stayed at the Waldorf-Astoria when he was in New York, so they'd made their way over to the hotel lobby. They'd been sitting nearly eight hours, waiting for Frank to finally go upstairs to bed.

When I went back into Peacock Alley, I told Frank about these people. He had me call room service and see if the women wanted food or anything. About a half hour or so later, he decided to call it a night. As we left Peacock Alley and were walking toward the entrance to the towers' elevators, the two women saw him and absolutely lit up. They stood up, and he walked over and gave them both a kiss on the cheek.

Then he pulled up another chair, sat down, and started talking to them. They were asking him questions, and he was telling them stories. They were absolutely over the moon. By then, it was close to six o'clock in the morning.

Frank said, "By the way, where do you guys live?"

"We live outside the city, about an hour's drive."

"How are you getting there?"

"Well, we took a taxi into the city because we didn't want to drive our car."

He looked at me and just nodded his head. I called Mattie, Frank's limo driver. Frank sent them home in his limo. Before I took them to the garage to get into the limousine, he told me to offer them as many tickets as they wanted, for whatever night they wanted, and take it out of his comp block. He also told me to make arrangements to have a car pick them up and take them home after the concert.

Frank's fans came from all walks of life, from the ordinary to the world famous. One of those fans was Madonna, who — like every Italian kid — had grown up worshipping Frank. In 1992, when Frank was performing at the Greek Theatre with Shirley MacLaine, I got a call from Freddy DeMann, who was Madonna's manager at the time. Madonna wanted to meet Frank while he was in town, and Freddy wanted to know if I could set something up. The situation was a little awkward since Shirley's brother, Warren Beatty, would be at the concert supporting his sister, and things were still a bit tense between Madonna and Warren, who'd broken up a few months earlier. I told Freddy I could make it happen and suggested Madonna visit Frank backstage while Shirley was onstage and Warren was out front watching her.

Backstage at the concert the next night, I got a call that Madonna was arriving and left Frank alone in his dressing room while I went to meet her. She'd arrived with her security detail. I introduced myself and told her that Frank was in his dressing room and was expecting her.

Visibly nervous, she said, "Give me a minute," and began pacing up and down. Aware that she was holding Frank up, she said, "I'm sorry. I'm just a little nervous."

I said, "No problem. The night I met him, I was just as nervous as you. But we really should try to get in there because Shirley only has so much time left on the stage, and she and Warren will be coming back here."

So she took a deep breath, let it out, and said, "Okay, I'm ready." I took her in, leaving her security outside.

When Frank lifted his head, I said, "Frank, look who's here." He stood up and came walking over. I said, "Frank Sinatra, meet Madonna Ciccone."

Frank gave her a big hug and said, "*Finally,* I get to meet you." She had a puzzled look on her face, so he continued. "I talk about you all the time. Tony, how many times a day do I say, 'Maronn', Maronn', Maronn'? [Madonna]" It was Frank's way of breaking the ice. We all laughed at the Italian joke, and she relaxed. They chatted a little while, until I heard Shirley's closing number and knew she was finishing.

I told Madonna, "I'm sorry, but we really should go." Frank gave her a kiss, and I walked her out.

Once we were outside, she thanked me and said, "It was nice to meet you both. I've always wanted to meet him." It was endearing to watch a world-class entertainer transform into a giddy little girl meeting her childhood idol. In Frank's presence, she became just another fan.

He was always generous with his fans — if people were polite. One good turn deserves another.

And one bad turn deserves another.

If a fan was rude, then he was rude. If someone walked over to him while we were eating and abruptly interrupted us, Frank would look up and say, "Excuse me, can't you see I'm in the middle of a conversation with a friend of mine?" I remember one night at Sir Harry's, five of us were sitting and eating. A fan kept coming over to the table and interrupting us. Frank was extremely kind to the guy, but the guy was pretty drunk by then and kept coming back. I was getting irritated, and so was Frank.

Finally, as I was about to stand up and meet the guy five feet or so away from the table, Frank grabbed my arm and said, "I got it this time."

Frank stood up and said to the guy, "What do you need?"

This time the guy asked for yet another autograph. Frank signed it and handed the guy the paper.

Then he took the guy's arm and said, "Now, don't f***ing come over here again."

Yes, Frank could be rude if he thought it was warranted, but it is flatly untrue that Frank Sinatra never apologized. Sometimes he did so directly. He'd look at you and say, "Hey, I'm sorry. Sometimes I'm a schmuck. Help me get my foot out of my mouth."

Other times, he was more indirect. He would do something above and beyond by way of either a gift or a kindness for someone you cared about. That was his way of saying, "I'm sorry. I guess I'm just a human being."

I said that to a reporter once, when the guy was talking about Frank's doing something that we all would have done in his place. I said, "At the end of the day, he's been portrayed as this superhuman creature all these years. Now, when you find out that he's just a human being like the rest of us, you're faulting him for it. Is that right, or is that wrong?"

For better or for worse, you always knew what you were dealing with when it came to Frank. He was a straightforward guy. If he was negotiating for something he wanted, and the other person was playing hardball, Frank would sit him down and say, "Listen. You have something I want. Let's explore this. Is there something you want or need that I may have? Let's make some kind of an arrangement."

Frank was always genuine. He told me, "I will never BS people. I'm always the same. I'm more relaxed with some people and more formal with others. But the essence of what I'm saying and what I'm doing is still the same." It was his approach with people that could be different. He spoke eloquently in some instances and used street lingo in others. Frank was part chameleon in that he could fit into almost any circumstance. He could be comfortable sitting with the queen of England and two hours later be in a hotel lounge chatting with a hooker, and neither one of the women would feel uncomfortable. You'd hear two different Franks, one if he was being interviewed by Walter Cronkite, and another if he was at his table at Jilly's, but you'd never get two stories. The stories stayed the same. How they were told might change to fit the crowd or circumstance.

That's not to say Frank couldn't be manipulative. When Frank got fed up, he'd use his reputation to his advantage, sometimes in a funny way. One time, we were at the Desert Inn in Las Vegas, and we'd been up very late the night before as usual. Barbara started giving him an earful for not taking better care of himself. His first defense was to make a joke. When the "little woman" didn't laugh, he turned it 180 degrees. You've heard the old saying that sometimes the best defense is a great offense? That's what he did. Frank went on a rant, saying things like, "You know what? I'm not a twelve-year-old. Screw you! I'll do what the hell I want. I didn't ask you to stay up with me. Nobody's going to tell me what I can or can't do."

I only heard about that part later. While this was going on, I was in the showroom, getting things ready. Frank liked to be backstage at least an hour before curtain, even though he didn't open the show. I was about to head up to the suite to walk Frank down when I got a call on the backstage phone. It was Vine.

"Don't bother coming up. He's on his way down, but watch it! He's really in a mood."

A few minutes later, here came Frank with his *Mind your own damn business* face and two security guards. Vine was walking behind him. They turned the corner and were walking toward me to go into the dressing room. Vine looked at me as if she were saying, *He's in a bad mood, so don't say anything.* Everyone was running for cover because the word had gotten out that Frank was hot. I didn't say anything to him. I just looked at him, and he looked back as he walked toward me. As he went into the dressing room past me, he flashed me a quick smile and gave me that George Burns look where he closes his eyes really tight. I was trying to keep from laughing. I finally got into the dressing room.

Frank went into the inner dressing room and said, "T," with a motion of his finger to tell me to come in. He quickly slammed the door.

I could only imagine what he was thinking, so I said, "How are you feeling?"

He said, "I'm fine, but don't let them know. They started giving me a bad time, and the easiest way to defuse it all was to make them believe I'm pissed off, so they'll leave the two of us alone. I don't want to hear their crap."

He knew how to work it whenever it was needed.

Frank's morality was grounded in his Catholicism. Religion was part of Frank's upbringing. Like me, he was raised by a Catholic mother and attended parochial school until he was a teenager. He attended church periodically, especially after his mother was killed, and he believed in the basic tenets of his faith all his life. For him, religion had less to do with rituals and faith than with how you treated people. Frank genuinely wanted to do the very best within his power to make other people's lives happier and better.

I remember one afternoon when Cardinal Mahony came over to the house to visit Frank, along with his monsignor. He'd requested an audience with Frank, and they were enjoying themselves. The cardinal was only supposed to stay half an hour at most, but once he and Frank got talking, time flew by. Frank's health wasn't too great by then, and about an hour and a half into the conversation, I could see that Frank was getting tired.

I pulled the monsignor into the kitchen and said, "Listen, Frank's having a really great time, but there are other things he has to do that we can't really put off." The monsignor understood completely, and when we went back in the other room, he figured out the right way to get the cardinal to make an exit. As we all stood up, the cardinal asked permission to give us a blessing and said a prayer over us.

As Frank and I were walking them to the front door, Frank put his hand on Cardinal Mahony's shoulder and said, "Now, listen, if anybody bothers you, call me. As a matter of fact, don't call me, have your guy [the monsignor] call him." And he pointed his index finger at me.

I had to bite my lip to keep from smiling. The cardinal chuckled and said his good-byes. Frank completely missed the irony of the situation. If a man of God has a problem, just call Sinatra. Better yet, call Tony O. He'll fix you right up.

Frank had a clear philosophy about the

purpose of money. He was well aware that he'd been fortunate beyond his wildest dreams and that others, through no fault of their own, struggled for the basic necessities. Frank believed that money was to be spent, not hoarded.

He told me countless times, "If you can't use money to make your life and the lives of people you care about better, whether they be friends, family, or friends you haven't met, then you're wasting your life. You come into this world with nothing. You leave with nothing. I've never seen a Brink's truck at a cemetery. You spend money doing the right thing, and you'll make more. You'll learn the way I learned, Tony."

Frank and I would joke sometimes about some of our wealthy but frugal friends. Bob Hope, for example, was charitable to a legendary degree when it came to giving his time. He dedicated his life to touring and entertaining soldiers all over the world. But when it came to cold hard cash, God bless the man, he could pinch every penny. I produced eight galas for him, so I learned about this quirk up close and personal. Frank adored Bob, but he'd lovingly joke about Bob's frugality.

"Son of a bitch, you know what? I don't care how old he gets. He's not leaving this planet until he finds a casket that's got pockets in it for his cash."

Frank also liked to kid about Los Angeles Dodgers manager Tommy Lasorda.

He said, "Tommy's idea of gambling is going out to dinner before he knows who's picking up the check." Then he continued, "Do you know how copper wire was invented?"

I knew it was a joke, so I said, "Okay, I'm listening."

"Tommy Lasorda and Bob Hope were arguing over a penny."

Frank Sinatra was by far the most generous human being I've ever known. He gave constantly, and most of the time, he gave without anyone's knowing that he'd done it. He often attached one important string to his giving. If it became public, he'd cut off the funds. If he knew I was writing about this, he'd pull the plug on my computer. Being thanked or praised for helping someone made Frank really uncomfortable. One time, when a friend insisted on repeatedly thanking him for a sizable favor Frank had done him, a frustrated Frank finally said, "Doing things for people makes me feel good, okay? It's got nothing to do with you. At the end of the day, I guess I'm a selfish prick. I did it for me. Not for you. For me."

After a brief moment of silence, we all broke up. Even onstage, when the applause would not stop, Frank could only take it for so long before he'd be overcome emotionally.

From the time he was a kid, Frank noticed when people needed help. One of Frank's childhood friends was a kid by the name of Billy Roemer. Billy's dad had a shop in town where he made furniture. Billy and Frank used to take scrap pieces of balsa wood from the business and make airplanes. They got so good at it that they entered a local contest for model airplanes sponsored by Ives McKinney, a local pilot. The two won first place. The prize was a ride for two in McKinney's open-cockpit biplane, which he kept at Teterboro Airport. Frank and Billy were over the moon in anticipation of their first real flight.

Frank had a cousin in Hoboken who was mentally disabled. These days he'd probably be diagnosed as autistic. Frank really felt for the boy. Nobody knew much about autism at the time, but Frank had read that sometimes a shock, like doing something as thrilling as flying in an airplane, could snap someone like his cousin out of his silent world. As much as Frank was looking forward to his first airplane ride, he thought that the opportunity might be a way for him to help his cousin. So he let his cousin take his place on the flight with Billy. Frank rode down to Teterboro with his cousin, the pilot, and Billy, and when they got there, Frank helped his cousin onto the plane and made sure he was safely buckled in. Then Frank stood and watched as the plane took off and soared out of sight over the ocean, reappearing a few minutes later. He waved at his cousin as the plane passed over, and he was there when it landed. Of course, the adventure had no permanent effect on his cousin's autism, but his cousin had the time of his life, and Frank never regretted his decision. This would be the shape of things to come; Frank would repeat that kind of quiet, often anonymous generosity over and over.

Frank was always there for Joe E. Lewis. A lot of people don't realize Joe didn't start out as a comedian. He started out as a singer in Chicago in the twenties, during Prohibition. The club he worked in was owned by the Mob. When Joe wanted to work at another club to move up in his career, the wiseguys weren't happy about that. One afternoon in his hotel room, a couple of guys busted in and slit his throat. Joe lived, but he couldn't sing anymore, so he started over as a comedian. Eventually,

Frank played Joe in a movie about his life called *The Joker Is Wild.*

Frank spoke with Joe on a regular basis and used to look out for him big-time. One time, Joe called Frank from Florida and said that he was really up against it financially. Joe was a genuine gambling addict at the dog tracks, at the horse tracks, and with bookies. He'd gotten up to his eyeballs in debt. Could Frank see his way clear to bailing him out?

Frank went to the bank and got $100,000 in cash. He also bought a parachute. Then he wrapped the cash in the parachute and sent it special delivery to Joe. That was Frank's way of keeping things light. He literally "bailed Joe out."

Frank also helped another friend named Joe Louis, this time the boxer. Joe was a national hero who had defeated white German fighter Max Schmeling at a time when Adolf Hitler was using Schmeling as a symbol of white superiority. Frank had loved boxing since he was a kid. One night, he went to see Joe fight at Madison Square Garden. Frank was sitting ringside, and the fight wasn't going well. Joe's opponent just wouldn't go down. Finally, Joe came back to his corner in between rounds and looked over at Frank. Then he leaned over and said to Frank, "Gee, this guy is tough. If I'm not able to knock him down within the next couple of rounds, I may have you come sing him to sleep."

In Joe's later years, he had a huge debt with the Internal Revenue Service. Joe was having serious financial difficulties because he couldn't box when he got older. He needed a job, so Frank got him hired as a greeter at Caesars Palace in Las Vegas. Joe walked around the casino, saying hello to people and taking pictures with them. Unbeknownst to Joe, Frank filtered the money for Joe's salary through his business office to the casino. Later, Frank hosted a fundraiser that raised hundreds of thousands of dollars for Joe's charity. Frank also paid for Joe's heart surgery, and eventually for Joe's funeral. He made sure Joe was given the care and dignity he deserved.

Frank came through when people needed him, even when the relationship between them had ended. He made sure Ava was all right later in life. It was done quietly through Sonny Golden, Frank's business manager. I'm not sure whether Ava knew where the money was coming from. He even helped his former valet George Jacobs, who wrote a very popular, scurrilous, and sometimes vindictive book about Frank after

Frank's death. During George's days as Frank's valet, George had been photographed dancing in a club with Mia Farrow when Frank and Mia's marriage was rocky. To Frank, that was a betrayal. He fired George, probably unfairly. I met George many years later, down in the desert. We hit it off. He got my phone number, and we were friends for a while. George called me one day and asked me if we could meet to talk about something. I met him at a friend's nightclub. George told me that he was having a serious health issue and needed brain surgery, for an aneurysm, if memory serves. It was a very expensive operation, and he had no health coverage.

George said, "Would you feel comfortable asking Frank? He's the only person I could think of. I've been kind of down on my luck."

"Well, I'm going to be seeing him in the next day or so. Let me see what I can do."

When I saw Frank shortly afterward, I said to him, "You'll never guess who I ran into the other night. George Jacobs."

Frank kind of laughed and said, "How's he doing?"

"Well, not so good, Frank. He needs brain surgery, he has no insurance, and he's broke."

302

Frank chuckled again and said, "I thought there was a prerequisite of having a brain." Then he continued, this time seriously. "Call Sonny Golden and take care of it," he said.

I called Sonny, who did the rest. Frank paid for everything, both the surgery and the recovery. This was about ten years before George got his book published. I was shocked by some of George's characterizations of Frank in the book. I was also saddened that George never mentioned that, long after he had left Frank's employ, Frank had paid for the medical care that saved George's life. The man George described in his book would never have done what Frank did for him.

Frank also treated many strangers like friends. So many times, he'd put a large amount of cash in an envelope and have me deliver it to someone in need. This happened frequently on the road. I was often the courier, something that was never discussed with anyone, even other members of Frank's team who were traveling with us. We rarely left Las Vegas or Atlantic City without Frank's sending me down to the cage in the casino to draw a $10,000 or $20,000 advance on his salary. People assumed it was for Frank's use, or so that Barbara could go shopping. Sometimes it was, but many times, the money was for someone in need. Other times, he'd have Sonny send him cash. Frank never wrote a check, because that would have identified him. I'd take a cab or a hotel limo so nobody would associate me with Frank. Sometimes one of Frank's staff or friends would notice my absence and ask, "Where the hell did Tony go?" My excuse was usually that there was a really good Italian delicatessen on the outskirts of town, and I was going to pick up some cannoli for Frank. In reality, I'd swing by the deli on the way back from bringing $10,000 in cash to a total stranger that Frank had read about in the paper.

I remember one December, there was a news clip about a family whose apartment had been robbed. The thieves had taken everything of value, including the children's Christmas presents. The family wasn't well-off and had no way to replace what had been taken. Frank dispatched me to their apartment with an envelope full of cash.

I knocked on the door, and a man answered, saying, "Can I help you?"

"Are you [so-and-so]?"

"Yes."

"This is for you."

I handed him the envelope, and when he

looked inside, he nearly passed out.

"I don't understand. Who is this from?"

"It's from a friend who wishes you a merry Christmas and tells you, 'Don't worry. Things will get better.' " Then I left.

Frank's favorite philanthropy was probably the Christmases at the desert compound with the local kids. Every Christmas, Frank would have children from underprivileged areas around the desert bused to the compound. There, they'd be treated to a luncheon, followed by an exhibition of trains. Frank had a whole bungalow dedicated to his model train sets. There were elaborate setups with miniature towns, intricate track patterns, even a solid-gold engine on a shelf suspended from the ceiling. He could run up to four trains at a time. It was a child's paradise, and nowhere was it more obvious that Frank was just a big kid himself. He'd put on his engineer's hat and run all four sets simultaneously while the kids watched in fascination. I doubt most of the children even knew who he was, just some nice old rich guy. When time was up, and they departed for home on the chartered bus, every child left the compound with a gift-wrapped toy. It gave Frank more joy than it gave the children.

They say charity begins at home, and

that's where Frank first learned it. His parents, in particular his mother, were active in raising money for charities in Frank's native Hoboken. It's easy to imagine that Dolly Sinatra wouldn't have been easy to say no to when she came knocking on the door. Dolly and Marty supported deaf and blind charities when Frank was a kid because of Frank's hearing damage at birth. He was significantly deaf in his left ear, and his parents wanted to help other boys with hearing problems. A small New Jersey charity for disabled children called Seeing Home originated as a place for kids with varying degrees of deafness and blindness to get help. The charity's website is dedicated to the Sinatra family, with pictures of Frank, Dolly, and Marty from the old days. There's also a tribute to Frank for his many unpublicized contributions. During Frank's lifetime, his donations were contingent on his not being acknowledged publicly as the donor. Since Frank's death, however, the small charity has been able to show its gratitude by memorializing the Sinatra family's kindness and generosity.

Frank donated, usually anonymously, to countless organizations. He raised over $1 billion for charity in the course of his lifetime — that I know of, at least — both in direct donations and through concerts and other events. Even in celebrity-generated dollars, that's an extraordinary amount. Since he also donated large amounts anonymously or in cash that was never tracked, it's impossible to know the full extent of his generosity.

Frank's love and support of Israel in particular are legendary. It all stemmed from his relationship with Mrs. Golden, the neighbor who had babysat him when his parents were gone. His love for Mrs. Golden instilled in him a special affinity for the Jewish people. For years, he kept a mezuzah Mrs. Golden had given him. When news of the Holocaust first began leaking out in 1942, he had hundreds of medallions made with St. Christopher on one side and the Star of David on the other, then had them delivered to soldiers and government leaders. In 1944, he endured the wrath of his Catholic priest when he named a Jewish friend, Manie Sacks, as godfather to Frankie Jr. It took a rather large donation to the church to quiet the priest's objections. On another occasion, when he heard a reporter call one of his friends a "Jew bastard" at a party, Frank decked him. And when Frank discovered that many golf clubs excluded Jews from membership, he became only the second Gentile to join a club whose membership was primarily Jewish.

Frank was never a bagman for the Mob, but on one occasion, he did serve as a bagman for Israelis. Frank became directly involved in the establishment of Israel as a sovereign nation when he got military aid to the Israelis through a Haganah agent in March of 1948. Haganah was Israel's paramilitary organization before Israel achieved statehood. The United States didn't support nationhood for Israel at the time and had placed an embargo on goods and money sent by Americans for the Zionist cause. Cut off from supplies, Israel was in desperate straits. American Jews had set up a base of operations for Haganah in Hotel 14 in New York, next to the Copacabana nightclub. Federal agents surveilled it constantly. Haganah agent Teddy Kollek tells what happened one night that March.

I had an Irish ship captain sitting in the port of New York with a ship full of munitions destined for Israel. But a large sum of money had to be handed over, and I didn't know how to get it to him. If I walked out the door carrying the cash, the Feds would intercept me.

I went downstairs to the bar and Sinatra

came over, and we were talking. I don't know what came over me, but I told him what I was doing in the United States and what my dilemma was. And in the early hours of the following morning I walked out the front door of the building with a satchel, and the Feds followed me. Out the back door went Frank Sinatra, carrying a paper bag filled with cash [estimated at $1 million in large bills]. He went down to the pier, handed it over, and watched the ship sail.

Frank told me he never even looked in the bag.

Decades later, on one of Frank's trips to Israel, Israeli prime minister Golda Meir told him, "The people of Israel owe you a debt of gratitude that they'll never be able to repay."

In classic Frank fashion, he said, "I'm sorry, but I don't know what you're talking about." He really didn't. He never thought of his efforts as anything special.

Though Frank's support of the Jewish people was lifelong, his passion for the oppressed wasn't restricted to the Jews. It came directly from his own boyhood. Frank knew what it felt like to be picked on, to bear the brunt of hate-fueled behavior. His childhood experiences made him passionate about any kind of prejudice, whether it be homophobia, religious intolerance, or racism. From the time he was young, the things he experienced shaped his views on how people should be treated. On March 21, 1945, Frank published an address to New York City youth caught up in racial conflict called "Thoughts of an American." Seventy-five years later, in the midst of national turmoil, it still resonates. Frank wrote, in part,

I know why, when I was going to school over in Jersey, a bunch of kids threw rocks at me and called me a little Dago. I know why they used to call the Jewish kids in the neighborhood "kikes" and "sheenies" and the colored kids "niggers." . . . Now this is our job, your job and my job and the job of generations growing up . . . to stamp out prejudices that are separating one group of American citizens from another.

Frank won his first Academy Award for a film on bigotry that he made the same year. The Oscar was an honorary one for his short film *The House I Live In*. The film has a simple premise. Frank is shown initially in a recording studio. A couple of minutes into the film, he goes out back into an alley to have a smoke, where he finds a group of boys ganging up on a Jewish boy. One of the kids has knocked the Jewish boy's belongings to the ground. Instead of scolding the kids, Frank explains why he thinks it's foolish to beat up on someone just because he's a different religion. Then he explains what America means to him. As the boys listen, he sings to them: "/ All races and religions / That's America to me." The film ends when the boy who knocked down the Jewish child's belongings picks them up and hands them back with a smile. Frank watches as the children walk away, now smiling and at peace.

*The House I Live In* was more than a film for Frank. It was a way of life. In these days of political correctness and legal terms like *hate crime,* it's easy to overlook how profoundly radical Frank's views were considered at the time. Long before it was socially acceptable, much less popular, Frank was advocating for African-American rights.

Throughout his performing career, Frank used his moxie, his music, and occasionally his fists to help bring African-Americans the respect they deserved. In 1961, with racial tensions at a peak and riots nationwide, he did a benefit concert for Martin Luther King at Carnegie Hall. King cried as Frank sang "Old Man River." Frank laid it on the line, saying, "We've got a hell of a long way to go in this racial situation. As long as most white men think of a Negro first and a man second, we're in trouble. I don't know why we can't grow up. It took us long enough to get past the stage where we were calling all Italians 'wops' and 'dagos,' but if we don't stop this 'nigger' thing, we just won't be around much longer."

Frank performed with virtually every prominent Black musician of his time: Billie Holiday, Ella Fitzgerald, Nat King Cole, Billy Eckstine, Count Basie, Duke Ellington, Lena Horne, and of course, Sammy. He brought Black music to white audiences and gave credit where credit was due, praising the greatness of Black composers and performers. Moreover, he performed with them as he would with any white performer, duetting with the women in sometimes sexually charged performances, openly embracing Black friends onstage, kissing and hugging them when such shows of interracial affection were taboo. More than that, he became friends with them, offstage and on, and you'd better watch how you treated Frank's friends.

When he was touring as a young man, and Southern café and hotel owners refused to let Frank's Black musicians eat or spend the night, he'd often punch them out before moving on. Ever the Hoboken kid, he knew better in theory — but in the heat of the moment, his reflex was to deck anybody who mistreated one of his friends. He forced Caesars Palace to feed and lodge Black entertainers and to start hiring people of color in the restaurants and casinos. If the owners resisted, he threatened to cancel his contracts, and the casinos couldn't afford to lose him. In 1955, he brought Nat King Cole into the dining room with him at the Sands and stared down the maître d' until he and Cole were both seated. Frank escorted Lena Horne to the whites-only Stork Club and insisted they admit her, watching the management sweat and squirm until they finally gave in. The principle was simple: If his friends couldn't eat there, he wouldn't eat there. If his friends couldn't sleep there, he wouldn't sleep there. If his friends couldn't do both, he wouldn't perform there. When the average person takes a stance like that, he might just get thrown out. But when you were Frank Sinatra and you took a stand, people had to pay attention. He wielded his star power like a weapon.

He helped Sammy break the color barrier at the Copacabana by way of Jack Entratter, who was running the place on behalf of mobster Frank Costello. Frank got Sammy the same featured billing as the white performers. One night after rehearsal at the Sands in Vegas, Frank said, "Come on, let's go have a drink or something."

Sammy replied, "I'll join you when I come back."

"Where you going?"

"I have to go downtown to the Moulin Rouge to check into my hotel."

"What do you mean, check into your hotel? You're here."

"No, Frank, I can't stay here. As a matter of fact, I'm not even allowed in the casino."

"*Really?* Okay." He told Sammy to come with him.

It was a New Year's gig, and Frank marched up to the manager's office. Once again, it was Jack Entratter, who'd been shipped from New York to the Sands to keep an eye on the wiseguys' investment there. Frank walked into Entratter's office with Sammy and said, "Listen, we can't stay long. I just wanted to wish you luck on your New Year's gigs with whoever is going to be appearing here." Then he turned around and started to leave.

Entratter said, "Wait, wait, wait. Where are you going?"

"Sam and I are going back to LA."

"Why?"

"Well, if he's not welcome here" — he gestured to Sammy — "neither am I."

Entratter responded irritably, "Oh geez, you're not going to start that crap again."

"Again? How about still? Don't you dare give me that. If Sam's not allowed to stay at this hotel and have free access to everything, including the swimming pool, then I'm gone, too, and I'm not coming back. And I don't want to hear that you're doing anything else like that to the rest of the people that are under contract here, like Nat King Cole and Ella Fitzgerald and Basie and Lena Horne."

Frank was the biggest name in Vegas at the time, the biggest singer in show business, and Jack Entratter knew what his bosses would say if he lost Frank. His bosses *loved* Frank. So he changed the policy, not only for Sammy, but for all the performers of color.

In an era when supporters of civil rights were considered Communists, Frank was tainted with the charge of Communism.

What bothered Frank even more than the label itself was that it prevented him from serving his country. The most glaring example is his military service.

Frank often told me about the day he found out America was at war. He was in the Roosevelt Hotel in Los Angeles on December 7, 1941, when he was awakened by the sound of banging pots and someone running up and down the halls, shouting, "Pearl Harbor has been attacked! We're at war!"

Like every other red-blooded American male, Frank signed up for the draft. He was refused because of his punctured left eardrum. Even though the disability had been in his medical records since birth, the press didn't believe it. Frank was widely reported to be a draft dodger. When a second attempt to join the army failed, he applied to join the USO to entertain the troops overseas. He was denied clearance, not allowed to go into combat zones until the war in Europe was over, when he was finally allowed to entertain our troops with his friend Phil Silvers. They'd purchase the ugliest, cheapest ties they could find and throw them to the cheering audience. The guys were a huge hit, but when war broke out in Korea, Frank encountered the same restrictions. In

1950 and again in 1954, Frank was denied clearance to entertain the troops.

Frank Sinatra was a dyed-in-the-wool patriot. As an entertainer, he was one of the biggest supporters of the United States of America. But in spite of his ardent patriotism, he often spoke to me about the fact that America was an imperfect country. Even though the press slammed him for saying it one night at Madison Square Garden, he truly felt that what makes this country work is not that it's perfect, but that we're all free to have a hand in making it better. Like his onetime-Democratic-ward-boss mother, Frank was always active in politics. He made his positions on issues known, and he wasn't afraid to roll up his sleeves to do whatever he could, if he felt he could make a difference.

Despite appearances, Frank's political views really never changed. The parties and candidates did. He always held the same basic beliefs about government. He loved Roosevelt because FDR was for the common man and fought oppression of all kinds. He loved John Kennedy in the beginning because he represented what he thought a politician should be as a man. Unfortunately, Kennedy disappointed him when politics changed their relationship. His friendship with Spiro Agnew convinced Frank to support Nixon. Later Frank became a big supporter of Ronald Reagan. They were good friends, and Frank believed much of what Reagan stood for. Though Frank remained a lifelong Democrat, he did become disillusioned when the Democratic Party turned its back on him. And he never got over JFK's treatment of Sammy Davis Jr. when, after Sammy's extensive fundraising efforts for the Kennedys, Kennedy had his secretary "uninvite" Sammy to the inaugural gala because of Sammy's engagement to a white woman. Sammy was told that his presence might offend some of the powerful Democrats in the South. Dean refused to attend because of it, but Frank had to go because he was producing it. The "Rat Pack" at the gala consisted of Frank, Joey Bishop, and Peter Lawford, with Dean and Sammy conspicuously missing. All of Frank's relationships with politicians were ultimately related to their integrity and the way they treated the powerless. In return for his efforts, he was awarded the Presidential Medal of Freedom in 1985, the NAACP Lifetime Achievement Award in 1987, and the Congressional Gold Medal, presented posthumously in 1998.

Each year on Frank's birthday, for the

twenty-three years since his passing, the Empire State Building has lit up in blue in honor of Ol' Blue Eyes. And each night at seven p.m. in the spring of 2020, while New York City sheltered in place at the peak of the coronavirus there, the citizens of NYC came out on their balconies to applaud the first responders and to listen to Frank. Frank's voice singing "New York, New York" issued from loudspeakers all over the city because, people told reporters, listening to Frank gave them strength. Now, that, ladies and gentlemen, is a life well lived.

# CHAPTER 8
## SEND IN THE CLOWNS
### THE FRIENDSHIPS

It was two in the morning, late for most people, early for Frank. We were in his suite in the Wyndham Hotel, overlooking the Manila Bay. It had been a successful tour, with Frank playing to sold-out audiences four nights in a row. It was a beautiful evening. The air was softer and cooler with the fading of the day, humid but no longer oppressive, the silence welcome after the noise of the concert. The moon lit the Manila Bay just outside the open French doors, and we could hear the soft rolling of waves. Every now and then, a World War II American PT boat, repurposed as a Philippine Coast Guard cruiser, briefly disturbed the stillness. We'd been talking quite a while when Frank remarked on the fact that from the time we were children, he and I had both been old souls. I agreed with him.

After a few moments' silence, Frank asked, "T, do you believe in reincarnation?"

I thought a moment. "I don't know. I've always had an affinity for older people, older music. I relate more to previous generations than my own. One thing I know is that there are a lot of things in my life I can't explain. I have knowledge of things that I've never personally experienced."

Taking another sip of Jack, Frank remarked, "You have to believe in reincarnation. I mean, look at you and me. What we have is far too intertwined for just this lifetime. We must have known each other before."

I didn't know if he was right about reincarnation, but he was right about us. In many ways, our relationship defied explanation. True, we had plenty in common, including our Italian heritage and passion for music. I'd always thought it was an odd coincidence that Frank and I had the exact same vocal range, note for note. That doesn't happen a lot. But none of that accounted for the instant chemistry between us. From the first night he heard me murmuring in Italian as he passed by me at Jilly's, we clicked. I've never been big on the term *kindred spirit,* but something connected us that went beyond the word *friend.*

Because friends held such a deep place in Frank's heart, he was very careful about letting people get close. His fall from grace in the early fifties taught him a lot about friendship. Very few of his "friends" stuck around when the money and fame disappeared. He used to say that sometimes, friends are like shadows. You only see them when the sun is shining. Jilly Rizzo and Nancy Sr. were the closest friends Frank ever had because they loved Francis Albert, not Frank Sinatra. He trusted them implicitly. When times were at their worst, when he was at his worst, they were there.

Friendship with Frank Sinatra ranged from the sublime to the ridiculous. For Frank, pranks were a form of bonding. If he played a prank on you, it was a sign you were in with him. One of his favorite victims was Mike Romanoff, whose real name was Hershel Geguzin. For decades, Romanoff's Beverly Hills restaurant was the place to be for people like Bogie and Bacall. *Time* magazine once described Romanoff as "one of the few genuine, 24-carat phonies." Whether you consider Romanoff an actor, a lunatic, or a con man doesn't make much difference, because everybody knew he wasn't the Russian prince he pretended to be. It's hard to know whether Romanoff believed his own fantasy, but everyone played along because they liked him. They called him "Emperor" while he regally presided over his private domain.

He and Frank became great pals. Romanoff smoked even more than Frank, and Frank soon had a running prank with him. He'd take cigarettes out of Romanoff's pack and cut them partway through with a razor blade, then put them back in the pack. When Romanoff took the cigarette out and put it in his mouth, half of it would be dangling. Around Frank, Romanoff was always wary when he took a cigarette out, fearing it was going to droop to his chin. Sometimes it did; sometimes it didn't.

Frank pulled the trick often on a trip to Europe with Romanoff. Romanoff finally got frustrated and told Frank, "I wish you wouldn't do that anymore. Please stop doing that."

Frank told him, "I really . . . I'm sorry."

When they got back, Frank sent him a carton of unopened cigarettes as an apology. What Romanoff had no way of knowing was that every single pack in the carton had been opened, every cigarette had been cut, and the packs had been resealed. No matter what cigarette he took out of the carton, they were all cut like that. He picked up the phone and called Frank.

When Frank picked up, Romanoff informed Frank in his most regal tone, "You, sir, are a chicken fucker." It was the prince's favorite insult.

Sometimes the pranks Frank pulled were simple and childish, as his close friend Don Rickles knew all too well. Frank had taken the younger comedian under his wing and started inviting him over to join the guys as sort of an unofficial member of the Rat Pack when they were both playing Vegas. He even had one of his signature Rat Pack bathrobes made for Don with the loving monogram "Bullet Head" on it. One afternoon Frank invited him over to join the guys in the steam room. Don was a bundle of nervous energy, telling Frank and the guys joke after joke. They were trying to unwind and sweat out some of the excesses of the night before, but instead of relaxing, they kept cracking up at Don. Frank loved Don's humor, but eventually, he needed Don to take it down a few notches so they could catch their breath. Everyone said, "Enough!" but Don kept going. Finally, Frank decided on a more direct way to get Don's attention. He pulled off Don's robe and towel and shoved him out the steam room door into the hotel pool area outside, totally naked in front of crowds of vacationers. Poor Don ended up pounding on the door with one hand while literally covering his butt with the other as giggling women passed by.

One of my favorite stories wasn't actually a prank; it was more of an unfortunate accident. Or fortunate, depending on your point of view. Frank was good friends with Jackie Gleason, whom he'd known since the early fifties, when they were both down on their luck. Gleason introduced Frank Sinatra to Jack Daniel's. Frank, in turn, introduced it to me, so I guess you could say Jack is kind of a Gleason legacy. They were both baseball fans, and one night in New York, they went to a Yankees game together. They were sitting in Yankee Stadium when an attendant brought them a note. It was from J. Edgar Hoover, who was at the game with his alleged partner Clyde Tolson. Since Hoover had been keeping a file on Frank for over a decade by then, it was an interesting invitation. Whatever his motive, Hoover saw Frank sitting in the stands and made the overture. Frank and Jackie went over to say hello.

The four chatted awhile, and then Hoover asked, "So where are you guys headed after the game?"

Frank said, "We're going back into the city."

"So are we. Why don't you come with me

in my limo?" Frank thanked him and accepted the offer, and he and Gleason went back to their seats.

When the game was over, they rendezvoused with Hoover and Tolson and climbed into J. Edgar's limo. The windows were blacked out and tightly shut, and the vehicle was bulletproofed. This was before air-conditioning, and since it was summertime, the interior was hot and stuffy. Frank and Jackie were riding in the jump seat, facing backward, and Gleason was starting to look a little queasy. He had consumed a dozen beers and nine hot dogs at the game, and he wasn't doing too well. After a few minutes, he was white as a sheet.

Frank said to him, "Are you okay?"

"Old pal of mine, I ain't feeling too well."

The words had no sooner come out of Jackie's mouth than he began projectile-vomiting. It splashed all over Hoover's clothes and shoes, and the stench was overpowering. J. Edgar pounded on the window for the driver to pull the limousine over. He threw Frank and Gleason out of the car and left them standing on a street corner in the middle of Harlem as Hoover drove away. They got a cab back to the hotel. As disgusting as the incident was, there was a certain satisfaction in it for

Frank. If Gleason was going to vomit, it might as well be on J. Edgar Hoover.

As much fun as Frank had with his friends, friendship with Frank wasn't all "Got ya!" and laughter. It wasn't a secret that Frank ran away from conflict with those close to him. People who were ambitious or manipulative used that weakness to drive wedges between Frank and his friends. Breaches sometimes occurred that took years to heal. A notable one was between Frank and the musician with whom he usually was most closely bonded.

Everyone who knows Sinatra's music knows Bill Miller. Bill was Frank's good friend and musical right hand for decades. Bill was a survivor in every sense of the word. Thirteen years into working together, one of the most touching tragedies in Frank's life involved Bill and his family. In 1964, Bill's home was destroyed in a matter of seconds when a local reservoir broke and released a giant wall of water. Bill's wife was killed, and his daughter barely escaped. Bill was critically injured. Frank camped at the hospital by Bill's bedside for days afterward so Bill would see a familiar face if he regained consciousness. When Bill finally came to, Frank broke the news to him of his wife's death. Frank had already identified her body so Bill wouldn't have to. Afterward, Frank made all the necessary arrangements, paid Bill's hospital bills, and took him home to Palm Springs to convalesce. When Bill was well enough, Frank got Bill into a new home, where Bill and I later became housemates for eight years. Frank and Bill seemed to have an unbreakable friendship.

Twenty-seven years after Frank and Bill started working together, they had a falling-out. It involved a man called Vinnie Falcone. Vinnie was a phenomenal piano player and a pretty damn good conductor, both things Bill was exceptional at. Vinnie was also very ambitious.

One night when Bill was scheduled for a long performance with no break, Vinnie told him, "You should let me conduct the overture tonight. No one will even know." The curtain would be drawn during the overture.

Bill foolishly said, "Okay," without mentioning the change to Frank. Not telling Frank was a fatal mistake on Bill's part. A couple of nights into the engagement, when Vinnie mentioned to Frank how much he was enjoying the new opportunity, bells went off in Frank's head. Why was Vinnie now conducting the overture instead of Bill, and more important, why hadn't anyone told him?

Afterward, when Bill got back to LA from the gig, he got a call from Mickey Rudin, telling him to come into the office. Mickey told Bill, "We're going to make a minor change. You're going to be making the same amount of money you've always made, but you're just going to be playing piano. From now on, Vinnie Falcone is going to be the conductor."

Bill was furious. "If that's the final word, then I'm out of here. After all these years, that's the kind of shit I'm getting?"

Mickey said, "Boy, you must have a lot of fuck-you money."

"If I had five dollars in the bank, my position would still be the same." Bill quit on the spot, and he wouldn't back down. Unfortunately, neither would Frank.

The breach between Frank and Bill lasted for years. It was like a cold war between a couple of stubborn kids. Frank wouldn't call Bill, and Bill wouldn't call him. Then a few years into the feud, Frank was asked by President Reagan to put together a party for Queen Elizabeth, who was visiting LA. The breach with Bill was starting to get to Frank by then, personally and professionally. He wanted Bill to play for the queen's reception, but he wasn't willing to risk Bill's saying no. Since Bill and I shared a house, Jilly sounded things out with me.

Jilly told me, "You know, the old man wants to get back with Bill. He wants to offer him a gig that would help pave the road to that. Do you think Bill would be agreeable to doing this thing for the queen?"

I said, "You know, Bill misses Frank as much as Frank misses Bill. I'm pretty confident he would say yes."

When I came home that evening, Bill had this "cat that ate the canary" look on his face. I said, "What's up? Something's up."

"Well, the mountain came to Muhammad." He explained that Frank's secretary had called, that the old man wanted him to put together a trio, and all the rest of it.

"That's terrific! What'd you say?"

"I said yes, of course."

On the night of the queen's reception, I met up with Bill after the gala. He arrived late, looking very satisfied with himself. He got a drink and then told me what had happened.

"I'm sitting at the piano, and this guy hands me a note and explains who it's from. Like I wasn't going to recognize Frank's handwriting. It was a request to play 'One for My Baby.' " Bill had played it with his trademark "stride piano," a rare and particularly difficult type of jazz piano that few musicians master.

When Bill finished, he heard Frank's voice: "That's what I've been missing all these years. Where the hell is that written?"

Bill told him, "It's not written. I created it."

Finally, Bill looked up. Frank was leaning on the piano with his chin in his hands, looking at Bill, like a kid posing for a picture.

Frank said, "It's good to see you, Suntan [his nickname for Bill, whose skin was pale white]."

"It's nice to see you, too."

"So what do you say?"

"I'm willing if you are." And that was it.

The Rat Pack was legendary, and a lot of what has been printed about it is just that — legend. What was always real, though, was the friendship that Frank, Sammy, and Dean shared.

Frank called Sammy Davis Jr. his little brother. Frank was ten years older than Sammy. The age difference, as well as the power differential when they first met, created the big brother/little brother dynamic between them. The fact that Frank watched out for Sammy cemented the connection. I don't think I'm overstating when I say that Frank was the single biggest driving force in not only Sammy's career but his life, period. Frank told me they met during Frank's early days at the Paramount Theatre, when Sammy stayed after the show to meet him. Sam must have been a standout: a dapper young Black man surrounded by screaming white bobby-soxers. Sammy was just eighteen then, a kid in Frank's eyes. Sammy and his uncle and dad, known as the Will Mastin Trio, did a show with Frank not long after. If memory serves, the first gig was somewhere in Saint Louis, and though Sammy wasn't well-known yet, Frank insisted that Sammy's name be in the billing. The new billing read, "Frank Sinatra with special guests the Will Mastin Trio, featuring Sammy Davis, Jr." The management fought it, for in those days, Black performers were supposed to be invisible unless they were actually onstage. But Frank wasn't having that, and from the beginning, he went to bat for Sammy.

When Sammy's life changed dramatically in November 1954, Frank was there for him once again. Sammy had a car accident driving to LA from Vegas after a show one night. His face was impaled on the center of the steering wheel, and he lost his eye. The accident only brought Frank and Sammy closer. Once Sammy got out of the hospital, he recuperated at Frank's home.

As Sam told me, "Everyone else, they meant well, but they were saying, 'It's no big deal, don't worry about it.' " Sammy said Frank was the only one who had a straight talk with him about it.

Frank told him, "It's going to affect your career if you let it. You have to get out there and do what you do, and don't let it stop you. Don't let it change you, because you're still the same guy. You still have the same immense amount of talent."

It took a while to get Sammy fitted with a glass eye, so he had to wear an eye patch. Even though Sammy didn't have his new eye yet, Frank convinced him that he needed to get onstage and get his sea legs back. So he helped Sammy get a booking for an engagement at Ciro's on the Sunset Strip. When the big night came, Sammy was very nervous and started to panic when Frank and Dean didn't show up. He didn't want to go on without them. Management held the curtain for nearly twenty minutes, but they ultimately insisted that Sammy go on.

As soon as Sam walked out on the stage, he noticed two men sitting at a table ringside. Even with only one eye, he couldn't miss them. They were both kicked back in their chairs, newspapers spread wide open in front of their faces, noses buried in the print, apparently engrossed in the latest news. Sammy started singing his opening tune. The whole time he was doing his first number, the men just sat there, paying no attention to the singer onstage, reading their papers. Neither one even looked up. When Sam finished the number and the applause died down, he greeted the audience.

Then he gestured toward the two men and said, "Ladies and gentlemen, let me introduce you to two men who are as close to being brothers as I will ever have. Ladies and gentlemen, Mr. Dean Martin and Mr. Frank Sinatra." When they finally put the newspapers down, both Dean and Frank were wearing eye patches that matched Sammy's.

All three shared the same adolescent sense of humor and the same love of pranks. The closer the friend, the bigger the prank. One time when they were working in Vegas, Frank had a special suite set up for Sammy. It wasn't Sammy's real suite, but Sammy didn't know that. When he arrived at the hotel, Sam was given the keys to the suite Frank had prepared for him. When he walked through the door, he looked around and saw that all the furniture, from the living room to the bedroom, was small. Tiny chairs, tiny tables, a toddler bed. Frank had had the whole suite furnished with preschool furniture for his "little friend," as he called Sam. Frank also had food services set the suite up with soul food: small steam tables with ribs, fried chicken, chitlins, greens. At some point, of course, someone showed Sammy to his real suite across the hall.

Sammy wasn't about to let that pass. Two days later, when Frank woke up at three in the afternoon as usual, he ordered room service. There was a knock, and Sammy ceremoniously served Frank's "breakfast" wearing nothing but a diaper.

I met Sammy in 1976, shortly after I came to California, but I didn't get to know him until the mid-eighties. One night I got to see him and Frank in action at the Greek Theatre, an outdoor amphitheater in the Hollywood Hills. Jilly and I were backstage, watching. Sammy was onstage when Frank asked Jilly to bring him a janitor's outfit. Frank put on the coveralls and hat, then took a broom and walked out onto the stage just beyond the wings. He started sweeping, and the audience began to laugh. Sammy, who was singing, couldn't figure out what the hell they were laughing at. Finally, people in the audience started pointing, and Sammy turned around. He cut the band off and walked over to Frank. When Frank noticed the silence, he turned around and looked at Sammy, not saying anything.

Sammy said, "Frank, what are you doing?"

Frank looked at him innocently and said, "What, you're going to do it?"

Sammy could be slyly funny at times. We were in a limousine one night, leaving a gig with Frank and Sammy. Jilly and I were sitting in the jump seat, and Frank and Sam were sitting facing forward. It had been the usual chaos as we left, with fans crowding around, asking Frank and Sammy for autographs and trying to take photos. As we pulled away, there was finally a quiet moment. Sammy gave me a little smile like, *Watch this.*

Then he said to Frank, "Leader?" Sammy called Frank that sometimes, tongue-in-cheek, since Frank was the "leader of the [Rat] pack."

"Yes, Sam?"

Sam said very earnestly, "Do you really believe that I'm a big star?"

"Of course. Why would you ask me a question like that?"

"I was just wondering." Pause. "Leader? If

I'm such a big star, why do I still have to ride in the back of the bus?" It was hilarious.

There were times, though, when Frank didn't know where to draw the line when it came to teasing. He was never cruel, and most of the time, we all enjoyed the ribbing. Every now and then, though, he kept it up just a little too long. One night, the four of us were at dinner: Frank, Jilly, me, and Sammy. Frank started teasing Sammy about his jewelry, as he often did.

"What the hell is it with a ring on each finger, all that stuff you're wearing? Jesus Christ, look at you. You look like a Mr. T starter kit!" At the time, an ex-wrestler-turned-actor who called himself "Mr. T" was known for his sleeveless, bare-biceps look and his piles of bling.

Sammy chuckled, so Frank went on ribbing him. After a while, I could tell Sammy was getting a little tired of it.

He said, "You know, Frank, I grew up in a tough neighborhood like you. And I learned the hard way that when you left the house, if you had anything of real value, you'd better take it with you because you didn't know if it was going to be there when you got back. That's what started all of this. I got in the habit of wearing all this stuff, all the jewelry." One of the things Sammy was wearing that night was a Superman pin on the lapel of his suit. It was the Superman *S* logo in diamonds and gold.

Frank said, "Okay, well, then what the hell is it with the goddamn Superman thing? What are you, twelve?"

I saw Sam flinch slightly and look down. It got quiet. Jilly didn't say anything. He just shook his head. I could see that Sammy was a little bit hurt, but I could also tell that Frank was oblivious to the discomfort he was causing his friend.

The silence seemed to drag on, and Sam remained quiet, so I finally said, "You know, Frank, everyone in their life has someone they look up to as their Superman. And in Sammy's case, and in my case, ironically enough, our Superman's last name also begins with an *S.*"

Frank looked at me. A moment passed, and I could see realization register on his face. He reached over and put his hand on Sammy's shoulder, squeezed it, and said, "I love you, Sam."

About two weeks later, I got a package in the mail from Sammy. Inside was a beautiful gold Superman tie tack, a miniature of the one in diamonds that Sammy always wore. It was Sammy's way of saying thank you.

Frank meant it when he said that friends are the family you choose. Jilly felt the same way. It's very Italian, this sense of connection. Because I was their good friend, I'd also become family in their eyes. We'd be there for each other in tough times. When my father began his long battle with heart disease and pneumonia, it was hard on me, especially since I couldn't be with him physically. One night at the compound, watching TV in the den with Frank, I was sober and preoccupied. My father was in the hospital with pneumonia. Frank knew about it, but we didn't say much. I left the room for a few minutes to use the restroom, and when I returned, there sat Frank, looking at me. He had put two or three cigarettes in each ear, two in each nostril, and a row of cigarettes in his mouth like bizarre, protruding teeth. He was sitting there casually, like nothing was unusual. I cracked up, and when I started laughing, he said innocently, "What's so funny?" Cigarettes fell from his mouth as he talked.

I said, "I hear there's a fine line between insanity and genius, and you just erased it!" That was the way Frank and I helped each other cope. One of our favorite things to say to each other was, "But I made you laugh!"

In 1989, two things occurred. Sammy was diagnosed with throat cancer. And my sister Angela, my kindred spirit since the day she'd come to us as a newborn, was killed on impact in a car accident. At the time of the accident, Angela was eight months pregnant with my niece, Stephanie. The paramedics performed an emergency C-section at the scene and rushed Stephanie to the hospital. She lived less than three hours.

The night I got the news, Frank and Jilly took me to dinner at Matteo's restaurant. I had no appetite, but I don't think they knew what else to do. I told them some of the details of what had happened, and Frank couldn't take it.

He looked at me and said, "You and your family got robbed." Then he left the table and went into the bathroom. He didn't come out for a while. Jilly and I sat there quietly, just the two of us, until he came back.

I flew to New York the next day for the wake and the funeral. My parents wanted my sister and niece to be buried together. The friends and family at the wake didn't know it, but the baby was in the casket with

Angela, covered up so the mourners couldn't see her. Mom and Dad couldn't face it, so I stayed behind after the service while the morticians closed the casket. I watched them gently place the baby in my sister's arms. I'd brought my sister's wedding photo and beautiful crystal rosary beads from Saint Patrick's Cathedral. I tucked them in the casket with Angela and Stephanie before they closed the lid. We were alone, just me and my sister and my niece, and the men from the mortuary.

I flew home three days later. When the elevator doors opened in the hallway next to my condo, there was a woman standing there. As I stepped out of the elevator, she said, "You must be Tony, Tony O."

I said, "Yeah."

"I'm Tarra. I'm Glenn Scarpelli's friend."

I said, "Oh. It's nice to meet you. I've heard a lot about you." Glenn was my friend and neighbor. He'd told me about Tarra. She was some kind of psychic who'd done a lot of work for the government and the Kennedys.

She said, "Listen. I have a message for you from your sister."

I said, "Excuse me?" I'd told almost no one about my sister's passing. Now here was this stranger with a "message."

"Your sister wanted me to thank you for putting the rosary beads and her wedding photograph in the casket." I felt like I'd been punched in the stomach. I hadn't told anyone, *anyone,* about that. I didn't know what to think.

At the same time, Frank was struggling with Sam's illness. Frank knew by then that Sammy wasn't going to be with us much longer. His diagnosis had devastated Frank. Sammy's friends wanted to do something to honor Sam before he passed away. The producer George Schlatter, Frank's close friend, came up with an idea. Sammy had started onstage as an entertainer when he was only four years old, so why not give him a sixtieth-anniversary celebration? Once word got out, celebrities got in line to be part of it. Frank told George he'd be performing first. He didn't ask George; he *told* him. Frank knew that if he didn't go first, he wouldn't be able to do it at all. The thought of waiting for hours while other performers praised Sammy was unbearable to him. He knew there was only a finite amount of time before Sam would be gone. Always a small man, by then, Sammy looked like a skeleton, and the skin around his neck had begun changing color from the intense radiation treatments. He was weak, and he had trouble speaking. Frank was committed to honoring his friend, but going first was the only way he'd be able to get through the performance.

The gala was held in the Shrine Auditorium on February 4, 1990, and recorded for broadcast worldwide. Frank was the first person to be introduced. When he walked downstage toward the audience, the bandstand behind him, his appearance was shocking. He was wearing his usual black tuxedo, but his face was gray. The flesh seemed to hang on his facial bones, and he looked twenty years older. Even his hair seemed to cling to his scalp. He appeared so exhausted that the audience must have wondered if he'd get through the performance.

Frank started by turning to Sammy, who was seated stage left on a circular riser ringed by a brass railing. He began speaking about Sam with a hint of a smile.

"I want to join in this celebration for my *little* friend." It was an old joke between them, and Sammy laughed. As Frank continued speaking, he addressed Sammy directly.

"The best friend I ever had. Sixty years. That's a lot of bourbon under the bridge, baby. And I knew that you were going to amount to *something,* but I didn't know you were going to amount to *everything.* And you did it all . . . Here's to you, Sam. I love you. I can't say it any more than that. You're my brother."

Sammy put his hand over his mouth to keep from crying as Frank began to sing: *"It seems we stood and talked like this before./ We looked at each other in the same way then . . ."* In his decades of friendship with Sammy, though some of the details had faded from memory, their times together were woven through the years like a golden thread. His voice was soft, and you could almost see his mind drift over the years of memories with Sam. So many places. So many times. Finally, Frank finished strong and walked off the stage. And kept walking.

He'd said to me and Jilly earlier, "I just can't. Even though I'm going to be backstage, I can't stand there and listen to what's going to be coming out of people's mouths. I can't deal with it." He left the building as fast as he could, with Jilly and me bringing up the rear. We went to La Dolce Vita and had a very liquid dinner.

George sent Frank a copy of the show before it aired, so we watched the rest of the show that way. At first, Frank sat there staring at the TV, silent and sullen, until the

344

high point of the gala arrived. Gregory Hines had been chosen to represent Sammy's background as an unparalleled tap dancer, and Sammy started to smile the moment Gregory began. Impeccable in a black tuxedo and red pocket handkerchief, Greg started off with a fairly standard routine. It had begun to build when he abruptly broke it off and came over to Sammy. Bending over to where Sammy was seated, he took Sam in his arms very emotionally. The audience and Sam both seemed to think he was done, but he said to Sammy, "I got more."

He returned to the platform center stage and told Sammy, "I feel so much love for you that I'm going to try to dance it out for you." And he did. He caught fire and poured all his emotion into a breathtaking performance. When he finished to a huge roar of applause, he again approached Sammy.

Then, just when you thought it couldn't get any better, the magic happened. Sammy turned to the person next to him and asked for something. He was handed a shoe box and bent down to slip off his street shoes and put on his tap shoes as the audience watched incredulously. Pulling his body upright, Sammy could barely be heard to mutter, "Stomp-off!"

Sammy made his way carefully up to the

platform with Gregory. Then suddenly, they were off, competing in the traditional way of tap dancers, each performing complicated staccatos for the other to imitate. They were time-stepping without music. Sammy had seemed to be holding himself up as he walked to the platform, but his rail-thin body relaxed the moment his first tap hit the stage. Suddenly he was Sammy Davis Jr. again, dancing as he was born to.

At first Frank perked up and began to laugh in the face of his friend's performance. But as the dancing continued, I watched Frank's mood change. Here was his dear friend, dying, but he could still summon the wherewithal to steal the stage. Frank's eyes welled up with tears. Finally, Sammy did a particularly difficult step with a complicated rhythm. Greg Hines didn't even try to follow. He fell onto his knees on the stage, crawled over to where Sammy was, and kissed Sammy's shoes. Afterward, Sammy and Frank's dear friend Ella Fitzgerald, in a glittering black floor-length gown, closed the show with "Too Close for Comfort." The rest of the performers gathered behind her. Sammy, his face beaming, moved from person to person, embracing them as the credits rolled. It was a worthy send-off for a remarkable man.

Less than three months later, Sammy passed away. Frank was in New York when he got the news. Waylaid by reporters leaving the Waldorf Towers by the underground parking lot, he looked distraught.

Sammy wanted a public funeral in the African-American tradition of the South. It was held on May 19, 1990, at Forest Lawn in the Hollywood Hills. A three-hundred-car procession briefly shut down parts of the LA freeways. Approximately three thousand mourners showed up that day. Dean and Frank, haggard in a black suit, were honorary pallbearers. Jilly and I went with Frank, Barbara, Nancy Jr., and Liza Minnelli. Frank and Barbara sat in the front row. Sammy's ornate bronze casket was heavily draped with yellow orchids and white roses. Prayers were given in English and Hebrew. Afterward, the strains of Sammy's singing "I've Gotta Be Me" filled the sanctuary. Gregory Hines said a few words, and Reverend Jesse Jackson gave a beautiful eulogy, ending with, "He has answered the curtain call over and over . . . encore no more. Let Mr. Bojangles rest." Sammy's wife, Altovise, lovely and fragile in a white suit, was escorted to the podium by Jesse Jackson. She said in a soft voice, "How lucky we all were to have Sammy in our lives. And how dearly I will miss him." The service ended with the strains of "Mr. Bojangles." Sammy was buried with his father and uncle, the original Will Mastin Trio, in a walled, forty-foot private plot.

Frank had been worried about the funeral since before Sammy passed, and not just because of his own grief. Sammy owed a huge amount of money to the IRS. Given the visibility of Sammy Davis Jr. and the publicity surrounding his funeral, Frank was worried that the IRS might raid Sammy's house while the family was at the service. To keep the IRS at bay, Frank gave Altovise a seven-figure check to pass on to the IRS, so that Sammy's family could have the funeral in peace. That night, the lights were dimmed on the Las Vegas Strip in Sammy's honor.

One postscript to the passing of Sammy Davis Jr. About a year and a half after Sam passed away, I took my friends Glenn and Tarra to see Frank perform. I can't remember whether it was at the Hollywood Bowl or the Greek Theatre, but it was one of the big outdoor amphitheaters.

When I talked to Glenn after the show, he was complaining about Tarra. He said, "I love Tarra, but sometimes she's a bit much."

I said, "What do you mean?"

"Well, you remember when Frank was doing 'Luck Be a Lady'?"

I said, "Yeah." It was a number Frank had often done with Sammy. That night he'd referred to Smokey before he started the song. "Smokey" was his private nickname for Sam. Sam was Smokey, and Dean was Dago. Frank was Leader. It was an insider thing. Glenn didn't know that, and neither did Tarra.

Glenn went on, "Tonight, when he started that number, Tarra said she saw Sammy Davis Jr. onstage, singing with Frank."

I felt a nervous chill. Part of me said the whole thing was ridiculous. But another part of me thought how wonderful it was to think that Sammy was still there, singing with Frank.

I met Dean Martin in the mid-eighties at a birthday party for Dean and Kirk Kerkorian, the man who built half of Las Vegas. I got to know him initially through Frank and Jilly.

Frank and Dean had been pals for decades. They'd hit it off from the beginning, with a shared Italian heritage and quirky sense of humor. Frank was there with Dean through the various marriages, becoming godfather to two of Dean's children. The two men had a very good, very solid relationship that lasted to the end. The stories claiming that Frank and Dean were feuding in the last years of Dean's life are a fabrication. It's absolutely untrue. In fact, Frank was the last friend Dean spoke to, when Frank called to wish him a merry Christmas on the night Dean died. I should know. I placed the call and stood there while Frank talked to him.

Frank and Dean had a natural chemistry and wit, and together with Sammy, they were kinetic onstage. When Frank talked about the Rat Pack years, he said they were rarely scripted because one would start something, and the others would pick it up. One of their most famous — and politically incorrect — bits happened at the Sands one night with the Count Basie Orchestra. Dean, who was much taller than Sammy, spontaneously picked Sammy up and carried him to the microphone in his arms. Completely poker-faced, Dean said to the audience, "I'd like to thank the NAACP for this beautiful trophy."

When a female heckler once shouted at Dean, "I'll leave my husband for you," he, always quick-witted, replied, "I don't want your husband!"

I only saw Frank, Sammy, and Dean do

their Rat Pack routine in person once, when they were doing their Together Again tour. It was in the Oakland Arena in 1988. Even though Dean struggled with his health throughout the tour, it was wonderful to watch them back to being adolescents on-stage. They seemed to be having a ball and just letting the audience in on it, which was always the secret of the Rat Pack's success.

Whenever they toured together, Frank and Dean bickered about their bedtime. Dean liked to get up shortly after sunrise, when Frank was just going to bed. One night on tour, Frank wanted to hang out, but Dean said, "No, I've got to get up in the morning and play golf." Dean was an avid golfer.

Frank said, "Okay," but he wasn't happy.

I don't know how the hell he did it, but somehow, Frank managed to get into Dean's golf bag and replace all his golf balls with Ping-Pong balls. To repay Frank, Dean paid one of the maids in the hotel to replace the shampoo with honey in the bottle in Frank's room. Frank found out the hard way — more accurately, the sticky way. Like Frank and Sammy, when they were together, Frank and Dean were a couple of kids.

In spite of his man-about-town image, Dean really didn't enjoy late nights, even at his own parties. Frank loved to tell me about the time Dean and his wife Jeanne had an anniversary party at their house. Frank said it was getting to be about eleven fifteen p.m. when he decided to wander away from the party to have a cigarette. He was out front, lighting up, when he saw police cars pulling up in front of the house and Jeanne Martin walking across the front lawn to meet them.

Frank said to her, "What the hell is going on?"

Jeanne said, "I don't know, but I can't find Dean."

Frank told her, "Okay, why don't you get back to your guests? I'll take care of this." Meanwhile, the cops were coming up the walk. Frank said, "Good evening, officer."

The sergeant replied, "Oh, hi, Mr. Sinatra."

"So what's going on, fellas?"

"Well, I hate to tell you this, but we got a call about the party disturbing the peace."

Frank looked at the cop and said, "Do you know whose house this is?"

"Yes, I do, sir. But we have to respond to every call that comes in."

Frank shook his head. "Who the hell would make a call like that?"

The sergeant turned around and told the other cops to go back to the squad cars.

Then he said to Frank, "I'm not really at liberty to say."

Frank took a couple of hundred-dollar bills and stuck them in the guy's shirt pocket. He told him, "Here's for the policemen's retirement fund. So tell me, who made the call?"

"Believe it or not, Mr. Sinatra, the call came from inside the house."

Frank told the officer he'd take care of it. Then Frank went upstairs to Dean's bedroom and opened the door. There was Dean in his pajamas, lying across the bed with a golf club on his shoulder, watching the eleven o'clock news.

Dean looked up and said, "Hey, pally."

Frank said, "I'll give you pally. What the hell did you do?"

Dean just shrugged. "Hey, they ate. They drank. They danced. Now let them go home. I got to get up and play golf in the morning."

Another night, Frank told me, he and Dean did a Christmas special together at NBC. Afterward, Dean said to him, "Why don't you come by the house? We're having an early Christmas gathering, and you could see all the kids. They're all starting to go their separate ways, you know. We don't get all of them together that often anymore. You should come over." Frank said okay.

They got into Dean's Stutz Blackhawk and headed for Bel Air. As they drove down Sunset Boulevard through Beverly Hills, a cop pulled them over. Dean had had a couple of drinks, and his breath smelled like booze.

Frank said, "Now, listen, when the cop comes, talk to the windshield, or talk to me. Don't talk to the cop." The cop came up, and Dean rolled down the window. By then it was seven o'clock, and it was dark outside.

When the cop shone his flashlight in Dean's face, Dean started singing to him. "I'd love to get you on a slow boat to China . . ."

The cop recognized him, and after a few bars, he said, "Okay, Mr. Martin." Then he looked at Frank. "I tell you what, Mr. Sinatra, would you ride in the car with my partner? And Mr. Martin, would you please sit in the passenger seat?" The cop got in Dean's car and drove him to the house while Frank rode in the police car because the Stutz was only a two-seater.

When they got to the house, they thanked the cops and walked up to the front porch. When they opened the door and got to the entrance of the dining room, it was wall-to-wall people. All seven of Dean's kids were there, with their spouses and their own children.

Dean looked a little blearily at Frank and said, "Can you believe this?"

Frank said, "What?"

Dean said, "Look at this room. I literally fucked myself out of a seat." That was Dean.

For most of their lives, Frank and Dean went out to dinner a lot. There'd typically be ten people at the restaurant. Frank told me that one night, they were having dinner at Chasen's when the conversation shifted away from him. After ten or fifteen minutes, Dean realized that Frank hadn't said a word. His mind had wandered off somewhere.

Dean said to him, "Hey, pally, where are you?"

Frank replied curtly, "Why don't you mind your own business?"

Dean wasn't sure if Frank meant it or was just joking. He said, "Hey, hey, take it easy." Frank was not in the mood.

About a week later, a package from Dean arrived for Frank. Frank opened it, and it was a beautiful gold pinky ring with letters spelling out *Love*. Puzzled, Frank turned the pinky ring around 180 degrees. On the other side, also in gold script, it said, *Fuck*.

Frank called Dean and said, "Thanks for

the jewelry, but what the hell is this?"

Dean said, "It's a mood ring. I did it so that the next time I'm in your company, and I approach the table, I can look down at your hand. You can turn the ring so the appropriate word is facing me, and I'll know whether I'm addressing Dr. Jekyll or Mr. Hyde."

Frank gave me that ring and told me the story himself. I still laugh every time I look at it. Frank also told me he did a reciprocal thing for Dean. He had a pair of cufflinks made with little gold sticks that were shaped like curb feelers, the things you put on your car so you won't hit the sidewalk. He said he told Dean, "So next time you go out drinking, you won't get hurt on the way home."

Everything changed for Dean the day his son Dino, Dean Martin Jr., was killed in a plane crash on San Gorgonio Mountain, the same mountain that had taken Dolly Sinatra's life a decade earlier. Dean Jr. was a member of the California Air National Guard. He died when the F-4C Phantom jet he was piloting hit the mountain in a severe snowstorm in March 1987. He was only thirty-five years old. As with Dolly's crash, it took days to find and recover the pieces of the plane and the remains because the impact was so severe.

One day after the plane went down, I found Frank sitting outside at the desert compound, staring at San Gorgonio, unmoving. After a few minutes of silence, he said, "If one day you're looking for me, and can't find me, and you hear a loud boom, and see that mountain blow up, you'll know it was me that did it."

Dean was devastated by Dino's death. Dean was always something of a loner, but he withdrew from everyone after Dino died. If someone approached him, he'd get uncomfortable after a few minutes and leave. Despite his public image, Dean was basically an introvert. He'd always been a private person. He kept walls up that no one, family or friend, ever got past. When Dino died, Dean blamed himself for not being closer to his son. Frank said that Dino's death became Dean's Rosebud, from the movie *Citizen Kane,* the symbol of all his longing and regret. Dean would beat himself up about not spending quality time with Dino. He started drinking in earnest. Before Dino's death, he really wasn't that much of a drinker. Playing a drunk was just part of his schtick. On the TV shows and onstage, more times than not, it was Martinelli's apple juice in his glass, not booze. After

Dino's passing, that changed.

As the months passed following Dino's death, Dean's friends became increasingly worried about him. Instead of moving past the initial grief, Dean was withdrawing further and further from the world. He tried to reconcile with Dino's mother, Jeanne, going so far as to propose to her again. She refused, which was probably a good decision, but she and Dean remained close for the rest of their lives. It was Frank who came up with the idea of a Rat Pack reunion tour in hopes it would cheer Dean up. He naively told Dean, "Let's get together and have some fun."

The whole idea was ill fated from the beginning. Dean was severely depressed and in poor health, and he didn't really want to do the tour. Instead of saying so, though, he agreed, because he didn't want to let Frank and Sammy down. Dean only made it through four performances. He just didn't have the wherewithal, physically or emotionally, to continue. Not only that, but he told Frank he didn't feel like he was holding up his end of the performance. He felt that he was being upstaged and overshadowed, and it was his own fault for not living up to the level of performance Frank and Sammy were meeting. Dean knew Frank was going to be blamed for his leaving, so Dean sent out a press statement that he was having some health issues. That wasn't really the main problem, but he checked into Cedars-Sinai Medical Center when he came back from the road just to cover the story.

In the years following the Together Again tour, Frank would make plans over and over again to have dinner with Dean. Dean would say, "Yeah, sure, pally, I'll meet you," but then he'd almost never show. Frank and I would be sitting at La Famiglia restaurant, waiting for him, but he'd never come.

When I called his house from the restaurant and asked for him, he'd never answer the phone. Instead, a staff member would pick up and say, "Oh, he's not here. Well, he's gone to such-and-such . . ." Afterward, I'd have to go back and tell Frank and see the hurt on his face.

One afternoon, I finally had a heart-to-heart talk with Dean. I said, "Frank loves you, buddy, and he really misses your company. He misses hanging out with you, and he misses all the laughs that you guys have shared all these years."

Dean said, "Yeah, I understand, pal. But you know, I've worked very hard all my life so that I can have my own space, and I just like staying home and watching television."

He used to watch Westerns all the time. He didn't want to leave the house.

Frank and Barbara and I tried to have dinner with Dean for what turned out to be his last birthday, in June, but again, he didn't show, so we decided to go have dinner at DaVinci's restaurant instead. Unfortunately, the press had spotted us waiting for Dean, so when we left for DaVinci's, they followed us. Frank was already feeling bad about Dean's not showing up, so when the paparazzi swarmed him the minute he got out of the Rolls, I got angry. I yelled at them to get out of his face, telling them that he was a private citizen just trying to have dinner on his personal time and should be left alone. We went inside and ate dinner, but by the time we got to dessert, with the paparazzi still waiting, I'd hatched a plan.

I knew that the owner, who was a friend of Frank's, drove a Rolls just like Frank's. It was parked behind the restaurant. He and I had a little conference, and about ten minutes before we were ready to leave, we had the valet bring Frank's car out front. The photographers swarmed around it. Meanwhile, another valet fired up the owner's Rolls and pulled around behind Frank's car. The photographers were momentarily confused. Just as the second Rolls arrived, the valet pulled Frank's car onto the street and went around the block, then behind the restaurant. A minute afterward, the second Rolls pulled out just as the first one arrived in front of the restaurant again. By then, the paparazzi were running around, some in back of the restaurant, some looking down the street, the ones in front trying to check the license plates to see which car was which. For about fifteen minutes, the merry-go-round continued. It was like a shell game. Then the valet pulled Frank's car in front and stopped. The press saw the Sinatra plates and rushed to the car. At this point, Frank and Barbara and I went out the back of the restaurant. Barbara got in the backseat of our friend's car, Frank rode shotgun, and I took the wheel. As I peeled out of the parking lot, the valet took off after us in Frank's Rolls and then turned another direction. By then the paparazzi were frustrated and hopelessly confused. We met up with the other car at Frank's house, swapped cars back, and pulled through the gates at home. When all was said and done, it had turned into a great evening.

The very last time we had dinner with Dean was a month or so afterward. This time, he showed up. It was Frank, myself, Dean, and Dean's close friend and manager,

Mort Viner. By this point in time, Dean was extremely withdrawn and would speak very softly. He was still sharp mentally, but he'd fallen into the habit that a lot of older people have of saying, "What? What'd you say? What did you say, pally?" He kept asking us to repeat ourselves. It was partly a hearing problem and partly just a habit.

By this time in his life, Frank, because of the punctured eardrum that had gotten worse over the years, was supposed to be wearing a hearing aid in his left ear. He hated wearing it and would only use it when he wanted to. This particular evening, he'd chosen to wear it. We were sitting in Dean's booth, which was right in the bar, so it was quite noisy. Frank and Dean were telling stories and reminiscing. Dean would start telling one story, and Frank would finish it. Then twenty minutes later, Frank would start telling the same story, and Dean would finish it. All the time they were talking, Dean kept saying, "What'd you say, pally? What'd you say? What'd you say?" It was beginning to drive Frank nuts.

Finally, Frank said to him, "For crying out loud, why don't you go to a doctor, for Christ's sake? Get a hearing test and get a goddamn earpiece!"

Dean looked at him and said, "What?

What'd you say?"

Frank said, "Goddamn it!" He reached across the table and grabbed Dean's shirt and pulled Dean toward him. Then he took the hearing aid out of his own ear and stuck it in Dean's. He turned the volume up to the point that it was beginning to squeal. Dean reached over and turned it down, then sat back. They just stared at each other for what seemed like an eternity but was really only seconds.

Finally, Frank very quietly said, "Now isn't that better?"

Dean looked at Frank and said, "Who the hell are you yelling at?" And they started laughing. That was their very last dinner together.

On Christmas Eve 1995, I was booked to take the red-eye to spend Christmas with my parents. Frank said, "Why don't you come over to the house in the afternoon, and we'll have our Christmas, and then I'll see you when you get back." That was the day Frank gave me my Cartier Pasha watch with the inscription on the back that says, *You're the best.*

We were sitting there together when Frank said to me, "Geez, I wonder what the Dago is doing."

"Well, why don't we call him?" I picked

363

up the phone and called Dean's private line.

I was glad when he picked up and said, "Hello."

"Dean, this is Tony O."

"Hey, pally. How are you?"

"Listen, I just wanted to wish you a merry Christmas. I'm probably not going to get to see you for Christmas, but I want to wish you the best. Meanwhile, the old man wants to talk to you."

"Oh, okay, pally. Take care and merry Christmas." And Frank got on the phone.

"Hey, Dago, how you doing?"

I heard bits and pieces of a weird conversation going back and forth. They were making no sense. Finally, Frank laughed and said, "I love you, Dago." He hung up the phone.

I said, "What the hell was that all about?"

"Can you believe this crazy bastard? You know his health condition, and he wants to tell me a joke."

"Yeah? So what was the joke?"

"The joke was, 'What did one casket say to the other casket?' I said, 'I don't know, what?' And the answer was, 'Is that you, coffin?'"

Of course, we laughed. Worst joke ever. And eerily appropriate.

I took the flight that night and walked into

my parents' house about seven the next morning. My mother was waiting at the door to hug me. I was going to say hello to my father and lie down a few minutes when my cell phone rang. I looked down and saw it was the private line at Frank's house. My heart fell.

I picked up the phone and said hello. It was Vine.

She said, "Listen, we just heard. We don't want you to hear it on the news, but we just got a call. Dean passed away."

Dean was gone? But I had talked to him less than twelve hours before.

I asked if Frank had the wherewithal to talk to me, and Vine put him on the phone. I said, "Listen, I don't know what to say. Words fail me."

"I know, I know."

"Do you want me to come back?"

"You know what, Ton', I really don't think that I'm going to be able to gather the strength to go to the funeral. If I change my mind, I'll send the plane for you." He added, "Outside of that, enjoy the holidays as best you can with your family, and I'll talk to you soon."

I said, "Okay," and I hung up.

Dean's funeral was held three days later at Pierce Brothers in Westwood. Barbara and Nancy Jr. represented the Sinatras. Frank was too devastated to attend. The Rickleses and the Newharts were there, and Angie Dickinson. The press was kept out, and no photos or video footage was taken. It was quiet and private, as Dean wanted. There was no casket, just a large picture of Dean next to a display of flowers and the flag of Italy. Dean had requested that the service be uplifting, and his friends did their best to comply. Jerry Lewis spoke, periodically overcome with tears. Shirley MacLaine, by that point as well-known for her spiritual journeying as for her performing, joked that she'd just talked to Dean an hour earlier. A special CD with several of Dean's songs was played over the loudspeaker. Rosemary Clooney closed the service, singing "Everybody Loves Somebody Sometime." Once again, as they had with Sammy's passing, Vegas dimmed its lights during Dean's service.

One of the greatest heartaches of old age is the gradual loss of your friends. One death at a time, in a relentless procession, your friends begin to disappear. You lose the people who were there at the time, who remember what you remember, who share your inside jokes. When Sammy and Dean died, Frank lost irreplaceable parts of himself. When Jilly Rizzo died, it was a loss of a whole new magnitude. There was no replacement for the man who'd shared his life for forty years. All either of us could do was treasure what we still had — share some laughs, some music, and some Jack Daniel's, and toast those we'd been privileged to know and those who remained.

■ ■ ■ ■

# PART III
# IN THE WINTER
# OF HIS YEARS

■ ■ ■ ■

I remember clearly the first time I walked into a room with Frank. It was the early eighties, at Matteo's restaurant in Los Angeles. When Frank came through the door, it seemed like the room stopped. People turned around, and there was a sudden silence. It was like one of those movie moments where they stop the film and everything goes quiet. Suspended animation. Then the room erupted into applause, and I could hear the whispers of excitement. It was like Frank created a vacuum, sucking all the energy and attention to himself. He had an aura about him that I was never able to explain. It wasn't something that he could consciously turn on or off, the way he could turn on the charm for a beautiful woman. His natural persona was larger than life. He dominated every room he entered without trying. People loved him, and they would go to great lengths just for a glimpse of him. Even as he aged and his health began to fail him, the persona remained. Audiences couldn't take their eyes off him.

In 1994, Frank was onstage at the MGM Grand in Las Vegas. Frankie Jr. was conducting. It was a song Frank knew like his own child, "Nancy with the Laughing Face," sung for his older daughter. And then it happened again. Frank went up on a lyric and lost the thread. He was far downstage, almost on the lip, within feet of the audience. Much too far away for Frankie to feed him the lyrics. Frank blinked in confusion at the teleprompter as I stood, helpless and dismayed, in the wings. Then something remarkable happened. Someone ringside leaned forward and began singing the lyric, trying to help him. Within moments, it caught on, and people around him joined in. Voices rose as the audience sang the words Frank could no longer remember, sang them to him. After a little while, he pulled the microphone from his mouth and just stood there, listening. When Frankie brought the orchestra to a close, the audience rose as one and gave Frank a standing ovation. He stood there, holding the microphone, with tears streaming down his face. That's how much his audience loved him.

That's how well they understood.

When the curtain finally went down and the audience left, the thin thread of composure that held Frank upright snapped. He began yelling at a terrifying volume that it was the worst show he'd ever done and that the audience should get their money back. People backstage faded back, fearful of what they saw only as rage. I saw something very different. I saw a man facing the realization that despite his best efforts, he was losing the battle with himself.

Frank was seventy-eight years old when he stood onstage that night. Unknown to anyone except Barbara and me, he'd already suffered five or six ministrokes in his sleep. He was also coping with Paget's disease of the skull. Barbara guarded the secret closely. I was sworn to secrecy.

She told me, "We have to protect him. We have to protect his career."

The thing Frank prized most was threatened — not his life, but his ability to perform. Without performing, it wouldn't be his life anymore.

It was in Richmond, Virginia, on March 7, 1994, that Frank's most dramatic onstage crisis occurred. It happened in an auditorium packed with fans and made every major newscast in America.

We arrived in Richmond after a long, exhausting tour. It was our last stop on the tour, and Barbara had flown ahead to Palm Springs, where we'd join her in a couple of days. Richmond was a two-night gig, with Frankie Jr. conducting. On the second night, I was in the wings offstage as usual, where I'd be visible to Frank. He looked tired out. We'd only been up until two or three the night before, which was early for Frank to go to bed, and he hadn't put away that much booze. He shouldn't have been that exhausted. I was glad when he started singing "My Way" because that meant he was just one song away from the end of the tour. He only had to sing "New York, New York" after that, and we'd be out of there. Suddenly, right in the middle of the song, Frank took a couple of steps upstage toward the piano.

He stopped singing and said to Frankie, "Where's the stool?"

Frankie couldn't make out what he'd said, so he ran into the wings to ask me what his father wanted. Just then, Frank collapsed. We both turned and watched as he seemed to melt into the stage, like he was in slow motion. His microphone bounced on the floor with a horrendous sound, and the band stopped on its own. I ran out and

374

turned him over, undid his tie, and opened his collar.

The first thing he said as he looked up at me was, "What happened?"

I was blocking the audience's view of him as I told him, "No big deal."

Frank asked, "Can the audience still see me?" I told him that they could. Then he said, "All right. Help me up. I want to wave to them." Several doctors from the audience had joined us onstage, and paramedics came onstage with a wheelchair. I was going to pull the drape, but Frank said, "Leave it open. I want to make sure they know I'm okay."

There was a hush in the audience. You could have heard a pin drop. I helped him to his feet and into the wheelchair, and as I lifted him, I felt the outer shell of his jacket. It was soaking wet. I thought to myself, *He's soaked right through, his shirt and everything.* Safely in the chair, Frank waved at the audience, and they all stood up and cheered. By the time we got him offstage, he was getting grumpy, a sure sign that he was feeling better. The paramedics checked his vitals and said he needed to go to the hospital for a couple of tests to make sure he was out of danger. In full Chairman of the Board style, he flatly refused. I took him aside.

"Look, Frank, it's not safe for us to get on a plane home without getting you a clean bill of health. Here are our options. We can either go to the hospital for an hour or so and have them check you out, or I can ask one of the doctors here to come with us on the plane. Your decision."

Frank knew I was right, and he wasn't about to bring a strange doctor on the plane. He reluctantly agreed to go to the hospital. He was in a better mood by then, and as we waited for the results of the tests, the situation morphed into something comical. Doctors began coming into Frank's room, one after another. Each time the doctor would look at the chart, say "Good morning, Mr. Sinatra," and then mumble something vaguely medical before leaving. The first few times it happened, I didn't think much of it, but as the long line of medical personnel continued, it was obvious what was going on. I'd wager every doctor in that hospital came by to see Frank that evening, and I wouldn't be surprised if some came by off shift. I thought, *I might as well have put in a turnstile and sold tickets.*

After what seemed like the tenth doctor, the routine started getting old, so when that doctor asked Frank one more time, "How's your head?" Frank replied, "How's your ass?

I want to get out of here!"

I said to the startled doctor, "I think he's feeling better!"

The tests confirmed that there was nothing seriously wrong with Frank. He'd just become dehydrated. The doctors thought it might be a problem with Frank's multiple medications, but by then, his electrolytes and oxygen level had stabilized, and the color had come back to his face. The doctor told Frank it was safe to discharge him and had a wheelchair brought in. Frank balked. There was no way he was going to get back in that thing.

The doctor, however, insisted. "It's our hospital policy to wheel you out —"

Frank stopped him and said, "You know where you can put your policy? I'm not sitting in another damn wheelchair. I can walk out of here under my own steam."

We finally compromised. Frank rode out of the hospital in the wheelchair, but the minute we reached the parking lot, he was out of there. When we got to the limo, Frank lit a cigarette, waved to the press and the people across the street, and got into the limo. We went straight to the airport. It was still dark when the plane landed back in Palm Springs. When we got off, I was shocked to see Barbara there waiting for

Frank. Barbara had never come to meet him at the airstrip before, much less in the middle of the night. She looked worse than he did.

She embraced him, saying, "Darling."

We drove back to the compound. When she knew he was okay, she said, "I'll leave you guys now. I'll see you tomorrow." She gave him a kiss, gave me a kiss, and went off to bed. Frank was thrilled that she'd come to the airport to meet him. It was better than any medicine that a doctor could have given him.

A couple of days later, I was sitting by the pool with Barbara while Frank was still sleeping.

She asked me, "Did you see any signs of this coming on the day of the concert? Were you guys up late that night?"

"Barbara, no, he was fine. He was joking."

"Wow. I guess I shouldn't have given him that stuff."

"What stuff? Barbara, what are you talking about?"

"Before I left, I noticed that his ankles looked a little swollen, so I gave him two more water pills." As part of Frank's regimen, he would take Diazide, a water pill, to regulate the water in his system.

"Barbara. Please don't do that without at

least telling Vine. She gives him his medication every day." Barbara started to cry, and I said, "I'm sorry if I upset you."

No wonder she'd been at the airport at the crack of dawn. She was terrified by what could have happened because of her mistake.

Frank, God bless him, never liked seeing doctors — in their professional capacity, that is. Privately, he liked some of them very much. But professionally, he could do without them. His affectionate nickname for any doctor, even a friend, was "croaker." When he needed to see a doctor, he'd tell me, "Call one of the croakers tomorrow and make an appointment."

I used to go with him for his physicals. Dr. Pat Picchione was the one who gave Frank his regular checkups. Frank would always walk into the office like he was running for president.

He'd greet everybody. "Hi. How are you, sweetheart?" Of course, with that tan, he looked like there was nothing ever wrong with him.

One time we were at Dr. Picchione's office for a checkup, and he gave Frank the normal series of tests, took some blood, and did an EKG. It took about forty-five minutes. When the doctor finished, Frank said,

"Okay. So how do things look?"

Pat said, "Well, you know, your blood pressure's a little high. But for the most part, God bless you, you're doing really well."

Frank was pleased, so his response was, "Great. Thanks. Okay." He got up to leave.

Then the doc said to him, "But . . ."

"What do you mean *but*?" Frank was halfway out the door.

"But as your friend, I really wish that you would cut back on your drinking."

Frank looked at me, looked back at Pat, and jokingly said, "Well, as *your* friend, why don't you go and fuck yourself? Because I see a lot more old drunks than I see old doctors."

There were times when a doctor would come to the house because Frank wasn't feeling up to par. After the doctor examined him, Frank would ask, "So what do you think?"

The doctor would say, "Well, I think maybe you have such-and-such."

If Frank didn't like what he heard, he'd say, "I don't want that. Give it to somebody else. What else you got?"

He had even stronger opinions about dentists, whom he called "choppers." We were at the beach house one morning when

380

Frank started fussing with his mouth. He kept rubbing his upper lip, massaging his gum.

I said, "What's the matter?"

He said, "Son of a bitch. Something's biting me up in here, and it hurts."

"Well, do you want to go see Choppers?"

"Yeah, that probably would be a good idea."

The next morning, I made the arrangements. Frank's longtime dentist, Dr. Lake, was in Palm Springs. A helicopter would pick us up at the Malibu sheriff's station five miles down the road and take us over the hill to Van Nuys Airport. There a jet would be waiting to fly us down to Palm Springs, where a limousine would take us to Dr. Lake's office. He'd do the examination and whatever procedure Frank needed. Meanwhile, the limo would be waiting to take us back to the jet, which would take us to the helicopter, where we'd be met by the limo to take us home. It was your basic $12,000 dental visit. Just a typical day in Frank's world.

On March 1, 1994, the Recording Academy was scheduled to honor Frank with the Grammy Legend Award. U2's Bono was going to present Frank with the award at

Radio City Music Hall. Bono was also up for a Grammy that night. He was a huge Sinatra fan who'd become a friend when he and Frank recorded "I've Got You Under My Skin" together for the first *Duets* album. Later, Bono had stayed a few days at the compound and done a video of the song with Frank, one of only two music videos Frank ever made. When he and Frank met up backstage on Grammy night, they picked up right where they'd left off. They were upstairs in Frank's dressing room, hanging out and having a couple of drinks during the show, when Bono's name was announced onstage as the winner. When someone came to tell him he needed to get downstairs and accept his award, he didn't want to leave.

Finally, we all told him, "Go down and get your Grammy, for God's sake."

When it was time for Frank's award a short while later, we went downstairs and took our places. There were two round baffles onstage. Frank and I were standing behind one, and Bono was standing behind the other. When they introduced Bono, he walked out and gave what Frank called "the best introduction" he'd ever gotten, a free-form poem Bono had written about Frank. It perfectly captured the complexity of the man I knew: *Turning on the right phrase and the right song / Which is where he lives . . . / His songs are his home, and he lets you in. . . .*

I was still standing behind the baffle when Frank walked out and gave his acceptance speech. He was very sentimental that night, showing a side of himself that he rarely did. He even got a little teary-eyed and was joking that no one had asked him to sing. It was touching, but it also took much longer than the producer anticipated. When Frank kept talking, the executive producer, Pierre Cossette, came to where I was hiding behind the baffle and said, "What do you think I should do?"

I said, "You're getting some great stuff here. But it's your show. Do what you feel you need to do."

"We really ought to cut to commercial."

"Well, Pierre, it's your choice, man."

At that point, in the words of the *Washington Post,* the evening turned into the great "Grammy Whammy." Pierre made the choice. The band started playing, and the show went to commercial. Frank looked at Bono and said, "What the hell is that?"

We left the building after Frank's speech, so we missed what came next. In one of the Grammys' all-time classic moments, Billy Joel, in the middle of singing "River of

Dreams," abruptly stopped, fell silent, and faced the audience. Still sitting on the piano bench, he looked at his watch and said, "Okay, that's ten seconds of valuable network time wasted. Twenty seconds of valuable network time wasted . . ." After about thirty seconds of that, he went back to whaling on the piano. It was very, very funny, and no one missed his point. The audience cheered. The next day, the decision to cut Frank off dominated entertainment news. Reviewers ripped the decision and applauded Billy Joel.

Frank's final concerts would be opening the Fukuoka Dome in Japan with Natalie Cole in December of 1994. People were flying in from all corners of the world to catch the shows. Even though no announcement had been made, the word was out that these would be Frank Sinatra's last concerts. Looking back, I can see that from the beginning, Frank acted in ways unusual for him. Normally, when we traveled that far and had to adapt to a major time change, we'd arrange the schedule to arrive two or three days before the first concert. It gave Frank a chance to rest and adapt to the new time zone. On this occasion, though, he insisted on leaving at the last minute. In retrospect,

I don't think he wanted to go. These would be the last concerts of his career. But in his heart of hearts, he knew he was postponing the inevitable. On the long flight to Japan, he was restless and preoccupied the whole time. When everyone else on the plane was asleep, Frank sat up with me, talking and drinking. We got no rest at all. When we got off the plane in Japan, it was dinnertime on Sunday, one day before his concert on Monday. We went to the hotel and then to dinner. Afterward, we stayed up until about five o'clock Monday morning. At that point, we had been up something like thirty-two hours. I was exhausted, and I could only imagine how it was affecting seventy-nine-year-old Frank.

Frank woke up late that afternoon, just a few hours before the show. Disoriented, he looked out the window.

"If I had a necktie for every time I took the ferry from Hoboken to here . . ."

I said, "Frank, we're in Fukuoka, Japan."

"We're what?"

I repeated, "You're in Japan."

"What did you let me drink last night?"

Two hours later, he was performing in front of forty thousand people. During the concert, he seemed to have trouble staying focused. He'd be thoroughly enjoying the performance one minute, but then his attention would wander off. He kept going up on the lyrics. Frank Jr. was physically staying closer to him onstage than usual, so if necessary, he could keep his dad lyrically on track.

As the show neared its end, he turned to Frankie and asked, "What else you got?" He had to have been exhausted, but he didn't want to leave the stage.

The performance was less than stellar. Yet the amazing thing about Frank was how forgiving people were if he made mistakes. His fans simply loved him. When he forgot lyrics, they stood up and cheered all the more. If he made any sort of apology, the audience would drown him out with applause. They were telling him that they didn't care if he made mistakes. All he had to do was come out and stand on the stage. They would have been happy even if he hadn't sung, as long as he talked to them. People still wanted to share the magic that was Frank Sinatra, even if it only meant looking at him.

On closing night, Frank performed like he was operating on remote control. Watching from the wings, I could see that he was struggling and emotionally detached. I had only witnessed his performing like that once before — in January 1977, at Caesars Palace, trying to sing for an audience while knowing that the airplane carrying his mother was missing. The performance wound its way down to the close.

Frankie Jr. had started the exit bows when again, Frank Sr. turned to his son and asked, "What else you got?"

This time, Junior responded, "That's it. We're done."

The impact of Junior's words on Frank was immediate. The robot was gone, and I watched a very conscious and emotional Frank Sr. return to the stage. The orchestra was still playing his bow music, and the audience was on their feet applauding. As he continued standing there, the audience quieted down, and Frank summoned the strength to address the crowd.

With a distinct melancholy in his voice, he said, "It has been my extreme pleasure to have made the journey . . . all this way . . . and to have entertained all of you. I dream of a day when we will meet like this once again. Until then, I wish each and every one of you . . . love, laughter . . . happiness, and peace . . . each and every day! I love you all . . . . *Thank you* . . . I love you all!" With that, he left the stage and headed into the wings, where I was waiting. Looking me in the eye, he put his hand on my shoulder. Together we turned, walked out of the theater, got into the limo, and went straight to the airport. Then we quietly boarded the jet for the journey home.

After Japan, Frank would only sing in public twice more. He was aware of his diminished performance ability. His cumulative health problems meant he could no longer consistently perform to the standard that he himself had set. He wasn't willing to perform as a shadow of his former self. He felt that his fans deserved better. He wanted to be remembered as the performer he'd been for sixty years. So he made the painful decision to walk away from the thing that he loved more than life.

His next-to-last performance was two months after we returned from Fukuoka, at the annual Frank Sinatra Celebrity Invitational golf tournament for Barbara's charity. Frank always performed at the Saturday gala. He was in a great mood that evening. When it was time, Frank went out onto the stage in a jubilant mood, and the place just went nuts, as expected. Frank was having a terrific time. He was at the top of his game that night.

After four planned tunes, he turned to

Junior and said, "What's next?"

Frankie said, "That's it. You're through."

"What do you mean, I'm through? You got no more tunes in the book?"

"No. Tony's waiting for you to go to the bar."

Frank turned to the audience and said, "Look at this. My son, who doesn't drink, is suggesting I go to the bar. Come on . . . you've got to have something else in the book."

Frankie pulled out the two alternates, and Frank finished with them. Even at that, he was disappointed. He knew it might be the last time he'd stand on a stage and sing like the man he'd been for sixty years. He wanted the moment to last forever, because once he left the stage, he might never return. So he held on, reveling in the moment. It was spellbinding and wonderful, and both Frank and the audience enjoyed every second of it.

With Frank's no longer performing, I told Sonny to take me off the payroll. It didn't seem right to take money to hang out with my friend. Sonny said, "Everyone else is getting paid."

"Well, it's not my style. Besides, I've got money coming in from Rickles now."

I'd already begun working with Don Rickles. I worked around Frank's schedule, sending someone else on the road with Don when Frank needed me. Don was one of Frank's oldest friends, and he understood. Working with Don only became an issue one time. Rickles was about to start a new deal at Caesars in Atlantic City, and I flew to New Jersey for his inaugural engagement. I didn't tell Frank, who was very uncomfortable with my absences, that I was leaving. He liked to have me close by. Whenever I left town, I always kept Vine apprised of my whereabouts just in case. Everyone on staff knew that if Frank asked where I was, they should defer the question and get word to me. Evidently, one of the gals on Frank's staff either forgot or was never told, and she told Frank that I was in Atlantic City that night.

The opening act was midway through their part of the show when the landline in Don's dressing room rang. It was the hotel operator.

She said, "Tony?"

"Yeah."

"Something strange is happening."

"What's the matter?"

"Some guy's on the phone, claiming to be Frank Sinatra, and he wants to talk to you."

"Oh, okay." I was standing next to Rickles, so I put my hand over the phone and looked at him.

Don said, "What the hell is going on?"

I said, "We've been busted."

"Oh, Jesus!"

I told the operator, "Put him on." The next thing I knew, I was talking to Frank. "How you doing?"

"What the hell is going on, man?"

"I'm here in Atlantic City. Don just started a new deal at Caesars, and I figured I'd come and support him, make sure everything went well. Why, what's going on there?"

"Well, I was wondering if you could come back. I wanted to talk to you about something. So when are you coming home?"

"Probably Monday."

"Okay, fine. So when you get back to LA, give me a buzz. Now, where's Bullet Head?"

"He's standing right here, why? We're about to go on."

"Don't worry about it. They can't start the show without him. Put him on the phone."

"Okay, hold on a second." I put Frank on hold, and Don was looking at me. "Frank wants to talk to you."

"Oh no, oh Jesus."

391

I put Don on speaker and said, "Frank, here's Don."

Frank's voice came over the speakerphone. "Hey, Rhino."

Rickles said, "How you doing, Frank?"

"I'll give you 'How you doing?' Why don't you find your own goddamn friends? You son of a bitch. What the hell is this bullshit?"

Rickles had developed this thing that he used to do because he never knew whether Frank was teasing or pissed off. He would keep repeating the phrase, "Oh, God bless you, Frank." Sometimes he had to repeat it twelve times before Frank would crack up.

That night he started saying, "Oh, God bless you, Frank. God bless you, Frank."

Eventually, Frank started laughing and said, "Have a good show, guys . . . we'll talk, T," and he hung up.

Don said to me, "So, what are you going to do?"

"Well, I'll probably hop a plane on Saturday and go home early."

"Oh geez, do you have to go?"

"I'll tell you what. The show will be coming down at about ten thirty. Before we have dinner, we'll call Frank. And you can tell him I'm not coming home."

Don started stuttering, "Oh no, no, no, no, no." Don couldn't always tell when I was joking, either. God bless you, Frank!

I knew Frank had gotten increasingly dependent on me. It sounds childish, but it was hard for Frank to hear I was now in Atlantic City with Rickles. I was supposed to be home with *him*. It was a difficult time. I was concerned about what it was doing to Frank to stop all his performing.

I suggested to him that he could just work in Vegas. "You could fly home every night if you wanted, and I'm sure a number of hotels would give a deal where you'd be a year at the same place. They'd be thrilled to be the exclusive venue in the world where Frank Sinatra is performing."

He responded, "It sounds good conceptually, but I don't know."

"Frank, I can't see you spending the rest of your life just waiting to go to dinner. You won't paint anymore. You don't want to play golf. You don't want to go swimming."

"Don't worry about me, kid. I'll be fine."

"I know you'll be fine. I'll be right here."

When I wasn't touring with Don, I was with Frank. We spent a lot of time in his den, playing with the dogs and watching television. I'd often put in a tape of one of his movies and say, "Hey, Frank. Look what I found!"

We'd sit and watch, and he'd have me

pause the movie to tell me some behind-the-scenes stories. It was like having your own personal set of special features. He'd be telling me things about the movie that only the people who'd been there knew. Once, when we were watching *Marriage on the Rocks,* there was a scene where Dean Martin got into an argument and went to the hall closet to grab his coat before storming out. When he opened the closet door, Frank was in the closet with his back to the camera. When Frank turned around, he only turned around about a quarter of the way. He was wearing a Hitler mustache, and he had his hands down by his privates as though he were urinating. Dean cracked up. Needless to say, that take didn't make it into the picture.

We spent most of the time at the compound. It was the only place Frank felt completely at home. It was a fascinating place, built over the years to Frank's specifications. At the entrance to the property was a large round grassy area with a distinctive sculpture of a horse in the center. It was originally designed as a helipad for President's Kennedy's visit, which he famously canceled at the last minute. Immediately north of the former helipad was Frank's pride and joy, the train house. To the west of the train house lay the theater. My room, in a round bungalow named for Frank's film *The Tender Trap,* was on the west side of the theater. The main house was between the former helipad and the pool. It was set up for entertaining with a huge, professional-grade kitchen and a butler's pantry, a breakfast nook with a pizza oven, and a slate wall with bronze Remington sculptures displayed along it. The living room had comfortable modern furniture and a piano covered with family pictures. The den had a full bar that divided it from the TV room. Frank and Barbara had adjacent suites with large, luxurious bathrooms and walk-in closets. The entire house was modern, open, and airy, decorated in white, yellow, and orange tones. The walls held family pictures and Frank's paintings. There was a lot of glass and beautiful views through windows that brought the outdoors in. The desert was part of the décor. The remainder of the property held a second pool and guest cottages, the largest being the New York house, with four guest suites.

Frank loved every inch of the property, indoors and out. We sat outside whenever we could. The light seems to change more often and more deeply in the desert, and the palm trees form black silhouettes like statues at dusk and dawn. Looking down on the compound is San Gorgonio Mountain. Though beautiful in itself, it was a towering symbol of loss for Frank after it claimed the lives of both his mother and Dean's son. Frank loved the desert with all its moods and nuances. It was his spiritual as well as his physical home, and he was happiest when he was there. He told me more than once that he hoped to draw his last breath in his beloved desert, drifting off to sleep in his home and never waking up.

The hot climate never bothered him. On the contrary, what kept most people from settling in the desert was one of its chief attractions for Frank. Frank loved the heat. He and I used to sit out by the pool in the middle of the summer when it was 114 degrees, without even a fan, just listening to music and chatting. He would be wearing only shorts, his skin covered with orange Bain de Soleil, his brand of suntan lotion. Frank even used a reflector to get more sun on his face. Sometimes I thought I could hear faint sizzling sounds coming from him, like a frying pan full of bacon. He just loved having a tan. The air of the desert agreed with Frank. He was his healthiest there.

The fall before his performing career wound to a close, I began hearing rumors that Barbara was considering selling the compound. She wanted to move into the city, where there was less upkeep. I didn't feel I could just ignore the rumors, so I began looking for some time alone to talk with Barbara. On Thanksgiving morning, I took advantage of an opportunity to discuss it with her. We were at the beach house, and as she and I walked down the beach after breakfast, I told Barbara that I had heard conversations with her business manager about selling the house in the desert.

I told her, "It would really pull a rug out from under his world if you did that. It's the one constant in his life, the place he's called home since the mid-fifties. He loves it. It's the only place where he truly relaxes."

Barbara answered me simply, "No, no. I'd never do that to him."

That was the end of 1994. Within three months, by February 1995, Barbara had convinced herself they should sell the property. She told a realtor friend of hers that it was going to be listed, so the friend put out a feeler in the local paper. The compound sold immediately, before it was officially on the market. I couldn't believe it, either that she'd done it or that Frank had allowed it.

As soon as she had his agreement to sell

the property, she started going through the house room by room, marking things with colored dots. She labeled everything in the house to indicate where it was to go: to storage, to the Foothill house in Los Angeles, to the beach house, to Bobby, or to Christie's auction house in New York. Unfortunately, Barbara didn't know the history behind some of the items she was labeling. When she didn't understand something, she'd sometimes ask me what it meant. I remember once she asked me about a Piaget pocket watch that was in one of the Plexiglas showcases. It was engraved on the back, *To Charlie Shoulders Love Smokey.*

Barbara asked, "Who is Charlie Shoulders?"

"It's Frank. They called him Charlie Shoulders because he would take everyone's problems onto his back."

"And Smokey?"

"Smokey was Frank's nickname for Sammy Davis." Barbara took detailed notes about all the pieces.

One afternoon, Frank asked me about the dots, so I told him. He said, "Christie's in New York? For what?"

I said, "She's having an auction." Frank accepted the news in silence. The reality of how far he'd gone to keep the peace was sinking in.

As Frank watched his possessions being marked with colored dots and taken away, he became increasingly uncomfortable. One night after dinner, long after Barbara had gone to bed, Frank and I were sitting out by the pool at about two thirty in the morning, talking.

Frank said, "I was wondering if you'd do me a very large personal favor."

"Of course, what's it about?"

"Let me get some stuff. I'll meet you in the theater."

I went into the theater to wait, and a few minutes later, he came walking into the theater with a black leather case, like an old-fashioned doctor's bag, but bigger. As Frank opened the bag, he told me, "These are very personal items to me. Given what's happening with the other stuff, I don't want them to be the subject of a tug-of-war between my kids and Barbara." Then he asked me to keep the items for him and give them to Nancy Sr. and his kids "when the time was right." We both knew what he meant.

One by one, Frank started removing the items from the bag and placing them on the table, explaining what each one was. One was the medal given to him by Golda Meir for his service to Israel. There were at least three or four gold-plated house keys the children had given him when they were young. One of the keys was for the house they'd lived in as children. They'd had it engraved with the words *Happy Father's Day. Nancy, Tina, Frankie.* There was a gold locket that I'd seen in many photographs of Frank. There was also a gorgeous gold pocket watch with a solid-gold fob from Mike Romanoff, Frank's old restaurateur friend. It was engraved with the seal of the Russian czar and said, *To Francis. Love, Your Emperor.*

After explaining the items to me, Frank carefully packed them back in the leather bag. When he finished, he began expressing to me how appreciative he was of my doing him this favor.

He said, "I've thought of you as family for quite a while now, almost as a son. I want to give you something to reinforce that statement and those feelings." I started to object, but he cut me off. He said, "No, no, no. Please let me do this."

Then he took a jewelry box out of his pocket and put it on the table. He slid it across the table and said, "This is for you. Go ahead, open it." I opened the box and saw that it contained his gold pinky ring with the Sinatra crest. He said, "Now, let me explain. That is actually the original. Because I used to wear that on my left hand."

"Yeah, I know."

"But when I married Barbara, I put a wedding ring on that hand." Then he made a little joke, saying, "Unlike Sam, I don't like wearing more than one ring on the same hand, and I couldn't put it on my right hand. As you know, I broke that hand. It never quite healed properly, and it got calcified."

"Yeah, during the fight scene in *Manchurian Candidate*."

"Right. I had to have a larger replica of the ring made so that it would fit over my calcified pinky, and I put this one away. I want you to have it because I think of you like a surrogate son."

He was choked up, and I was getting as emotional as he was. I thought, *If he starts to lose it, I'm going to lose it, and it's not going to be pretty. What can I say that will crack him up?* So I did something very irreverent.

I looked at the ring and said, "May I?"

"Yeah. It's yours."

I took the ring out of the box. I held it for a few seconds, just looking at it. Then I said, "So, let me get this right. This was the ring that was on your hand through . . . oh, my

God . . . all those women? Lauren Bacall and Juliet Prowse and Victoria Principal and Mia and Ava and Marilyn Maxwell and . . ."

"Yeah. Why?"

"Excuse me." Then I held the ring up to my nose, and I sniffed it.

He looked at me and started laughing. "You crazy bastard!"

"Yeah, but I made you laugh!" When I put the ring on my right pinky, it fit perfectly. It remains there to this day.

I hid the leather bag in my bungalow and stayed in the desert with Frank another week before I had to get back to LA. Eventually, I put Frank's bag of treasures in a safe-deposit box, where it remained until Frank's estate was settled years later. When I went to my business address to check my mail the day after I got home, there was a box from the compound. I thought, *I just left there a day ago. What the hell?* I took the box home to open it. There was a note from Frank. It said, *T., this is for you. There's no discussion.*

To appreciate the gift, you have to understand that Frank knew how difficult it had been for me to give up my performing career. He'd also made it clear to me that he respected me as a musician and as a singer. He knew that I lamented the fact I'd never have the career I'd dreamed of. The moment I opened the box, I knew that besides saying thank you, the gift was his way of acknowledging all that. Inside was a gold record. I picked it up and read it. It was Frank's gold record for "My Way."

I was speechless. Almost out of reflex, I picked up the phone and called the private number in the desert. Vine answered. It was still "morning" for Frank.

I said, "Is the gorilla up?"

She said, "Yeah. He's having his breakfast." She was in the bar. I knew he'd be at the backgammon table nearby having his breakfast like he always did.

"Tell him I'm on the phone. I'd like to speak with him."

She pulled the phone away from her ear and said, "Mr. S?"

"Yeah, sweetheart?"

"Tony O is on the phone. He wants to talk with you."

I heard Frank chuckle. Then he said, "Tell the kid to read the fucking note again." He wouldn't talk to me. He wouldn't even get on the phone. He wouldn't let me thank him. For Frank, it was nothing to make a fuss about. He wanted to show his appreciation for me. He'd done it. End of story. If I'd insisted on thanking him, he'd have told me he hadn't done it for me, that he was really just a selfish prick who'd given me the record to make *himself* feel good. Frank joked like that to avert situations that were very emotional for him. He found it painful to listen to praise or gratitude directed at him.

The day the sale of the property was finalized, Frank got up really early for him — ten in the morning. He was trying to get out of the house before Barbara found him. He said to me, "Come on. We gotta get out of here!"

I went into the butler's pantry, but he wasn't quite fast enough. As he was starting to leave, I heard Barbara say, "Oh, sweetheart! Wait a minute."

Frank answered, "No, no. I gotta go. Tony's waiting for me. We've got an appointment downtown."

"I need you to sign this."

"No. Tony's going to get mad. That's why I'm up so early, 'cause he wanted to get the hell out of here. We gotta go."

That was it for Barbara, who said firmly, "You're going to come back here, and you're going to sign these papers before you go. It'll take two minutes. Where *is* Tony? I need him to witness them."

Frank said, "He's already in the car."

All that time I was in the butler's pantry, listening. Frank finally called me back, and I watched as he reluctantly signed the papers. I could see his anger mounting as he signed the final paper and said to me, "Let's get the hell out of here."

Signing those papers was a fatal turning point for Frank. He was deeply troubled that he'd done it. I know that he kicked himself over and over again for agreeing to sell his compound. He tried to rationalize the decision by taking in some of Barbara's logic — that it was expensive and that he'd have better access in Los Angeles to his children and friends. Frank and I talked a lot about what was going on. He wasn't unaware of what was happening, but he allowed it because he didn't like conflict. The truth was that signing the papers was a terrible mistake, and he knew it, but he couldn't take it back.

The pain from the loss of the desert compound would never leave him. As the date to leave the desert approached, Frank made himself so ill physically that Barbara had to pay two months' rent to the man who bought the compound because I could not physically get Frank to leave that property till the end of May. We had a skeleton staff, and with so many of his possessions boxed up and carted away, the place looked empty. When the dreaded departure finally came, Frank and Vine and I went back to LA by limo. I had some music on, but it was a pretty quiet trip. Frank was staring out the window most of the way, not saying very much. We stopped only once, near where Jilly's daughter lived, so Frank could stretch his legs and have a soda. Then we drove on to the house on Foothill Road in Beverly Hills. I wouldn't call it his home, for that house was never Frank's home. His home lay one hundred miles to the east.

Frank may have lost the battle for the desert, but he still managed to needle Barbara about it. We'd be sitting in the Foothill house, watching TV, while Barbara was thumbing through magazines.

Suddenly, Frank would say to her, "Sweetheart?"

"Yes, dear?"

"When are we going home?"

"You *are* home."

"No, this is *your* home. When are we going to *my* home?"

She'd answer a little irritably, "I don't want to discuss this."

Putting on his innocent face, Frank would say, "It's just a question, dear." He did it to

406

get under her skin. It was the only power he had left by then.

The big excitement that summer was the eightieth-birthday special for Frank that our friend producer George Schlatter had sold to a network. Frank hated that kind of thing and had refused to do it until George offered to donate a large sum of money to Barbara's children's center. The special would be called *80 Years My Way*. Barbara was very excited about both the donation and the publicity.

About this time, Frank began suffering pain in his neck. It came on gradually, and at first, we thought it might be a strained muscle. He was given some simple pain pills, which helped a little, but only temporarily.

He told me, "You know what it feels like when you hit your funny bone on the corner of a desk or something?"

"Yeah."

"Amplify that by about a hundred, and that's the kind of shooting pains I'm getting down my back."

I was up with him day and night, doing double and triple duty. I was mentally and physically exhausted. One night, at about three o'clock in the morning, I told Frank I was going to bed and to call me if he needed anything. I remember falling down onto the bedspread and just lying there with my clothes and shoes on, something I never do. I couldn't seem to move my body to change clothes. I must have drifted off. I don't know how much time passed, but I remember sensing that someone was in the room. I opened my eyes, and there was Frank, standing next to my bed.

I started and said, "What? What's the matter? Everything okay?" As I came to, I noticed he had a blanket in his hand.

He said, "I thought you might be cold." Then he reached over and put the blanket over me like I was a child being tucked in. In the middle of all his pain, he'd thought about me.

Barbara didn't want Frank on heavy painkillers for fear he might get addicted. I knew Frank might need surgery, but Barbara wouldn't allow it until after the special. It was the longest summer of my life since I'd cared for my uncle Joe when I was sixteen.

The birthday celebration, *80 Years My Way*, was taped at the Shrine Auditorium on November 19, 1995, three weeks before Frank's actual birthday. Frank wasn't happy. In addition to the pain issues he was having, he said, "How the hell am I going to sit there for two or three hours and listen to these people tell me how wonderful I am?" That kind of praise, especially publicly, was sheer torture for Frank.

As the taping of the show approached, I pulled George aside and told him, "George, it's going to be difficult for even me to keep him seated there for three hours. Do me a favor. I need to have a complete copy of the script so that when you go to video clips that run for a few minutes, I can sneak him out in the darkness where he can have a cigarette and a bit of a break. I'm going to need a cooler under my seat in the auditorium. I'm going to need a couple of bottles of Jack. I'm going to need water and ice. I'm going to have to be in as close proximity to him as possible so that I can keep him well lubricated." George provided everything I'd asked for, and that's exactly how I got Frank through the night.

There was a big list of performers that evening. Patti LaBelle sang the hell out of "The House I Live In." Frank was the first one to stand up and applaud when she got done. Ray Charles sang "Old Man River," and Little Richard did "That Old Black Magic." Tony Bennett, Steve and Eydie, and Natalie Cole all performed. Rickles tore it up. Gregory Peck spoke. As a thank-you for helping Frank get through the evening, George gave me a disc that had nothing on it but what they call ISO footage. It was from the camera that was trained on Frank with me behind him, because I was always in the shot when he was.

At the end of November, after the special was shot, Frank was finally evaluated for his back problem. It turned out to be a bone spur that was pushing on a nerve. They were going to schedule a deep spinal injection in Frank's neck. Basically, they were preparing to give him an epidural, which had to be injected at the precise location of the nerve pain.

When we got to the hospital the day of the procedure, the first thing they did was to put Frank on a CAT scan machine to find the exact place to target the needle. Frank had to be sedated for the procedure.

The nurse administering the anesthesia asked me, "How is he with medication?" I told her that he wasn't allergic to anything, but that he did have a high tolerance for anesthetics, so she might want to make certain that she gave him enough so he'd be truly out. She replied, "This is a standard thing. We do this all the time."

I said, "Hey, I'm not trying to tell you how

to do your job. You asked me, so I'm telling you what I know."

Barbara was busy signing papers, so I stayed with Frank as we went into a control room next to the machine. They attached a series of wires to Frank's body and put him on something that looked like a conveyor belt. The conveyor belt slowly took him into the cavernous part of the machine where the scan would take place. From the control room, it was almost like looking through a periscope with crosshairs where they were going to inject the needle. As they were lining up the crosshairs, there was movement on the screen, and then some more movement.

The doctor was busy concentrating on the screen when all of a sudden, he said, "Oh, no!"

Frank had managed to back out of the machine and was sitting up on the conveyor belt, looking confused and cross-eyed from the medication. It was like the scene from *Gulliver's Travels* where Gulliver pulls up all the ropes that the Lilliputians put on him. As Frank sat there with all those wires hanging from him, he called out, "Tony!?"

The nurse was frantic. I looked at her and said, "I warned you."

Once they calmed him down, they had to

start all over again. After all that chaos, the procedure that followed was a whopping success. It took only twenty minutes to alleviate months of pain.

Ten days later, in early December, we flew to New York. Capitol Records had taken advantage of its being Frank's eightieth birthday and coordinated the Tower Award with a birthday party at the Waldorf. While we were in New York, the long-awaited Christie's auction of the items from the desert took place. Barbara and Bobby were the only ones who went to the auction. Frank stayed in the suite all day in his pajamas. It was a very painful day for him. He wouldn't let me out of his sight. I couldn't even sneak away from him long enough to take a shower. Barbara came back from the auction around seven o'clock in the evening. We were in his bedroom, and he was lying on the bed, staring at the ceiling, when she arrived. We had the TV on, and I was sitting next to him. Barbara was bubbling over with good news, telling Frank about all of her triumphs. If memory serves, she cleared a total of $2,800,000 that day. She was jubilant.

The auction didn't put an end to the struggle over Frank's assets. Instead, the property war that had erupted between

Frank's wife and children steadily escalated. I was sometimes put in the middle of it. Sonny Golden, Frank's longtime business manager and old friend, would often call on me to help with sensitive issues. Sonny was competent and honest, and Frank trusted him completely. He diligently protected Frank's best interests. Knowing Sonny would always side with Frank caused Barbara to see Sonny as a threat. Eventually, she kept Sonny from seeing Frank. If Sonny showed up at the house with anything that vaguely resembled a portfolio, she'd tell him that Frank was in the shower or asleep and turn him away. She no longer trusted Frank's judgment and worried constantly that he'd side with his children.

Often, that just left me. Sonny would give me papers and say, "She's cut off my access to him. You need to get them to him to review and sign." It became my responsibility to swing by Sonny's office whenever I was on my way to any of Frank's houses and pick up a stack of papers for Frank. Sonny would say, "When the opportunity presents itself, ask Frank what he wants to do about this."

"This" usually referred to Frank's businesses. Being in a position of trust with Frank wasn't always comfortable for me. If

Barbara had found out, I'd have lost access to Frank, too.

One of the rationales for moving to LA was so that Frank could see his children more. I was cautiously hopeful that would happen, but I wasn't optimistic. When Frank first moved from the desert, an attempt was made to have a regular family dinner, usually at La Dolce Vita. That didn't last long. The dinners ranged from long and uncomfortable to downright toxic. I was frustrated with both Barbara and Frank's children. The kids needed to call him more often, call me if they needed to, and visit more, no matter what Barbara said. For a while, things would go smoothly, but then the cycle of war and peace, recrimination and reconciliation, would start all over again. By now, both sides were so entrenched in their positions, so certain they were right, that communication had broken down almost completely. Frank's daughters and wife were fighting a civil war, and Frank was the battleground.

Barbara was an expert at pushing Nancy and Tina's buttons, and vice versa. For example, when we got back from the Waldorf party in New York, Barbara planned an eightieth-birthday party for Frank in LA. It was to be a family dinner party. But when George Schlatter offered to host the party at L'Orangerie, one of Beverly Hills's most exclusive restaurants, Barbara immediately took him up on it. The guests were to include the Pecks, the Lemmons (Jack and Felicia), the Douglases (Kurt and Anne), Frank, Barbara, and me. Frank's children weren't invited to the party.

I vividly remember the day they found out about it. Both girls went ballistic and repeatedly called the house. Nancy Jr. kept calling, crying uncontrollably. Tina was livid. Frankie was nowhere to be found. Frank was very stressed, confused, and beaten up because of all the arguing between Barbara and the kids, so he didn't take the calls.

He asked me, "What the hell is going on? The whole world is caving in on me."

I told him, "Frank, Barbara's saying the kids never got back to her about a family gathering, so she took George up on his offer of hosting a dinner party for you. The kids weren't invited to George's party."

Frank said, "Then why didn't *she* invite them? After all, they're my blood. How can you have a birthday party for me and not invite my children?" Frank finally confronted Barbara about the situation.

She responded innocently, "What seems

415

to be the problem here?"

Frank answered, "The problem is that a birthday party is being thrown for me, and my children have not been invited. What kind of crap is that?"

She said, "Oh, it's not a birthday party. It's just a dinner party."

Frank said, "Yes, but it just happens to be falling on my birthday." Barbara didn't seem to take his meaning.

Barbara couldn't see the kids' point of view, and they couldn't see hers. All the Sinatra women were at war at that point.

Frustrated by the endless back-and-forth between his wife and daughters, Frank just shook his head and said to me, "You do know that the snake that bit them died, right?"

The day before the party, someone leaked to the press the name of the restaurant where the dinner party was being held to ensure a deluge of paparazzi. The party George was planning would be ruined.

As the time for the party approached the next afternoon, we got a call from L'Orangerie, telling us that the press were all over the place. I went outside and walked around the side of the house to look over the wall. The press were there in force, waiting for Frank's limo to pull out of the driveway.

After a few minutes of thought, I called George and told him about the paparazzi. He agreed to change the party from the restaurant to his house and have L'Orangerie deliver the food there. He lived only a few blocks from Frank.

When I got off the phone, I talked privately to Vine. I told Frank I had a plan and not to worry. Then I had the limousine pull up where the press couldn't see. Vine and I got in the limousine, which had tinted windows. We had the driver pull out and take the long way to the restaurant. Just as I hoped, all of the press followed our limo. After a few blocks, I called the house on my cell and said, "The coast is clear. You can leave now."

Everyone at Foothill got in the Rolls-Royce and drove over to George Schlatter's. Nobody followed them. When Frank's limo pulled up at L'Orangerie, the press crowded around it with cameras. The driver opened the door for us, and Vine and I got out. At first, the photographers were snapping pictures furiously, their cameras flashing. Then it registered what they were looking at: a redheaded man with a beard and a tall Creole woman. They all stopped at the same time, like a freeze frame. I wish I had a copy of one of those photos. I remember saying to them, "Hi, guys. What's going on?"

Vine and I had some great times together over the years, but that one may have been the best. The paparazzi never did find Frank.

The next day, Frank had a party with the kids at Nancy Jr.'s house. Nancy Jr., Tina, Frankie Jr., A. J. and Amanda, Nancy Sr., Frank, and I were there. It was a nice evening, but it took a toll on Frank emotionally. He was trying to enjoy himself, but the pain of knowing that an abyss existed between his wife and his flesh-and-blood family wouldn't go away.

The last time Frank sang in public was early the next year, at his charity golf tournament. That year, Vic Damone, Jack Jones, Andy Williams, and Steve and Eydie were performing at the closing gala on Saturday night. The evening didn't go well from the beginning. Frank was out of sorts. It was the first time he'd attended the tournament since he'd left the desert, and he was uneasy. We were staying in a Rancho Mirage rented house in the Thunderbird Country Club, and Frank wasn't comfortable with it. We stayed up all night Friday with Frank's pistol on the table because he didn't feel secure without all the protection he was used to at his former compound.

He was worn out the next night, but he came because it was benefiting Barbara's charity. When it was time for the show, we went out to the main dining room to sit down. The performers were going to sing Frank's tunes; then for the finale, Frank was going to join them while they all sang "New York, New York" together. The performances went as planned. Frank was enjoying himself by then, listening to all his great tunes with his arrangements. I was to move Frank backstage when Andy Williams was in the middle of "Moon River." Then Frank was going to walk onstage and join the other performers. It was a terrific idea, except for one minor detail. Nobody had told Frank.

When Andy started "Moon River," I leaned over to Frank and said, "It's time for us to make our move."

He said, "What move? Where are we going?"

"We're going backstage."

"Why?"

"Well, because you're supposed to sing with them for the finale."

"What? I'm supposed to what? This is news to me."

Barbara heard us talking and said, "What's going on?"

I said, "Barbara, didn't you tell him about singing 'New York, New York' with the rest of the singers?"

She calmly said, "Oh yeah, sweetheart. I meant to mention it."

He turned to me and said, "Why am I the last one to know? I'm the one that's got to get up and do this. I haven't warmed up. I haven't sung in I don't know how long." Frank was getting hot, and I knew I had to defuse it before he caused a scene.

I got him outside, and we walked toward the rear of the stage. Frank was angry and swearing by then. It took a bit of coaxing, but I finally got him into the backstage area. When we got there, he said, "So what is this BS I've got to do again?"

By that time, even I had reached my limit. I said, "You know what? Do whatever you want." I'd never spoken to him like that before.

Startled, Frank responded, "What?"

"Do whatever you want. You want to sing, sing. You don't want to sing, don't sing. I'm going to the car."

Frank said, "Wait a minute. Where're *you* going?"

"I just told you."

"Well, what am *I* supposed to do?"

"Do whatever you want. I don't care at

this point."

I walked away. I could feel his eyes burning a hole in the back of my head. Finally, he said, "T."

I stopped in my tracks. I didn't turn around. "What?"

I could feel him staring at me. Meanwhile, I heard the opening bars of "New York, New York" playing onstage.

Finally, Frank said, "Okay, so tell me again. What do I have to do?"

"Frank, you don't have to do anything, but it would be nice if you would sing the last couple bars of this tune. These people paid a thousand dollars each and have been sitting here all night just to see you."

"All right, all right. Which way? You coming with me?"

"Of course, I'll come with you." I led him to the wing and pointed to a spot onstage. "Right there."

Frank walked out onto the stage. The place went nuts. He sang the last four bars by himself. The other singers all had the presence of mind to let him, and at the end, he held that last note forever. He didn't want to let it go. In some respects, it was a way for him to let out all that anxiety. He knew that the road was finally ending for him. That was the very last time Frank Sinatra sang in public.

# Chapter 10
## Softly, as I Leave You
### THE PASSING OF A LEGEND

Frank was "lying in state" in the mortuary, perfectly dressed in his favorite suit. I was on the kneeler in front of his open coffin, immersed in thought. All of a sudden, I sensed movement. When I opened my eyes, Frank was sitting up in his casket. He was in a foul temper. I tried to stop him, but he climbed over the edge of the coffin while I watched helplessly. Then he walked past me like I wasn't there and headed toward the door.

I couldn't let him leave like that, so I called after him, "Where do you think you're going?"

He said, "Well, somebody's got to sort out this crap between my wife and my kids."

I awoke in a sweat. It had felt so real. The nightmare of waking had spilled over into sleep. I felt as though Frank and I were in the eye of a tornado, with Barbara and his children spinning around us in the wind and

423

the dark, and I was helpless to stop it. I had no way to protect him from, ironically, the people who loved him the most. I kept having the nightmare over and over again. I never shared it with anyone. It was too painful.

If you had to guess, you'd think it was either cigarettes or whiskey that took Frank Sinatra's life. If you knew about his habit of baking under a reflector in 110-degree weather, you'd guess skin cancer. In all cases, you'd be wrong. Those sins never caught up with Frank. Even though he smoked a pack a day of unfiltered Camels his whole life, his doctors declared that his lungs were clear until the end. About the only time he drew deeply on a cigarette was when he was using it as a prop onstage. He'd light the cigarette, inhale the smoke, then sing. He could sing a phrase that was nine bars long, and there'd be a continuous stream of smoke coming out of his mouth the whole time. I swear the smoke must have gone all the way down to his shoes.

The last two years of Frank's life, I spent a lot of time at hospitals. In November of 1996, Frank was admitted to Cedars-Sinai in Beverly Hills with heart problems. He was put on the eighth floor at Cedars.

Celebrities were usually put there, partially for privacy, partially because the accommodations were more luxurious. By a weird stroke of fate, my father, who now lived near me in California, was admitted to a Burbank hospital twenty miles away at the same time, with the same condition. I was spending the day at Providence St. Joseph's hospital with my father, going by my condo afterward to take a shower and change clothes, then spending the night at Cedars with Frank. Meantime, my father lay in bed, lamenting that he couldn't go visit Frank.

One night, I was by Frank's bed while Barbara and Tina sat on the settee in an adjacent room of his suite. At about seven o'clock that night, a public relations executive at the hospital came in to make sure that everything was okay and to find out if they needed anything.

Barbara jokingly said, "What I could really go for is a drink."

Tina said, "Oh, me too."

So the woman said, "Well, if you had a choice, what would you drink?"

Barbara said, "I'd settle for a glass of wine."

"What do you prefer, red or white?"

Tina said, "I like red."

Barbara said, "Me too."

"You know, we do have some wine here at the hospital."

Barbara said, "Really? Could we see a wine list?"

The whole incident was like a preview for *Keeping Up with the Kardashians.*

Early the next morning, when Frank was taken downstairs for tests, I returned to his room and found a stranger in a hospital gown searching Frank's suite. When I challenged him, it turned out he was a reporter who'd convinced a doctor to admit him so he could get the scoop on Frank. How low could you go? Hospital security escorted him off the premises. I wonder if the doctor who admitted him kept his job.

It was a stressful time. One night I was sitting with Frank when he started to complain that Jilly was looking at him through the window. On the eighth floor, nobody could have been outside the window, apart from the obvious fact that Jilly was dead. Frank's hallucination made me wonder about his condition. I didn't believe the stories about people's seeing deceased loved ones before they passed away, but I'd heard enough stories in my family to feel a little uncomfortable.

When the hospital hadn't discharged Frank after several days, he started getting desperate to leave. I agreed to help him "escape" and started walking him around the eighth floor. We walked up and around the halls in various directions and around the nurses' station until Frank was exhausted. When I knew he couldn't go much farther, I suggested we return to his room. He finally let me get him back to bed. He was almost tearfully happy when he was finally released. It was only when my father was also safely home that I could breathe a sigh of relief.

The respite was brief. Less than two months later, in January 1997, Frank's urologist diagnosed him with cancer of the ureter. The doctor wanted to operate immediately, so he performed surgery that day. Fortunately, the press didn't get wind of it. Frank came home after a twenty-four-hour hospital stay.

For the first few days, I stayed at the house. I slept in a bedroom near Frank's in case he needed me at night. I knew the surgery had been serious, so I was being extra vigilant. An overnight nurse was hired to monitor Frank. I'd just gone to sleep at one a.m. on the second night home when the nurse roused me an hour later, saying, "Mr. Sinatra! He's on the bathroom floor!"

I ran into the bathroom and found Frank

shivering on the floor, holding his left arm. He was conscious but very pale and clearly frightened, his pulse racing. I covered him with towels and asked him how he felt.

He said, "I'm a bit nauseous. I got this pain in my arm."

I reassured him that he'd be all right and told the nurse to get Rex Kennamer, Frank's longtime physician and friend, on the phone. Rex said he was sending a paramedic ambulance immediately. I picked up the intercom and told Barbara that Frank was being transported to Cedars Emergency. When the ambulance arrived, I told the driver, "Please turn the lights and siren off." I'd already called the Beverly Hills PD to escort us with lights only. If I hadn't done that, by the time we got to Cedars, we'd have had a greeting party with a John Philip Sousa marching band. Our security guy escorted Barbara behind the ambulance.

The doctors who examined Frank told us there had been post-surgical complications that caused fluid to back up in Frank's system, bringing on a heart attack. This heart attack was much more serious than the previous one. Unfortunately, this time the press found out. The papers immediately started accusing us of withholding information. I didn't really care what they thought.

I was focused on Frank. He spent several days back on the eighth floor before they released him.

Frank was too ill to go to the annual golf tournament in February, but Barbara still had to go because it was for her charity. She was very worried about what might happen while she was gone, so she asked a buddy of mine to install a surveillance system. She had him put a small camera lens in the den, where Frank spent most of the day, and another next to the TV, across the room from the foot of his bed. There was a direct feed from those cameras into her bedroom upstairs. She explained to me that she wanted to keep an eye on how Frank was doing. She didn't tell Frank about it. She was already monitoring the private telephone line from upstairs. She kept track of every call. If we pushed the privacy button on the phone downstairs, we'd hear her immediately on the intercom. I told Frank about the surveillance system and explained Barbara's rationale. He listened in silence and then accepted it as just another fact of his life by then. That same month, Frank did a short hospital stay while he underwent further testing. There was no sign the cancer was coming back, and there'd been no further incidents with his heart. My relief was short-lived.

In March, my father fell at home and broke his tibia. It was a bad break, and he was admitted to St. Joseph's for surgery. About a week later, he lost all feeling from the waist down. Exhausted from the pain and the stress of hospitalization, Dad just wanted to go home. The doctor, whom my father grew to dislike, wanted to keep Dad in the hospital.

He told my father, "If you go home, you're going home to die!" I had to get in his face and tell him what I thought about his "bedside manner." Dad knew the risk if he went home, but he just wanted to get the hell out of there and be in familiar surroundings. So I put everything in place to care for him at home. We brought him home in an ambulance, and I set up his bedroom with a hospital bed and all the things he needed to make himself comfortable. Less than a week later, he passed away.

I made arrangements at Forest Lawn cemetery in the Hollywood Hills, a beautiful memorial park not far from my home. There was only one problem. My father's doctor, out of sheer spite, refused to sign the death certificate, which meant we couldn't bury my father. I didn't know what the hell I was going to tell my mother. We had a Catholic service in the little chapel on site. Don and Barbara Rickles flew back from Atlantic City, where he was performing, to be there for the funeral. They offered to pick up Barbara Sinatra on the way to the service, but Barbara didn't feel she could leave Frank on his own. She sent a huge funeral wreath. We received flowers and condolences from many friends, both the famous and the not-so-famous.

I made sure I was the only one at the graveside ceremony afterward to watch the attendants take my father's coffin *back* to the funeral home. I don't know what I would have done if I hadn't run into Frank's lawyer, Harvey Silbert, the next day. Harvey was a friend and a major player in the entertainment industry. I told Harvey what was going on, and the following morning, the doctor signed the death certificate. It was a Hollywood miracle.

I was under strict orders not to tell Frank yet. When I finally did tell him about my father, he sent Mom another huge bouquet.

By the way, I don't believe I ever mentioned my father's name. He was also named Frank. Frank Anthony Oppedisano.

At eighty-one, after two heart attacks, Frank's age was showing, both physically and mentally. In contrast, Barbara was an energetic, vital seventy-year-old who was still leading the life she'd been living for decades. As Frank grew increasingly frail and homebound, it created strains on the marriage. Whenever they quarreled, Barbara stopped speaking to him, and the quarrels happened more and more. There was little to lift Frank's spirits. He was no longer performing. Often, there was no one around him except the household staff and me. Frank's world was growing increasingly silent. I'd take sanity breaks at my condo in Toluca Lake, but by then I was staying at the Foothill house 80 percent of the time. Frank didn't want me out of his sight, and we never knew when there'd be another health crisis.

As he rotated in and out of the challenges that everyone faces in old age, his world got smaller and smaller. By this time, most of Frank's friends had passed away. It got to where I dreaded watching the news to find out who was next. As each one died, I saw another small piece of Frank fall away. The family was still around, but the deep divide between his daughters and Barbara had only grown worse. Frankie Jr. was usually away touring, but Nancy and Tina still came by, especially when Frank had a health crisis.

But even when they were there, it was uncomfortable having them and Barbara in the house at the same time.

For a while, Frank was able to keep some sense of balance. I'd see occasional glimpses of the old sparkle in his eyes. He loved talking about the old days. Certain things like catchphrases that he and the guys used to use could bring the old Frank Sinatra back. One trick that worked like a reflex was reciting a line from *Amos 'n' Andy,* the old radio show.

I'd say, "If all the women in Texas is ugly as Sapphire's mama . . ."

And Frank would finish it: ". . . the Lone Ranger's going to be alone for a long time."

Another thing that always worked was putting on an old comedy recording by Jo Stafford and her husband Paul Weston, who went by the stage names Jonathan and Darlene Edwards. Frank knew Jo from the Tommy Dorsey band days. Jo and Paul did comedy numbers where Paul would play a tune with the wrong beat and in the wrong key on the piano. Jo would sing along, off-key and out of meter. Paul often played melodies that had nothing to do with Jo's song. He might be playing "Chopsticks" while she sang "April in Paris." If Frank was really down, I'd slip one of Jo's CDs in the player. As soon as the recording started, he'd crack up, and for a while, he'd be happy again.

The only singing Frank did anymore was just fooling around. He and I used to sing fractured lyrics. He'd do a takeoff on the old joke about a guy that meets a girl in a bar. She takes him to her apartment, where he watches her get undressed. First, she takes off her wig and throws it in a drawer. Then she takes her teeth and falsies out and puts them in the drawer. Frank would sing, *"You went upstairs to get undressed. / You came down without your chest. / It's magic . . ."* And we'd both laugh like it was the funniest thing we'd ever heard.

One time I was sitting next to the bed with the TV on low while Frank dozed. Suddenly, Frank started singing, *"Boop boop ba loop, dubba dooby dooby doo."* Then he opened his eyes and stopped. I said, "That's very nice."

"You like that? Wait till you hear the second verse!" That was Frank Sinatra. You never really knew what to expect, even then.

The toughest challenge was when he and Barbara would squabble. Frank would look at me and say, "What do *you* think?"

Instead of replying, I'd start with my own *Amos 'n' Andy:* "Well, ah, I havta splain it to you . . ." Most of the time he'd crack up, and the squabble would be forgotten.

There were a lot of times when Frank wanted desperately to go out for dinner, but Barbara worried about his being out in public now that he no longer looked like "Ol' Blue Eyes." The tabloid press would have loved to get a shot of him when he wasn't looking his best. Barbara was trying to protect him, but it ended up hurting him. It was robbing him of being Frank Sinatra.

I knew that trying to hold on to the old Sinatra was a losing battle. Frank was clearly changing. Not surprisingly, music was his solace. At night, he'd listen to a channel that played classical music and opera until dawn. Sometimes, he'd stare at the ceiling in silence and process what was on his mind. I sensed a growing awareness that the road was taking him to a new destination. Time was pulling him forward, and he was no longer struggling against it. He'd let it play out as it was meant to.

One afternoon, Frank was lying on the bed, with the TV on as background noise, when he said to me, "Tony?"

"Yeah?"

"Can you make my mother leave? She keeps staring at me, and I'm trying to get some rest here."

Dolly had been dead for twenty years by then, but I just said, "Sure." After all, Dolly was one of the last people you'd want in the room if you were trying to relax.

Another late night when Mario, the night nurse, was there, Frank woke up and asked Mario to get his mother on the phone. When Mario replied that she was dead, Frank went ballistic.

From my room, I could hear Frank yelling, "Get out of my house!" I went down the hall to Frank's room and told Mario to go in the other room.

Then I asked Frank, "Do you really want to call your mother in New Jersey at five o'clock in the morning? You'll scare the hell out of her!"

When it finally sank in, Frank said, "Okay. We'll call her tomorrow."

We chatted for a few more minutes, and finally, he said, "You know, T, I think I'll put it in the bag."

"Good idea, Frank. Sleep warm."

The week of May 11, 1998, was one of the longest of my life. That Monday, Frank and I had a conversation about how he was feeling. I sat down on the side of his bed, and he said to me, "Tony, you know me. This is not me. I'm not happy, and I don't like what

436

I've become."

I didn't know how to comfort him, because what he said was true. He wasn't that Frank anymore, no longer the man who could mesmerize a room just by walking through the door, who lit up a stage like it was a building with blazing lights, who stuck cigarettes in his ears and laughed with his whole soul. His biggest passion in life — performing — was gone. Nothing that had brought him joy, that had made him Frank Sinatra, was there anymore.

Barbara continued to see that he was given the best care possible, but her own life was also important to her. Their age difference hadn't mattered when she'd married Frank. He was still strong and vital then, at the top of his game. But as he steadily faded away, the gap between them widened. He felt trapped in a world that had been constructed for him by someone else. His life no longer belonged to him. He began to gradually give up the existence that had been forced on him. It was the only power he had left. Subconsciously, I knew what was happening, but I wasn't ready to let him go.

Barbara was scheduled to be out three nights that week. Frank wasn't happy about her being gone so much. He couldn't understand why she was still going out while he was stuck at home.

On Monday night, once Barbara left, I did my best to keep him in a good mood without violating the doctors' orders. He really missed drinking, so I said, "You know, Frank, I feel like having a drink. Why don't we have a beer?"

Frank perked up and said, "Sounds great. What the hell! She's not home anyway. She'll never know!"

I poured the beer into two tall glasses filled with ice and put a little salt in it to give it some body, just the way we liked it.

When he finished the first glass, he looked at me and said, "Jeez!"

"What's the matter?"

"Can you believe it? This beer kicked my ass!" We both were laughing, but I was laughing harder. Frank didn't know we were drinking O'Doul's, which is nonalcoholic beer. I knew that it was alcohol free, but in his mind, he was getting drunk and having a ball without his wife's yelling at him. He said, "I haven't had booze for so long. Can you believe it? A lousy beer kicked my ass!"

I never told him the truth. I just let him enjoy the high he was having in his mind.

The next evening was another social engagement for Barbara. She didn't see him that day until three thirty, when she came down the stairs for a forty-five-minute visit. Frank was thrilled to have some time with her. Then she went back upstairs and came down again two hours later, all dressed up.

Frank said, "Where are you going?"

Barbara told him that she was meeting two of her girlfriends for dinner.

Frank said, "What about me?"

"Tony's here with you."

"Yeah, but what is this BS?"

Before it got heated, she said, "I've got to run, sweetheart. I'm going to be late."

She left. I calmed Frank down, and we had dinner together. He drifted off to sleep around midnight. Just after he fell asleep, Barbara came home. She walked in just as I was leaving Frank's room and said loudly, "Hey, Tony!"

I said, "Shh, Barbara. He just fell asleep."

"Oh, okay. I want to say good night to him. I'm going to give him a kiss." She went in, and a moment later, I heard him yelling. She'd woken him up to say good night, which was never a good idea with Frank. Suddenly jolted out of a deep sleep, he remembered she'd gone out without him and got angry. Then she got angry.

I heard her saying, "Well, if that's the way you're going to be, then good night. I'll see you when I see you!"

She turned around and went upstairs to her bedroom. It took me over an hour to calm Frank down. He finally drifted back to sleep at about two.

I said to Mario, who'd arrived a short while earlier, "I'm going to run back to my place real quick. If you need me, call my cell phone." About an hour and a half later, my cell started ringing. It was Mario, and he was panicking. I told him, "Just calm down. Tell me what's going on."

Frank had awakened out of a sound sleep and become angry all over again.

Mario said, "Tony, I'm scared. His face is very red, and his pulse is way elevated, and this is not good."

I said, "Mario, put the phone down and get in his face. Tell him what time of day it is, that I'm on the phone, and that I need to talk to him."

"Okay, I'll try."

"Don't try. Do it." I understood Mario's apprehension. God bless him, when Frank yelled, he could shake a house, even then. I heard Mario talking to Frank.

At first Frank kept yelling, but Mario said again, more loudly, "It's *three* o'clock in the morning, and *Tony* is on the phone, and he needs to *talk* to you."

It finally registered. Frank said, "Three in the morning! Tony's calling? Something must be wrong. Where's the phone? Give me the damn phone!"

When Frank got on the phone with me, I made up a story to divert his attention and kept talking until he began to calm down. When he was back to normal, he said to me, "Listen, T, I think I'm going to stretch out now and put it in the bag for a little bit. You coming around later?"

"Yeah, I'll see you in the morning. Get a good night's sleep."

"Okay, kid, see you."

On Wednesday, I returned to the house and spent the day with Frank. That evening, Barbara went out again. This time, I made sure to have some friends come over, and Frank had a good time. It didn't bother him as much that she'd gone out for a third night in a row because he had friends of his own over. Thursday, however, would be a whole different matter.

On Thursday, May 14, the sun struggled to shine through the clouds of what LA residents call "May gray." When Frank woke up in the early afternoon, it was still cool and gloomy, but we decided to put on jackets and sit out by the pool anyway. I was relieved that Frank appeared relaxed.

With the storms of the week apparently behind us, I decided Frank was stable enough for me to go ahead with my plans for that night. I'd invited Glenn Scarpelli and his business partner to dinner. Barbara was still there when I left about five that afternoon. I started helping my mom prepare for dinner, and my guests arrived, but I had a nagging feeling I should check on Frank. When I couldn't shake it by seven thirty, I called Vine and said, "How's he doing?"

Vine sounded worried. She told me Frank wasn't feeling very well. I told her I'd come back as soon as my guests left. About an hour later, Vine called again, so panic stricken she could hardly speak. I could hear Frank in a tirade because Barbara had gone out without him for a fourth night. Suddenly, Vine screamed.

"Vine! Tell me what's happening!" She told me Frank's face had turned dark red, his eyes had rolled back, and he'd fallen onto the bed.

I called Frank's physician, Rex Kennamer, who called the ambulance. Vine went with the ambulance while I raced over the dark canyon road to Beverly Hills. When I arrived at Cedars-Sinai, Vine was in the lobby, pale with fear, clutching Frank's little travel bag. I rushed past her and straight to the emergency desk, where the nurse on duty pointed to a draped area and told me to take a seat. Somebody handed me Frank's socks and glasses, and I absentmindedly put them in my jacket pocket. After a few minutes, Rex came out of the draped area and found me. He told me Frank was having a serious heart attack and then pulled the curtain back and showed me in. I saw what was clearly a major emergency under way. Frank's cardiologist, Dr. Helfenstein, was there, along with what looked like a dozen other medical personnel, all working furiously. Machines with wires and tubes were hooked up to the familiar figure in the bed.

Frank was conscious, clearly in deep shock, his face as white as the hospital sheets. I remember wondering how someone with such a deep tan could be that pale. I don't think he was in pain, but he was terrified, his eyes wide with fear. He knew exactly how much trouble he was in. I went toward the bed, and the moment he saw me, he reached for my hand. As he clutched my fingers, he managed to whisper, "Hey, T."

We held tightly to each other's hands as I said, "Just relax, breathe. You're gonna be okay. Just breathe. Nobody breathes like you do, Frank." He tried to smile at that. I told him I loved him. He kept his eyes fixed on my face.

His hand was ice cold. He'd start to slip away, and each time he did, I repeated, "Stay with me. Stay with me," until he seemed to be coming back. I was grateful he wasn't in pain, but all I could think of at that moment was, "Stay." As long as his eyes were fastened on me, everything would be all right. I told myself that it was nothing we hadn't been through before. He was going to be fine. He had the best medical help money could buy.

Dr. Helfenstein stayed close, directing the procedures. Rex was in and out, helping me deal with the increasingly complicated situation as the minutes ticked by. He told me Frank's publicist, Susan, had arrived. I thought, *Vine called her.*

I stepped outside just long enough to let Susan know what the situation was and asked, "Did you get ahold of Barbara?" She said that Barbara had forgotten to leave a contact number, and her cell phone was off. It had taken a while to track her down, but Susan had finally gotten ahold of her. Barbara was on her way. Susan went back to making calls, and I thought, *Good, she's calling the kids.* One less thing to worry about. I was running the list of what had to be done through my mind, in tight control of my emotions.

I went back in and took hold of Frank's hand again. He seemed slightly calmer, but he still clung to my fingers like a frightened child.

About an hour after I got there, the drape was pulled back again, and Rex brought Barbara in. I could see the shock on her face as she registered what she was looking at. I realized immediately that I was where she should have been, holding her husband's hand. I braced myself to let go, but in an act of grace I'll always be grateful for, she didn't ask me to. She looked at me, looked at Frank, then moved past me with a touch of my shoulder. She went to the head of the bed, next to me. She began to stroke her husband's hair and forehead, murmuring comfortingly as he looked at her and continued to cling to my hand. On one side of the gurney, the medical staff worked; on the other, Barbara and I stood side by side. We could see that he wasn't responding to the treatment.

Barbara whispered intently, "Fight, darling, you must fight. You mustn't give in."

He looked back at us and whispered matter-of-factly, "I'm losing." Then he fell silent.

Barbara, pale and shaken, told me, "I'm nauseated." She looked like she was about to pass out. I helped her out of the tented area to a nearby chair, fetched her some cold water, and sat next to her. She rallied after a few minutes, and we went back inside. Frank had been intubated while we were gone and could no longer speak, but he was still conscious.

We took our places at his side again. Barbara resumed talking softly and stroking his brow while I took hold of his hand once more. His eyes were closed, but he squeezed my hand weakly. He knew I was there. Another few minutes went by, and Barbara began to look really ill. I knew that shock was setting in. I helped her out to a chair again, got her more water, and sat beside her, doing my best to comfort her. A few feet away, Susan was still on the phone. I thought surely she'd reached the kids by then and vaguely wondered why it was taking them so long.

Then the drape was pulled back once more, and Rex came out. He said kindly to Barbara, "Are you okay?"

She nodded and said, "Yes."

"Then you'd better get back in there now. He's having another heart attack, and I can't stop it. We're going to lose him."

Rex looked helpless, exhausted, and frustrated. I could see the grief in his eyes as he delivered the news about his friend. Lose Frank? Frank was a force of nature. I couldn't take it in.

Rex took Barbara and me inside once again. Only one nurse was there now. The feverish activity had stopped. Out of respect for our privacy, Rex had asked the rest of the medical staff to leave. When I took Frank's hand, he squeezed it weakly and held on a short while longer. Then slowly, it went limp. He took one last, soft breath, and then expelled it, the final mortal act of a man who'd controlled his breathing with extraordinary skill for seven decades. At the end, he went out of this life quietly, peacefully. The singer of the century, the man I loved like a second father, was gone. It was 10:50 p.m., less than three hours since Vine had first called me. Rex and the nurse quietly left me and Barbara alone.

Barbara had begun crying softly, holding a tissue under her nose with one hand, her other arm wrapped around her torso to comfort herself. Neither of us said a word. I continued to hold Frank's hand, but I reached out with the other and put my arm gently around Barbara. My eyes were dry. Somewhere in the back of my mind, I knew I didn't have the luxury of crying. I thought, *Not now. There are things you have to do.* After a few minutes, I placed Frank's hand gently on his chest. Rex came back in with a couple of nurses, who began disconnecting the tubes and wires that had failed to keep Frank connected to life. Frank had a "do not resuscitate" order in place, so there was nothing more to be done for him.

I helped Barbara back to a chair, and Susan moved over to be with her. I heard Barbara tell Susan, "You should probably call the kids now."

I couldn't believe what I was hearing. No one had called Frank's children?

When I had a chance for a private moment, I took Susan aside and said, "Why didn't you call the kids?"

Susan replied that Barbara had told her not to call anybody until she had gotten ahold of Bobby.

"Are you kidding me? Bobby's in New York. The kids are right here. They could've been here in ten minutes."

She repeated, "Barbara told me not to call anyone until I reached Bobby."

448

I could only imagine the repercussions with the family. I told her, "Well, you'd better call them now."

She said, "I just did, and Nancy and Tina are on their way."

I could tell Susan felt bad about it, but like everyone else, she knew that Barbara was in charge. I pushed my feelings aside. I didn't have time to be angry any more than I had time to grieve. I told Rex I needed to tell Vine what had happened but not to move Frank until I could go with him.

Rex replied, "Don't worry. He's staying right here. Come and get me when you've told Vine."

I walked back out to the waiting room to give Vine the news. She collapsed in sobs. I offered to walk her back in to see Frank, but she couldn't do it. I did my best to comfort her and then asked for the personal grooming items she always carried for Frank. I took them and went back inside.

Rex had arranged for Frank to be moved to a private room and given orders that I was to stay with the body at all times. I didn't want Frank's kids to see him in the middle of that zoo, and I was already worried about the press. I would remain with Frank while Barbara waited for Nancy and Tina. There was no word of Frankie Jr. Two orderlies came and took Frank to a private examining room on the same floor. I walked by the gurney, my hand on Frank the whole time. Once the orderlies left, I opened the grooming kit Vine had brought. I didn't want anyone seeing Frank Sinatra looking like that. I washed his face, combed and brushed his hair, and made him look as presentable as I could. Absentmindedly, I stuck the brush and comb in my empty jacket pocket. Once Frank was presentable, Barbara came in and sat next to him. A few minutes later, Nancy Jr. and Tina arrived.

They were stunned by shock and grief. It was obvious that Nancy was also furious. She glared at me and demanded, "Why weren't we told?" I could see this was going to get ugly, and I had to stop it before it went out of control.

"This is not the time or the place. Your father's not even gone a half hour." Telling her Barbara's orders would have set off a bomb, so I told them that Susan had had a lot of things to do because she didn't want the press to find out. Susan had to postpone releasing the news as long as possible so we could make arrangements before the on- slaught of paparazzi. I said I had also called Elite Security, our private security guys, and told them, "This is going to turn into an absolute circus."

That helped turned the focus back to where it was supposed to be — spending time with their father. I left the room so Nancy and Tina could have time with Poppa. A short while later, they went back to the Foothill house. Barbara was gone by then, so it was only me left behind to see to the remaining tasks. Adrenaline was flooding my body. It was the only way I could deal with all the details and not break down.

I called our security staff again and said, "I'm going to need you to be wherever they're releasing the body from. You'll need to run interference. I'll call you as soon as I know when and where."

Rex informed me that, unfortunately, Frank's body couldn't stay where it was. He'd have to be moved downstairs to the morgue. Mortuaries were only allowed to receive bodies from the morgue, not from hospital rooms. Rex had kindly arranged for me to accompany Frank there as well. Someone, probably Rex, told me that arrangements were in place to take Frank to the McCormick mortuary in Inglewood. Our security company put a strict protocol in place for the transfer. Frank's body would be the only one in that part of the mortuary, and access would be closely monitored.

If they'd taken him to a Beverly Hills mortuary, the security issues would have been much more complicated. The press would be staking those out as soon as word spread of Frank's passing.

The orderlies came back to take Frank down to the morgue. I walked with him through the silent halls until we reached a cold, sterile room filled with slabs and refrigerators. It was well past midnight by then. The chilly room was the place nightmares are made of. The morgue attendants turned to me and said, "We have to do what we do."

I told them to go ahead. They cut off the wristband and handed it to me. I stuck the wristband in the pocket of my windbreaker with his comb and brush. They put a toe tag on him with the name "Ramsey," a name Barbara wanted him to use in hospitals to maintain anonymity. It had always seemed ridiculous to me because it's not as if people would be fooled by a wristband. They told me that they had to put him in a body bag and into a freezer.

I told them, "You can put him in a body bag, but you're not putting him in a freezer drawer. He wouldn't let you do it to me, and I'm not going to let you do it to him." I told them that he'd only be there about an hour, and that nothing was going to happen in that amount of time. I added, "And I'm staying by his side."

I was wearing what Frank always called my "Don't fuck with me" face. They finally said, "Okay."

Oddly enough, they put him in a white body bag. Usually body bags are black. For some reason that image, of the white bag in the metal room, has stuck in my mind ever since.

Within an hour, two guys showed up from the mortuary, driving a vehicle that looked more like a station wagon than a hearse. I checked their IDs, but neither one was the person I'd been told to expect. I said, "You know what, guys? With all due respect, I am not releasing the body to you. Stranger things have happened when famous people's bodies have been given to the wrong people." I told them that when their boss showed up, I'd sign the papers. "Until then, Mr. Sinatra's staying right here." They were surprisingly understanding.

About one a.m., their boss finally showed up, and I signed the papers. Then I walked with the gurney out to the hearse. Between the hospital security, the Beverly Hills police, and our guys, there were no cameras there to violate Frank's privacy. I felt good that we'd been able to do that for him. I stood there until the hearse pulled away into the darkness. I left the hospital soon afterward and got back to the Foothill house at about one thirty in the morning. There was one news van there. I called up to the house on my cell, and the housekeeper told me there were already too many cars there for me to park inside the gates.

I said, "No problem," and parked a short way down the block. I walked to the gate, ignoring the reporter, and punched in the code. When the gates opened, I walked wearily up the steep driveway to the house. Nancy, Tina; friends Jerry and Rita Vale, Jerry Weintraub, George and Jolene Schlatter, Steve and Eydie; and, of course, Barbara were there already.

Everyone was in the living room. I went to the bar and made myself a drink, which I desperately needed by then. When I looked up, I saw Nancy and Tina sitting on the couch. Nancy was glaring at me. I didn't want a public scene, so I asked Nancy and Tina to come in the den where we could talk. As I shut the door behind us, I got an uncomfortable feeling. This was the room in which I'd been talking with Frank just a few hours earlier. Nancy looked at me and said accusingly, "Why didn't you call me?"

I said, "Nancy, you're upset."

"Yes, I'm upset!"

I looked her in the eyes and said, "Nancy, in all the times we've rushed your father to the hospital, in any of those instances, did you ever once get a call from me?"

"No."

"Who called you?"

"Vine or Susan."

"Why is it then that tonight, *I* should have called you? I had no way of knowing this would be the last night. I was doing what I always do. I was comforting your father. He was scared, and I needed to keep him calm. Don't do this. There are things to do. There are a lot of people you should be calling. You need to talk to your mom." I thought of Nancy Sr. *Oh, God.*

Tina said to her sister, "He's right. He was there for Poppa. That's the main thing."

I said, "I'm so sorry, Tina," and gave her a hug. She hugged me back, crying deeply. Then I hugged Nancy, too. She let me hug her, but her body was stiff. I knew she was struggling.

Afterward, both girls were subdued. The realization was sinking in that their poppa was actually gone. Surprisingly, there was no visible tension between the girls and Barbara. In the face of such loss, they'd called a temporary truce.

Somewhere around three a.m., I said to everyone, "It's going to be a very long weekend for everybody. We need to let Barbara get some rest." Everyone took the cue. People immediately began gathering their things, hugging each other, saying goodbye. I saw everyone to the door. Then I went back in the house and walked Barbara upstairs.

I told her, "I'll be back in the morning." She hugged me and then shut the door.

I went back downstairs to check on Vine. She was already in her room off the kitchen, sobbing inconsolably. I didn't know how to comfort her. Eventually, she cried herself to sleep.

The house was completely silent for the first time that day. It was hard to believe that less than eight hours earlier, the walls had been echoing with Frank's screams of rage and frustration. I turned off the lights and walked back down the driveway to my car. By then, the street was teeming with news vans. I was besieged by reporters as I walked to my car under the artificial glare of news lights. I stared resolutely ahead, ignoring them, willing myself to just keep going.

Finally, one reporter shoved himself in my

face with lights and a microphone and said, "Obviously, you must be a friend of Mr. Sinatra's. Can you tell us what you're feeling right now?"

What I was feeling? Seriously? I guess I had reached my limit, because I looked at him and said, "Take a f\*\*\*ing wild guess, asshole! Put that on the news if you want to. Now get out of my way!" My remarks did not make it on television, though I have no doubt Frank would have enjoyed hearing them.

As I threaded my car through the crush of reporters, to the outskirts of Beverly Hills, and then on to the darkness of the canyon road toward home, my mind kept circling back to the same thought.

Frank Sinatra hadn't really died. He'd escaped.

When the news of his passing broke, the lights on the Vegas Strip were dimmed, and casinos stopped spinning for a minute's tribute. The lights on the Empire State Building were switched to blue. Those things were meaningful to me only in retrospect. I couldn't allow myself to feel anything. Not yet.

When I got home, I stretched out on the bed to rest for about two hours. I don't even know if I slept. Before long, I got up, took a shower, and went back to the Foothill house. When I entered Frank's room, the maids were already there. They were going through his room with a fine-toothed comb, changing and disinfecting everything. I looked around in bewilderment.

The housekeeper told me, "Barbara has people flying out for the funeral. She needs all the rooms ready." It was a gut punch for me. Frank had been gone less than twelve hours, and I felt like he was already being erased.

Until the funeral, it was important that nobody know where Frank's body was. So after the usual mortuary services, we took over McCormick's. Until the memorial services, a very limited number of people would be informed of Frank's location and allowed to visit. We had him in an open casket. Frank's head of security, Lou Palumbo of Elite Security, was providing twenty-four-hour armed security on the property, and Frank was the only one there. The people who visited were family and extremely close friends. I called Lou in advance each time to tell him who was coming. I also made sure they had security in front of and behind the vehicles the visitors drove, so we could make sure they weren't tailed. Not one reporter found out where

Frank was in the four days he was in Inglewood. I'm very proud of that.

The next task at hand was to begin planning the funeral. I was with the family all day Friday, Saturday, and Sunday, helping with the arrangements. It was to be a private funeral. The service was going to be at Good Shepherd in Beverly Hills, and it was going to be a big event. Not only would we have to send invitations, but we'd also have to call people and print tickets. Tuesday was going to be the rosary service, which would last a couple of hours. Tickets for the rosary were blue. The following day, in the early afternoon, there'd be a high mass with Cardinal Mahony and four other priests. This would be the actual memorial service. Those tickets would be lavender. Barbara and the girls decided on the speakers. Greg Peck would fly back from Paris to deliver a eulogy. There was a big discussion about which of Frank's songs they were going to play. We talked it over, and it was unanimous: "Put Your Dreams Away."

By Monday evening, I was worn out. I desperately needed a break from dealing with so many people's needs. I had dinner at Morton's with my close friends Michael Guarnera and Eric Kunze. I was actually able to laugh at dinner, but afterward, I felt

I needed to see Frank again. Mike and Eric insisted on going with me. I said, "You can't come in," but they said, "We don't care about that. We just want to be there to support you."

I spent about an hour with Frank at the mortuary that evening. I was on the kneeler, completely immersed in thought. My mind was going 150 miles an hour, over all the things that had happened with Frank. There was so much that it was overwhelming.

I was the last person to see Frank in the casket. The mortician wouldn't open the casket without someone in authority's being present, and I was the one. We had him dressed in a midnight-blue suit with very fine pinstripes, a white shirt, and a pink tie with blue fans on it. Barbara had asked that his watch, his wedding band, and his newer (1976) pinky ring with the family crest be removed from his body. The kids wanted to put some special things in Frank's pockets before he was buried. They couldn't bring themselves to do it, so I volunteered. I put his handkerchief in his left pocket, put his reading glasses in his breast pocket, and tucked in a pack of Camels, an airline-size bottle of Jack Daniel's, and a roll of dimes. The roll of dimes went back to the days when Frankie Jr. was kidnapped and you could make a phone call for a dime. After I placed the items in the casket with Frank, I kissed him on the forehead and said my final goodbye. That was the last time the casket was opened. When it was closed, it was closed for good.

Tuesday I was back in Inglewood early. We loaded the casket into the hearse, and I went to Good Shepherd and had a staging meeting about the way the processions were going to go. It was eerily like producing an all-star show for Frank. Before the rosary service that evening, I began marking off the pews, placing cards to show who'd sit where. The pallbearers, including myself, would be in the front row on the right. The family would sit across the aisle from us. Tradition dictated that as Frank's wife, Barbara would be in the first row, with her son and his fiancée and those closest to them. Nancy Sr. and Frank's children and grandchildren, with their loved ones, would be in the second row. Nancy Jr. had arrived by then. When she saw me placing the card with Barbara's name in the first row and hers in the second, she lashed out at me.

"What are you, on *her* side?"

I was near the end of my rope at that point, physically and emotionally. I felt like I couldn't take one more second of the feuding that had cast a shadow over Frank's final years. In a sharper tone than I'd ever used with her, I said, "You know what, Nancy? At the end of the day, right now, I'm on *my* side. Okay? I know you lost your father, but try to put yourself in my shoes, would you please? Just once." And I turned and walked away.

The rosary service went as planned. The music was beautiful. Afterward, people gathered around the casket. Peggy Lee was there in her wheelchair, and Rickles, looking pale and strained, was leaning on the casket with one arm as he talked to her.

Peggy kept staring at his arm, and finally he said, "What's the matter? What are you looking at?"

"You're leaning on the casket."

"Why should things change now? I've been leaning on Frank all my life."

Afterward, everyone left because Frank's body was supposed to lie in state in the church. As I was getting ready to leave, the sexton and two men came up and started to move the casket.

I said, "Excuse me. What are you doing?"

The sexton said, "We're just going to put him in the back of the church, and —"

I interrupted him and said, "Wait a minute. What do you mean you're going to put him in the back of the church? He's supposed to be lying in state here in front of the altar all night long. The church will be locked up, right?"

The sexton answered, "Well, yes, we were going to lock the church, but they forgot to cancel seven thirty mass tomorrow morning, so people are going to be coming here. Don't worry, though, nobody will know he's back there. We'll cover him up with a white drape."

In my head, I could hear Frank laughing. After everything I'd been through to keep Frank's body safe, they were actually going to put him in the back of the church, with a white cloth draped over the casket, and expect that nobody would notice?

I said, "Well, guess what? *I* would know he's back there, and that's not the way it's going to go down. If you do, in fact, have to move him, we're going to have to find another secure place for him. I don't want people walking in here at seven thirty tomorrow morning and saying, 'What's that over there? A piece of furniture?' Someone else might answer, 'No, it's Frank Sinatra. Just ignore him.' "

I looked around and saw that there was a small annex next to the church that was used for choir rehearsals.

I said, "How about in here? Can it be locked and alarmed?"

They said, "Sure."

"Then this is where we're going to put the casket." That's what they did. What better place for Frank than the music room?

The next day was the funeral. It was a beautiful day, but the beauty was lost on me. Though the guest list itself was carefully controlled, the streets leading to the church were thronged with people who'd come to pay their respects, many dressed soberly for the occasion. Overhead, a skywriter soared, drawing the initials *FS* and tracing them in a heart as onlookers watched. The press crowded forward to snap pictures of the celebrities entering the church.

The mourners were an eclectic group, to say the least, and very appropriate for Frank. There were the crème de la crème of celebrities, political figures like former first lady Nancy Reagan and former New York governor Hugh Carey, and a host of friends. Vine and Roland and Frank's closest staff were also there, along with Frank's favorite bartender at Chasen's. The crowd was like Jilly's club on a Saturday night decades before. One of the people taking up considerable space in a pew was comedian Joey

Villa, my old and dear friend and an early client of Jilly's.

I was seated with the other pallbearers next to the casket, which was blanketed with white gardenias, Frank's favorite flower. Each pallbearer wore a white gardenia and the Elite Security logo on his lapel. Barbara was seated with Bobby in the front row across the aisle from me with Bobby's fiancée, Hillary; Vine; and Frankie Jr. Frankie Jr., nominally one of the pallbearers, couldn't bring himself to touch his father's casket. He sat in the front row instead, where he could move directly to the podium when his turn came to speak. Directly behind him sat Frank's daughters and grandchildren, with Nancy Sr. and Tina's friend and family attorney Bob Finkelstein. Nancy Sr. looked stoic and spent. Her face reminded me of a photo I'd seen of her when Frankie Jr. was kidnapped. She was somber, the lines in her face etched deeply, as she stared straight ahead. She'd cried her tears in private. There'd be no Hollywood movie ending now for Frank and Nancy. Mia Farrow was seated behind her, dressed in black, accompanied by her young son Ronan. She looked ten years older than her years that day, ashen and distraught.

Ava had preceded Frank in death eight years earlier.

A trio of Frank's old friends, with Al Viola on guitar and Bill Miller on piano, played as the guests were seated. It was a high mass, conducted by Cardinal Roger Mahony and four priests. After the Introductory Rites, there was a musical tribute to Frank by the trio before Cardinal Mahony welcomed everyone. More prayers and songs followed, leading up to communion. At a specific moment before communion, the cardinal nodded to me, and I went to the rear of the church. The family wanted me to participate, and I said I'd be honored. So what did they pick for me to do? They wanted me to bring in the wine. As I carried the gold decanter down the aisle to the altar, I stared at Frank's casket and thought, *Look at us. He's gone, and I'm still bringing him booze.*

Afterward, during communion, people came up and formed two lines, one on either side of the casket. Because I was in the front aisle seat, people were filing past me. I sat there, staring at the casket, and didn't look up.

All of a sudden, I felt a hand on my shoulder. I glanced up, and it was Joey Villa. He patted my shoulder, then went up and took communion. Four or five minutes later, people were still passing by me. I was looking down, lost in my thoughts, when I smelled Dunhill cologne. I knew only two people in the world who used that cologne: Jerry Lewis and Joey Villa. I looked down at the shoes next to me, and it was Joey again. He was in line for communion a second time. I looked up and frowned at him, but he ignored me. Another five minutes went by, and there he was, passing by me again. I looked up at him, puzzled, and held my hands out like, *What are you doing?*

He leaned over and whispered in my ear. "I didn't have any breakfast." I guess three communion wafers were going to hold him over till dinner. I swear I could hear Frank laughing a few feet away.

When communion finally ended, the choir sang the twenty-third psalm. Then Frank's voice filled the church, the notes of "Put Your Dreams Away" bringing people to tears. Afterward, the speakers delivered their tributes. Kirk Douglas, R. J. Wagner, Bobby Marx, and Frankie Jr. all spoke briefly. I had to smile when our dear friend producer George Schlatter told the assembled mourners that Frank's two favorite words were "Jack" and "Daniel's." Cardinal Mahony made a formal statement released to the press by the diocese. The speaker that stands out in my mind, though, is Gregory Peck, reprising the eloquent, moving tribute for Frank that he'd given two and a half years earlier, on Frank's eightieth birthday:

> Sentimental softy, reckless rogue,
> Weaving a musical garment of the
>     threads of his life
> Golden threads from the golden years.
> The gold record years, the gold statuette
>     years.
> Blue threads woven into the cloth from
>     the "where-has-she-gone" years.
> And the "one-for-the-road" years.
> And the pure white thread of the decent
>     deeds
> Done in the name of the nameless needy
>     years.
> And the threads worked their way into the
>     pattern of his life,
> Forming a garment for protection and a
>     banner of defiance.

Across the aisle from me, on the other side of the casket, an unrehearsed family drama was going on. In the extremity of the moment, emotions had finally spilled over. Cardinal Mahony and the priests were handing out memorial crucifixes to family and close friends seated in the family section. As Tina reached over Barbara's shoulder to take a crucifix for her friend Bob, seated to her left, Barbara grabbed Tina's hand and asked who it was for. When Tina said, "Bob," Barbara said, "No." A literal tug-of-war ensued, a painful embodiment of the emotional tug-of-war that had been going on for years between them. Barbara succeeded in pulling the crucifix from Tina's hand, leaving Tina's palm bleeding. As much as I wished Frank were there with us that day, I could only hope he didn't see that. There is a photograph of Barbara in the doorway of the church at the end of the service, several crucifixes clutched in her hand.

The eulogies were followed by the signs of farewell, the holy water and incense, the prayer of commendation, and finally the choir and congregation singing "May the Angels Lead You to Paradise" while the recessional took place.

There were seven of us pallbearers, including Don Rickles, Sonny Golden, Steve Lawrence, and Bobby Marx. As we brought the casket out of the church into the sunlight at the top of the stairs, the honorary pallbearers formed two lines below us, standing as if at attention between the bottom step and the open doors of the hearse. Tony

Bennett, Kirk Douglas, Quincy Jones, Wayne Newton, and Gregory Peck were among them. Afterward, Wayne Newton expressed what a lot of people felt when he said he didn't want the service to end because he wasn't ready to let go of Frank.

In news footage taken after the service that day, I'm easy to spot in my charcoal gray suit, standing at the front of the casket on the right side. Though I had a viselike grip on my emotions, I look much like Frank did at Sammy's funeral: gray-faced, grief-stricken, seeming to have aged overnight. I struggled down the steps, bearing not only the weight of Frank's casket but the weight of my own grief. It's a terrible thing to face the death of those you love under the glare of the public eye, with cameras in your face. It was an extraordinary feeling saying goodbye to my best friend and at the same time having to deal with the family craziness that still surrounded us. The chaos and the insanity of the overheated emotions and old rivalries that had bubbled up in the face of such loss felt like an assault.

The funeral over, Frank's body was being flown east for burial in the desert. With Frank's casket safely in the hearse, I rode with Frank to Sky Trails Aviation at Van

470

Nuys Airport, where we put Frank's body on Kirk Kerkorian's jet. I helped put the casket on the conveyor belt and watched it go up into the belly of the plane and disappear from sight. It was the same jet that we'd flown to Japan and Manila for Frank's concerts. Now it was taking him on his final flight. Nancy Jr., Tina, Frankie, Barbara, and Bobby were already on the plane. I was invited to join them, but I elected not to go. I was exhausted by all the drama and desperate to make my own escape so I could finally begin to mourn. The graveside service was to be private, conducted by a priest from St. Louis Church, the same church Frank's mother had attended, where Jilly's funeral had been held. Frank would be buried in Desert Memorial Park, next to his parents and Jilly. He'd intentionally chosen a very ordinary grave site, just yards from the road, where fans could visit him any time they wanted. To the very end, he felt a profound sense of obligation and gratitude to the people who'd given Francis Albert from Hoboken the extraordinary life of Frank Sinatra.

Frank always told me that he hoped to draw his last breath in the desert. He didn't get that wish, but it comforted me to know that his final journey was to the place he loved best. He rests there, now and for eternity, beneath the heat and the wind and the brilliant blue skies, next to the people he loved. He is finally home. Sleep warm, Frank.

■ ■ ■ ■ ■

# PART IV
# CODA

■ ■ ■ ■ ■

PART IV
CODA

This time I was the one seeing Jilly, not outside the window of a hospital room, but in my dreams. In the dream, I was on a beach in Southern California, somewhere south near San Diego, walking along the sand where the edge of the surf packs it hard. It was a beautiful day, and at first, I seemed to be alone. Then I looked up and realized there was somebody about thirty yards ahead of me, walking in the same direction. He was a tall man wearing a baseball cap, walking with an odd and familiar gait. He looked like Jilly. I began calling to him, but there was no response. He didn't turn around or even slow down; he kept walking. Finally, I sprinted across the sand until I could get in front of him, blocking his path.

It was Jilly, healthy and unhurt and very much alive. I cried out, "What the hell! What are you doing here?"

Jilly looked down at me with sorrow and said, "Tony, I'm so sorry for what I put you through. I can't apologize to you enough. But I just couldn't take it anymore. I couldn't stand watching Frank deteriorate. I had to get away. I couldn't figure out another way of escaping, so I faked my death."

And then, with a start, I'd always wake up. To this day, I don't know whether I was processing what I'd been through when Jilly died or whether Jilly was trying to help me process Frank's passing. So much had happened at the end. In reality, I've spent the last twenty years trying to work it all through.

When Frank became ill, to use a phrase from "My Way," I did what I had to do. Once he was gone, and there was nothing left for me to do, I found myself faced with an overpowering grief. It was so overwhelming that I ran from it. When Frank passed, my mind endlessly cycled through the same thought: *I just lost my father all over again.* It was different, though, because Frank Sinatra was a combination of many things to me: part dad, part uncle, part mentor, and part best friend. He'd also been the focus of my professional life for over a decade. No matter how many people called, no matter how close they were, I knew my world was never, ever going to be the same.

In the months after Frank's passing, I lived the truth of his saying "Sometimes friends are like shadows." When Frank was alive, I had ten thousand new best friends every week. After he passed away, I sometimes felt like I was talking into a dead phone. A little while after Frank died, I called a producer friend to ask for help with talent I was representing. I heard his secretary tell him that I was on the phone.

In the background, I heard, "What does *he* want? Doesn't he realize Frank is dead?"

When she came back on the phone, I interrupted her and said, "You can tell him from me that I am painfully aware of where Mr. Sinatra is. I helped carry him to his grave."

Fortunately, many of the people whom I enjoyed being around with Frank — people like the Pecks, the Wagners, the Douglases, and many more — remained my friends. Our relationships weren't based on money, or power, or station in life, but on simple human emotion.

Inevitably, there was a long and fierce battle over Frank's estate. It took a couple of years for the tumult to finally die down and the legal issues to settle. I waited patiently until both sides ran out of things to argue about. Then I went to my bank and picked up the leather bag Frank had entrusted me with over five years earlier. I called Nancy Sr. and the kids and let them know I had something for them from Frank. At the time, Tina had a house on Linda Crest in Beverly Hills. I was invited there for dinner, and when I arrived, the whole family was waiting: Nancy Sr., Nancy Jr., Tina, and Frankie Jr. We shared a nice dinner, and when we adjourned to the next room afterward, I retrieved the bag from the car. I set it on the table and told everyone Frank had given me these things five years earlier to keep for them. I explained that he'd wanted to make sure they got them because everything he'd saved was very special to him. There was no legal problem, for everything predated his marriage to Barbara.

The family gathered around the table, and I proceeded to do exactly what Frank had done years before. I took the items out one at a time and set them on the table, explaining what each one was.

"This is the kazoo you gave him, Nancy, when you were a little girl. This is the rose gold watch Danny Thomas gave him with the twelve turned a quarter of the way so he didn't have to turn his wrist to read it. This is the silver Medal of Valor Golda Meir gave Poppa. It's shaped like the Star of David, with a sword and an olive branch on one side. These are the keys you kids gave him for Father's Day. This is the locket he always took on tour with him. It has pictures of two of you, but not you, Tina, because you hadn't been born yet. This is the diamond watch some guys from Chicago gave your dad. You can see it has a map of Sicily on it . . ."

As I set each item on the table, they picked it up and looked at it with wonder. They couldn't believe some of the things he'd kept. They laughed at some of the items, but they did it with tears in their eyes. By the time I finished, everything was laid out on the table, just as it had been that night in the theater when Frank put the items into my keeping. The evening was warm, welcoming, and deeply emotional. For his family, it was exactly what Frank had hoped it would be. For me, it was a promise kept.

I'd been deferring my grief for years by then. I kept putting it off to another day so I could survive the one I was living. I kept busy. I was on the road with Rickles full-time at that point. I continued producing, now with Michael Guarnera, a gifted actor who'd started as my client and became my producing partner and surrogate family. And I drank, a lot more. Too much. I never lost the ability to function, but for a long time, Jack Daniel's was my closest friend.

It all took its toll. The most obvious manifestation was physical, for I could suppress my emotions, but my body had a will of its own. Bell's palsy, an illness that had first afflicted me after Jilly died, came back with a vengeance after Frank passed away. It was my body's payback for everything I'd put it through. I'd flown to Atlantic City to produce a show for Rickles and Joan Rivers when it struck. When I got up in the morning, the right half of my face appeared to have melted, like wax near an open flame. I already knew that the condition was caused by stress and fatigue. There was no medication that would make it go away. The only cure was time. I went to rehearsal that afternoon anyway and tweaked everything for the show. I got some strange looks, but nobody said anything. That evening, I went back to the hotel, changed for the performance, and then went to get Don. When he opened the door at my knock, he looked at me but just asked his normal preshow questions: *How's the house? How's the band? How are the lights?* We drove to the theater as usual, and Don and Joan were great. It was a terrific show. Still, nobody said anything about my face.

After the show, we were in Don's dressing room, having a couple of drinks with some casino executives. Joan was there, along with some friends who'd come to see the show. I was doing my best to act normal as everyone chatted.

About fifteen minutes into the socializing, Don said, "Well, I suppose it falls to me to address the elephant in the room." Everyone immediately looked uncomfortable, glancing at me and Don like, *Oh, geez, what's he going to do? Poor Tony.* After all, this was Rickles, the king of insults. I just stood there, doing my best to smile. Don turned to me and continued, "You know, Ton', you're in a room full of people who love, admire, and respect you. You know that, right?" I nodded yes. "However, we took a vote, and the results are unanimous. I guess it falls to me to break the news to you. We, who love, admire, and respect you, all still agree that you are too short to play the lead in *The Phantom of the Opera.*"

I started laughing, hard, the way you do when you finally get relief from unbearable

481

tension. God bless Don Rickles. That was Don's philosophy of life: the best disinfectant for the most sensitive subjects is humor. As I laughed, a little bit of the pain started to seep away. There'd be more laughter, more friends, more moments, and little by little, my world righted itself.

It felt like the blink of an eye until 2015, the centennial of Frank's birth. In May of that year, Don Rickles turned eighty-nine. His wife, Barbara, decided to throw a big bash for him instead of waiting for the round number, ninety. Rickles told me, "I'd like for you to give me a birthday present that only you can give me. I want you to sing that night. My son-in-law is putting together his sextet, and I want you to be the only vocalist." I was honored and touched.

Half of Hollywood was there that night, including many of Frank's old crowd. Barbara Sinatra had a table with Steve Lawrence and other old friends. It was like the old days when Frank was still alive. When it was my turn to speak about Don that night, I told the guests, "Long before anyone came up with the concept of the Twin Towers, as an Italian-American kid growing up in Brooklyn, with my eyes securely on becoming an entertainer, I had my own vision of the Twin Towers — the Twin Towers in entertainment. One in music and one in comedy. Music, obviously, is Frank Sinatra, and comedy, Don Rickles. Even in my wildest dreams, I could never have envisioned not only working with these two American originals, but becoming close personal friends and family with both of them." I had a ball singing Frank's old tunes that night.

Almost two years later, Don — nicknamed Bullet Head by Frank but known as Mr. Warmth to the rest of us who loved him — passed away peacefully. One of the last of Frank's surviving friends joined him in death. His beloved wife, Barbara, recently passed away as well. Barbara Rickles was a force of nature, a very classy lady and an absolute Rock of Gibraltar. Don chose wisely when he chose her.

When Frank's hundredth arrived in December, it was the ultimate party. I'm only sorry Frank missed it. Everybody competed to honor him. There were Grammy specials, and network specials, and his very favorite (I'm sure), the Jack Daniel's Sinatra Select limited edition. From Vegas to New York to London to Tokyo, the world celebrated. I imagined his being there while we watched the fireworks together on TV. At some point, he would have made me turn off the television. Frank would have been overwhelmed and humbled, wondering aloud once again what he'd done to deserve all the fuss. He was just a singer from Hoboken who'd gotten lucky.

I had the time of my life celebrating Frank's one hundredth. I ended up as a regular feature on *Sundays with Sinatra,* a show on WGN radio in Chicago. I was also approached by highly respected rock and roll manager Simon Napier-Bell to coproduce a documentary on Frank. It's called *To Be Frank: Sinatra at 100.* It ran on Netflix for three years. I was interviewed on radio and in newspapers, and I enjoyed it all. I was honored to share my years with Frank with the public. Turns out "the kid" had become one of the last living experts on "the old man." Time will do that for you.

By far the best part of the centennial for me, though, was getting to perform again in a full-blown Sinatra tribute. There's a charitable foundation called Big City Broadway in the unlikely location of Jackson Hole, Wyoming. I was approached through my producing partner, Michael, to do a concert there honoring Frank's one hundredth. Michael would produce and direct. There'd be a small jazz orchestra, a trio, and two Broadway stars — friends Eric Kunze and his gal pal Gina Feliccia. And me, singing a couple of hours' worth of pure Sinatra. The thousand-seat theater sold out almost immediately.

That night, I did about ten of Frank's songs with the jazz orchestra in the first half of the show. Each time I introduced a song, I told the audience the backstory. Eric and Gina sang "Darn It, Baby, That's Love," the same way Frankie Jr. and Deana Martin did it when they were teenagers on their fathers' shows. There was a Q-and-A on Frank with me and the audience, and I showed stills and clips of Frank from my personal collection. I told a few jokes. Then I brought both Eric and Gina back onto the stage at the end, for the three of us to sing "New York, New York" together. I closed the show with "Put Your Dreams Away," as Frank so often had. It was only then, as Frank's music drew to an end, that I felt Frank's presence. I knew he was there with me once again, filled with pride and with love. Doing the show was the best gift I could have gotten for Frank's birthday.

We lost Frankie Jr. three months later, in March 2016, may he rest in peace. Bill Miller had died on tour with Frankie a decade earlier. Frankie had a long career after his father's passing, traveling with many of his father's musicians and singing his dad's arrangements. He died on the road the way he wanted to, doing what he loved. He never escaped his father's shadow; he never expected to. Frankie was in the middle of a very successful tour in Florida when he passed away. He was walking down a corridor to a ballroom for rehearsal when he had a heart attack. He collapsed and died instantly. Merrill Kellem, one of Frank Sr.'s old security guys, was with him when he passed, so Junior didn't die alone. Within an hour of Frankie's passing, Merrill called to tell me what had happened. After a decent interval, I called Nancy Sr. and then the girls. They told me they didn't plan to have a memorial because Frankie hadn't wanted one. He was mourned privately, as he would have preferred.

Barbara Sinatra remained a part of my life until the end. We enjoyed a unique relationship. I didn't always agree with the decisions she made about Frank, but I loved her despite that, and she loved me. We had our share of confrontations while Frank was alive, but none that were insurmountable. There were times when she'd storm away from me, frustrated and angry, yet she wasn't so much angry with me as with the situation. She always knew where my heart was. Besides, Frank had loved her, and that was enough for me.

I saw her often over the years. Whenever I ran into her, she gave me a big hug and a kiss on the cheek. When we parted company, she'd always say, "When the hell are you going to come out and spend a week with me at the beach? We'll have some food, and we'll have some laughs." Somehow, it never seemed to happen. I had no doubt she meant what she said, but I guess you just can't go back. Those days were over.

The last time I spoke with Barbara was when I called her on July 11, 2017. It would have been her and Frank's forty-first wedding anniversary. We spoke for a good twenty minutes or so. She sounded good, and we enjoyed a couple of laughs. She passed away exactly two weeks later, at ninety years old. I was very moved that Barbara selected me as an honorary pallbearer for her memorial service. R. J. Wagner and Dick Van Dyke were among the speakers, but the most touching tribute was from Bobby's daughter, Carina. Carina was deeply proud of the philanthropist her grandmother had become. Barbara had been equally proud of Carina.

Nancy Jr. and Tina are doing well. Tina continues to work in the entertainment industry and runs the family trust. She was always the business head in the family. She wrote movingly about Frank in her memoir, *My Father's Daughter,* two years after his passing. Nancy Jr., who also chronicled her father's life, has moved back to Rancho Mirage, where she lives down the block from her dad's old compound. Though both of Frank's daughters mourned him deeply, his passing may have been the hardest on Nancy Jr. She was the oldest, Poppa's big girl, and I believe she's missed him more and more as the years have passed. She does, however, have her two beautiful girls and two granddaughters of her own.

I've kept good relationships with both of Frank's granddaughters, A. J. and Amanda, and I do what I can to keep their grandfather alive for them. A. J. is the singer in her generation. She does some of her grandfather's tunes from his *Only the Lonely* album. It's an intimate show, just her and a piano. A. J. and I have had many conversations about music over the years. She misses being able to talk to her grandfather, so I've tried my best to pass on the things he taught me about music. A. J.'s daughter, Miranda, turned eight years old in May. I wish Frank could have known her. Amanda, Frank's younger granddaughter, is the most level-headed sweetheart of a young lady you'll ever meet. She reminds me a great deal of her grandmother Nancy Sr., whom both girls were very close to. Amanda is an artist, like her grandpa, and like him, she paints abstracts in bold, bright colors. Amanda lives in the artists' colony in Laguna Beach with her husband and small daughter, Annie.

Nancy Sr. was the latest one to leave us, two decades after Frank's passing. She and I had a very special relationship. It was hard for me to see her go. I had badly wanted her to have her happy ending, but it wasn't to be. I spoke with her last in June 2018, a month before she passed away. We were attempting to make plans to get together.

She apologetically said, "Tony, I wish we could just put a date on the calendar, but I never know from one day to the next when I'm going to be feeling good. So we're just going to have to try and roll the dice. If I'm up to it, I'd love to see you."

Sadly, it never came to pass. She died in July at the impressive age of 101. Amanda called to tell me the news. A. J. was too torn up to talk about it. One of the things I said to Amanda that made her laugh through the tears was, "Well, you know, Grandma achieved a lot in her life, including one of her primary goals as she got older."

Amanda said, "What was that?"

"She was determined to outlive Barbara. And she sure as hell did!"

It was about six months after Frank's death before I could bring myself to visit his grave. I wanted to wait until there was a headstone, and until some of the furor died down. I didn't want to be rubbing elbows with his fans at his grave site. Frank was buried next to his parents, just four plots down from Jilly, so I was able to visit them both. I was very fortunate that day. I had the place to myself. I wasn't sure how I'd feel when I got there, but there was a peacefulness about standing there, a resolute peace, a solace. It was like all of the craziness was finally done.

The marker was simple. It read, "THE BEST IS YET TO COME. FRANCIS ALBERT SINATRA. 1915–1998. BELOVED HUSBAND & FATHER."

It was a beautiful day, warm, with a nice breeze. The perfect place to rest under the sun after the chaos of Frank's life. I still go back there when I can, though not as often as I used to.

Time doesn't heal everything, but it helps a hell of a lot. I have reflected so often over the years on the roles Frank Sinatra and I played in each other's lives. I have wondered sometimes if part of my purpose in life has been to help people at the end of their earthly journeys. I helped my uncle Joe through his final illness when I was only sixteen years old. I was with my sister and my niece at the end, doing what I could so they could rest, trying to keep my parents' pain bearable. I was with Jilly shortly after the moment of his death, and I stayed with him and his family until they could find some peace. I helped my parents to the grave. I took the final journey, a journey of years, with Frank. If I dwell on the losses, my life seems like a series of tragedies. But I dwell on the laughs. I remember the good times. Frank loved to say, "You only live once, but if you do it right, once is enough." For all his failings, Frank did it right. So, I hope, have I. Maybe that's what my dream of Jilly was really about. Maybe he was thanking me for doing what he couldn't.

The only good dream I had about Frank after his passing stayed with me for a long time. It recurred night after night, and I couldn't make any sense of it. It was so persistent that I came to believe Frank was trying to get a message to me. In the dream, I was sitting in a bar, drinking by myself. There was a band playing. All of a sudden,

491

the side door opened, the one the musicians use to haul their equipment in and out. When I turned to look, in walked Frank, heading straight for me. As he got closer, I stared at him in disbelief. It was really him.

When he got to my booth, he said, "When the hell did you start drinking alone? What kind of crap is that?"

I answered, "I didn't —"

He interrupted me. "Well, are you going to order me a drink, or are you just going to sit there?"

"Yeah. Sure, Frank. I, uh, didn't expect to see you."

I called the waiter over and said, "Bring him a Jack and water." Frank sat down in the booth with me, and the waiter brought his drink.

We were sitting there, drinking together, when Frank said, "Excuse me a second. I've got to go say hello to somebody." I still didn't know what was going on. Frank walked across the room to another booth, where there was a guy sitting by himself with his back to me. Frank slid into the booth opposite this guy and obviously asked him to turn around and wave. The guy turned around, and of all the people in the world, it was Arthur Godfrey, the popular broadcaster of the fifties and sixties. At that point in the dream, I always woke up.

The first time the dream came, it bothered me so much that I called Vine and said, "Vine, something really weird happened. I had the strangest dream. You know all the conversations Frank and I had with people around the world. Did he ever mention to you that he had a friendship with Arthur Godfrey?"

Vine said, "What? Did you have a pepperoni pizza before you went to sleep? I don't remember him ever talking about Arthur Godfrey."

I told her, "Me, either. It's the damnedest thing, and I can't figure it out."

I kept having the dream over and over, and it was really beginning to drive me crazy. Then, a couple of weeks after I had the dream for the first time, the cable went out on my TV in the middle of the night. I needed something to pass the time till sunup, so I pulled out some videotapes to watch. Since I was about to leave again the next day to go on the road with Don, I settled on a tape of a TV special that Rickles had done over twenty-five years earlier, shortly after I met Frank. I'd never seen it. It was still in its original shrink-wrap. As I put it in the machine, I thought, *I'll watch this damn thing, and maybe I can tease Don about it on the road.*

The program was shot at Caesars Palace. It brought back all kinds of memories because it was shot in the room where Frank had held court for much of the seventies and early eighties. There were two Dons in the program: "Evil Don" onstage and "Good Don" offstage. It was kind of like the old Donald Duck cartoons with Bad Donald on one shoulder and Good Donald on the other. Evil Don was about to take Rickles's usual shots at the audience while Good Don stood in the wings, stage-whispering things like, "No! Don't do it! Not the fat lady!" Partway through the program, the scene changed. Don was in a tuxedo, walking in the desert with the wind blowing in his face. He was wandering aimlessly, trying to figure out where he was. Suddenly, he looked up, and on top of a hill in front of him was a pair of gates. A man was standing at the gates, wearing flowing white robes. He had long white hair and a beard. There was a podium in front of him with a large book on it. As Don neared the podium, the camera cut to the man's point of view, looking down at Rickles.

Don looked up at him and said, "Who are you?"

"You may have heard of me. I'm Saint Peter. What are you doing here?"

Rickles said, "I don't think it's my time yet. Look in the book, would you?" Apparently, "Saint Peter" was about to decide which was the real Don, Good Don or Evil Don.

Suddenly, the camera cut to a reverse angle over Rickles's shoulder and focused on the face of Saint Peter. And who was it? Arthur Godfrey. I almost dropped my glass.

An idea suddenly hit me in the gut. Was it possible that Frank had been trying to tell me through the dream that Saint Peter had welcomed him through the gates to heaven? It seemed preposterous, but it also felt like too big of a coincidence not to mean something. It's one of the most bizarre things that has ever happened to me in a life filled with amazing events.

After that night, I never had the dream again. It was as if its mission had been accomplished. I felt like Frank was telling me, in the only way he could, "Don't worry. I'm okay." For me, it will always be a sign that my friend is back to being the real Frank Sinatra, in a place where the sun is a perpetual glory and a jubilation, singing once again.

For though the nights grew long

In the winter of his years,
On a soft summer night, in the warm
    moonlight,
I can still hear him there
In the perfumed air.
His voice sweet and clear
Through the seasons of his years.

# SOURCE NOTES

Unlike most Sinatra biographers, I lived this book. It is based almost entirely on direct personal experience and on thousands of conversations that occurred over decades with Frank, Jilly Rizzo, Nancy Sinatra Sr., and others close to Frank. I expect that I have been consulted on so many other Sinatra books because, in some cases, I have the only living memory of what occurred. I have become something of a keeper of the flame.

Over twenty-five years ago, Nancy Sinatra Sr. first floated the idea that I write this book. She wanted the true story told. When Frank and I would talk about all the garbage that had been written about him, I would ask him why he never corrected the record himself. His answer was always that the romanticized version had taken on a life of its own, and he'd learned the hard way to pick his battles with the press.

I'd say, "But Frank, the truth is the truth."

He'd tell me, "If you feel that passionately about it, then *you* fix it," and I said, "I will."

Once the seed of that idea was planted, it grew steadily as time passed. This book has been decades in the planning. Because I am what my collaborator describes as an "obsessively organized pack rat" (as opposed to Rat Pack), I have kept every scrap of paper and item I accumulated during my years with Frank, right down to his orange luggage tags that read A.F.P.O.L. (Another F***ing Piece Of Luggage). I have concert schedules, hotel bills, menus for Frank's Boys' Nights, letters, and personal notes — a collection so large that it would add another chapter to this book if I listed everything. I also made hundreds of notations at the time things happened, so I'd be certain to remember. They're scribbled on hotel notepads, napkins, scraps of paper, and eventually, on my phone. I possess extensive archival footage of Frank's concerts and public events, in some cases unedited and never released to the public. I also have hundreds of photographs and what amounts to a Sinatra archeological treasure trove. Most important, I possess an uncommon sensory memory that has enabled me to recall almost every song and a plethora of the conversations I've heard. It got me A's throughout school without ever taking a note and enabled me to perform as a musician and vocalist without a scrap of sheet music. When I was five, it embedded songs I heard on the radio so deeply in my mind that I could remember and reproduce them on a piano. Over my lifetime, having this unique memory has clearly preserved fond reminiscences, but it has also seared into my mind things I'd rather forget. My memory is both a blessing and a curse.

Because so much of what has been written about Frank is erroneous, my collaborator and I fact-checked everything possible, to support the accuracy of both my and Frank's recollections. In addition to my own archive, we used primary sources such as transcripts, recordings, and first-hand accounts. We scoured the Internet and YouTube for recordings, as well as contemporary and contemporaneous reports. For example, we looked at Teddy Kollek's first-person account of Frank's role in getting money to Israel one night, which perfectly mirrored Frank's version of the story. When the issue of Frank's involvement with Natalie Wood came up, I called R. J. Wagner to verify Frank's version. We consulted Frank's copy of Richard Gambino's book *Vendetta,* a history of Italians in America, which Frank at one time had hoped to produce as a film. We looked at the Giancana family's account of their involvement with Frank in *Double Cross,* a book by Sam Giancana Sr.'s brother and nephew. Tom and Phil Kuntz's *The Sinatra Files* provided government memos related to Frank and transcripts of federal wiretaps of Sam Giancana. My collaborator read every word of Frank's 1275-page FBI file, a PDF nightmare with heavy redactions that would make anybody sleep warm. We also read Marilyn Monroe's FBI file. Both files were, to say the least, enlightening. Allowing for some inevitable human error, this book is as painstakingly compiled and rigorously researched as possible.

It was important to me to get it right for Frank's sake. It's the least I owe him, and it fulfills the promise I made to him.

# ACKNOWLEDGMENTS

I would like to acknowledge and extend my heartfelt thanks to:

My mom and dad, my brothers Peter and Paul, and my sister Angela, first and foremost, for a loving and supportive home environment . . . but especially my mom, whose staunch encouragement of my pursuit of a life and career in the entertainment industry overshadowed the well-meaning, yet overprotective concerns of my dad, who, in the early years, kept telling me to "get a REAL job!"

My "other brother" and partner in Winbrook Entertainment, Michael Guarnera, for his ever-present, unwavering dedication, support, and friendship, as well as his family, Antonello Stornelli, and the entire Guarnera clan.

Jilly Rizzo, for his belief in me early on, his

501

friendship and that of his sons Willie and Joey.

My fellow musicians and friends Les Stanco, Richie Scollo, Dominic Famularo, Frank Goldstein, John Bonelli, Gary Berzolla, Joe Costanzo, Wayne Sabella, and the Jimenez brothers, Eddie and Joe. It was an honor sharing the stage with you all over the years.

Barbara and Don Rickles, Angie Dickinson, R. J. Wagner, George Schlatter, Tony Danza, Lorna Luft, Deana Martin, Michael Bublé, Randy Taraborrelli, James Kaplan, John Landis, Michael Frondelli, JoAnn Tominaga, and Sandee Bathgate.

Jimmy Kimmel, his family, and our friends Bob Saget and John Stamos.

Mrs. Nancy Sinatra Sr., for her friendship, deep loyalty, and for being the first person to strongly encourage me to write this book!

Conrad Denke of Victory Studios and, again, Michael Guarnera, for their resilient diligence in pushing me to see the book through to fruition.

Alan Nevins of Renaissance Management,

whose tremendous expertise in the literary world, along with his belief in me, made this book a reality.

My extremely talented collaborator, Mary Jane Ross. She made this work a very pleasurable journey and a profound labor of love.

My friends and associates at Simon & Schuster and Scribner, specifically Nan Graham, Rick Horgan, Beckett Rueda, and Clare Maurer.

# ABOUT THE AUTHORS

**Tony Oppedisano** — a.k.a. "Tony O" — is a former professional musician and singer who went on to become an award-winning producer and personal manager to entertainment icons Frank Sinatra and Don Rickles. Tony met and befriended the singing legend when the younger man was only twenty-one years old. He later became Sinatra's best friend and road manager, a contributor to two of the singer's platinum albums, and a producer of the documentary *To Be Frank: Sinatra at 100*. Tony grew up in Brooklyn, New York, and currently lives in Los Angeles. He is the author of *Sinatra and Me*.

**Mary Jane Ross** has collaborated on numerous bestselling memoirs, including books by Albert DeMeo, Ray Charles Robinson Jr., Nancy Mace, and Piper Laurie.